'The American economy relies on a startup culture to create new goods and services, provide job opportunities, and raise living standards. Eric Ries's *The Startup Way* provides a compelling roadmap to guide all organizations – old and new, big and small, high-tech and low-tech – to build a startup culture to experiment, iterate and innovate'

Alan Krueger, chairman of the President's Council of Economic Advisers under President Obama and Bendheim Professor of Economics and Public Affairs at Princeton

'As someone who is deeply committed to the public sector, I was heartened to see that the entrepreneurial principles and practices that Eric Ries describes in his new book, *The Startup Way*, apply equally effectively to governments and non-profits, as well as for established for-profit businesses. If you want to visit the future of the modern organization, read this compelling book'

'A 21st-century toolkit that will allow any company to flourish'

Ron Conway, founder of SV Angel

'Eric Ries does it again – brilliantly. In his new book, *The Startup Way*, Ries argues that established businesses need to build a new entrepreneurial capability in order to innovate continuously. Most large companies are missing this fundamental piece of the corporate innovation puzzle. Neglect his advice at your peril'

Thales S. Teixeira, Harvard Business School

'In *The Startup Way*, Eric Ries offers leaders across the public, private and non-profit sectors a road map for managing continuous innovation, regardless of organizational size or complexity. As someone who helped introduce some of these practices to the US government, I've seen first-hand the improvement in people's lives'

Aneesh Chopra, former CTO of the United States

'My research has focused on what causes established companies to maintain success, and *The Startup Way* provides practical guidance on how to do just that'

Clayton Christensen, author, entrepreneur, and Kim B. Clark Professor of Business Administration at Harvard Business School

'*The Startup Way* creates a vision and blueprint for a new form of management that combines entrepreneurial and general management skills and practices. The inspirational examples across multiple, diverse organizations show that integrating the highly iterative, experimental mindset and skills of startups into established organizations is key to unlocking continuous innovation and sustainable growth . . . Provides clear and useful guidance for tackling the toughest challenges'

Kathy Fish, CTO, Procter & Gamble

'Big companies are struggling as never before. They need a brand-new stem-to-stern game plan, and they get exactly that in Eric Ries's new *The Startup Way*. It keys off *The Lean Startup* and makes a great leap forward. The game plan Eric suggests is "not optio[...] find a way. Well done!'

Tom Peters

'If the Startup Way can transform the federal government – and it has – it can transform your company. For everyone who's thought "there has to be a better way," here's your proof and a playbook to make it happen'

'In *The Startup Way*, Eric Ries uses his years of work with companies like GE and Toyota to show us what the company of the future will look like. If you want to know how companies can become more agile, more innovative, and more resilient in the face of today's relentless pace of change, read this compelling book

'Eric Ries shows that entrepreneurial management is a key to success in this fast-changing world. At ING we've embedded Lean Startup principles into the way we innovate. *The Startup Way* brings new and valuable insights.'

'Eric brilliantly describes the limitations of old management thinking in a time where competitors bring out new products in an order of magnitude faster than legacy companies. *The Startup Way* describes how to foster entrepreneurial leadership essential to corporate survival in the twenty-first century'

'Eric has done it again! Every company can benefit from these startup principles – and should – because if they don't, a startup is probably going to drink up all their milkshake. This is the Internet revolution and if your company isn't adapting to *The Startup Way*, it's failing'

ABOUT THE AUTHOR

Eric Ries is an entrepreneur and the author of the *New York Times* bestseller *The Lean Startup*, which has sold over one million copies and has been translated into more than thirty languages. He is the creator of the Lean Startup methodology, which has become a global movement in business, practised by individuals and companies around the world. He has founded a number of startups, including IMVU, where he served as CTO, and he has advised on business and product strategy for startups, venture capital firms, and large companies, including GE, with whom he partnered to create the FastWorks program. Ries has served as an entrepreneur-in-residence at Harvard Business School, IDEO, and Pivotal, and he is the founder and CEO of the Long-Term Stock Exchange.

THESTARTUPWAY.COM | @ERICRIES

THE
STARTUP
WAY

How Entrepreneurial
Management Transforms
Culture and Drives Growth

ERIC RIES

PORTFOLIO
PENGUIN

PORTFOLIO PENGUIN

UK | USA | Canada | Ireland | Australia
India | New Zealand | South Africa

Portfolio Penguin is part of the Penguin Random House group of companies
whose addresses can be found at global.penguinrandomhouse.com.

First published in the United States of America by Currency 2017
First published in Great Britain by Portfolio 2017
001

Copyright © Eric Ries, 2017

The moral right of the author has been asserted

Set in 13.08/16.10pt by Adobe Garamond by Jouve (UK), Milton Keynes
Printed in Great Britain by Clays Ltd, St Ives plc

A CIP catalogue record for this book is available from the British Library

Hardback ISBN: 978–0–241–19724–0
Trade Paperback ISBN: 978–0–241–19726–4

For Gabriel and Clara

CONTENTS

INTRODUCTION

ON A SUMMER AFTERNOON, a team of engineers and a group of executives at one of America's largest companies met in a classroom deep in the heart of their sprawling executive training facility to discuss their multi-hundred-million-dollar five-year plan for developing a new diesel and natural gas engine. Their goal was to enter a new market space; excitement was running high. The engine, named Series X, had broad applications in many industries, from energy generation to locomotive power.

All of this was very clear to those assembled in the room. Except to one person, who had joined the meeting with no prior knowledge of engines, energy, or industrial product production and was therefore reduced to asking a series of questions Dr. Seuss might have posed:

"What is this used for again? It's in a boat? On a plane? By sea and by land? On a train?"

The executives and engineers alike were no doubt wondering, "Who is this guy?"

That guy was me. The company was GE, one of America's

oldest, most venerable organizations, with a market cap (at the time) of $220.47 billion and no fewer than 300,000 employees.

So what was I doing there at GE in the summer of 2012? I'm not a corporate executive. My background is not in energy or health care or any of GE's myriad industrial businesses.

I am an entrepreneur.

GE Chairman and CEO Jeffrey Immelt and Vice Chair Beth Comstock had invited me to Crotonville, New York, that day because they were intrigued by an idea proposed in my first book, *The Lean Startup*: that the principles of *entrepreneurial management* could be applied in any industry, size of company, or sector of the economy. And they believed their company needed to start working according to those principles. The goal was to set GE on a path for growth and adaptability, and for Immelt to leave a legacy that would allow the company to flourish long term.

That day we took a fresh look at the plan for the Series X engine and realized that it could get to market radically faster by building a simpler engine in a matter of months, not years. It was the first of many such sessions (some of which you'll hear more about).

The next day I had a conversation that seemed—on its surface—very different. It was with the founder and CEO of one of the next generation of hypergrowth tech startups. The two companies couldn't be much more different: one old and one new, one the market leader in many of the businesses it's in, the other fighting to get traction. One building massive physical products, the other building the kind of software infrastructure that powers the Internet. One East Coast, one West Coast. One where executives wear suits and the other where they wear ripped jeans.

The CEO of this company, an early adopter of *The Lean Startup,* was confronting a new set of challenges: How could they scale beyond their first, successful innovation? How could they empower their employees to think like entrepreneurs? And, most of all, how could they find new sources of sustainable growth?

I was stunned by how, despite all the surface differences, these two conversations were surprisingly similar. GE—like many successful companies—was looking to reinvigorate its culture with entrepreneurial energy so it could continue to grow. The startup I'd met with that afternoon was trying to figure out how to maintain its entrepreneurial culture as it grew up.

Over the past few years, I've had many such moments, when I've been struck by the parallel challenges faced by organizations we typically think of as very different. Out of these conversations with leaders and founders, I have come to realize that today's organizations—both established and emerging—are missing capabilities that are needed for every organization to thrive in the century ahead: the ability to experiment rapidly with new products and new business models, the ability to empower their most creative people, and the ability to engage again and again in an innovation process—and manage it with rigor and accountability—so that they can unlock new sources of growth and productivity.

That process—and how to take it from "missing" to "thriving" in *any* company or organization—is the focus of this book.

WHO AM I?

My journey to that meeting in Crotonville was an unlikely—not to mention unexpected—one. Early in my career, I trained as a software engineer, after which I became an entrepreneur. If you've ever pictured a stereotypical tech entrepreneur as a kid, laboring away in their parents' basement—well, that was me. My first foray in entrepreneurship, during the dot-com bubble, was an abject failure. My first published writing, 1996's scintillating *The Black Art of Java Game Programming,* is, last time I checked, available used on Amazon.com for $0.99. None of these projects seemed, at the time, like harbingers of the future years that would be spent advocating for a new system of management.

After I moved to Silicon Valley, though, I started to see patterns in what was driving both successes and failures. And, along the way, I started to formulate a model for how to make the practice of entrepreneurship more rigorous. Then I began writing about it, first online beginning in 2008, and then in a book, *The Lean Startup*, published in 2011. What happened from there exceeded my wildest expectations. The Lean Startup movement spread worldwide. More than a million people around the world read the book. Odds are, no matter where on the globe you are right now, there's a local Lean Startup Meetup group nearby.[1] Thousands of founders, investors, and others in the startup ecosystem rallied to embrace the ideas and practices of Lean Startup.

In the book, I made a claim that seemed radical at the time. I argued that a startup should be properly understood as "a human institution designed to create a new product or service under conditions of extreme uncertainty." This definition was purposefully general. It didn't specify anything about the size of the organization, the form it took (company, nonprofit, or other), or the industry or sector of which it was a part. According to this broad definition, anyone—no matter their official job title—can be cast unexpectedly into the waters of entrepreneurship if the context of their work becomes highly uncertain. I argued that entrepreneurs are everywhere—in small businesses, mammoth corporations, health care systems, and schools, even inside government agencies. They are anywhere that people are doing the honorable and often unheralded labor of testing a novel idea, creating a better way to work, or serving new customers by extending a product or service into new markets.

In the six years since *The Lean Startup* was published, the diverse organizations adopting its methods have proven this claim time and again. I have had the chance to travel all over the world, working with companies of just about every size you can imagine. Three founders working on a new app? Check. Small business? Check. Religious nonprofits? Certainly. Medium-sized manufacturing companies? Check. Hypergrowth pre-IPO tech startups? Definitely. Massive government bureaucracies? Check. Some of the largest and slowest multinational companies in the world? You bet. All these kinds of organizations can use the Lean Startup methodology to do more effective work and accelerate their progress.

BUILDING THE MISSING CAPABILITIES

These travels are ultimately what brought me to that GE classroom. The success of the Series X engine, along with a number of other similar pilot projects, led to something extraordinary. GE and I forged a partnership to develop a program called Fast-Works,[2] which enacted a major cultural and managerial change. Over several years, we trained thousands of leaders throughout the company. I personally coached more than a hundred project teams, spanning every function, region, and business unit in the company. Within GE, every business CEO and top manager has been trained in entrepreneurial ways of working, and internal functions have been transformed so that they facilitate—rather than hinder—innovation.

But I've been surprised to discover that startups, too, need this kind of training and transformation work. Like many of my peers in Silicon Valley, I came up in my career with a belief that "big company" people were fundamentally different from creative, disruptive entrepreneurs like us.[3] That once organizations reach a certain size, they start dying slowly, from the inside. They cease to innovate. The most creative people choose to leave. Big companies inevitably become sclerotic, bureaucratic, political.

This belief creates a strange paradox, a kind of cognitive dissonance that affects all of us who aspire to high-growth entrepreneurship. Having worked with literally hundreds of entrepreneurs, I've become used to asking them:

"If you hate big companies so much, why are you trying to create a new one?"

They're often stumped by the question, since in their mind's eye, the company they are busy building will be different. It won't be dragged down by inane meetings and nosy middle managers. It will remain dynamic, scrappy, a perpetual startup. But how often is this ideal organization actually what they end up creating?

Over the past several years, founders and CEOs who had been early adopters of the Lean Startup method began to get back in touch with me. In the early days, they had been excited about the parts of Lean Startup that are about getting started quickly, like *minimum viable product* and *pivot*. But they hadn't been as focused on the parts that are, frankly, a little more boring: the science of management and the discipline of accounting. Now that their companies had scaled to hundreds, thousands, or, in some cases, tens of thousands of employees, they realized they had to find a way to hold on to their entrepreneurial way of working, even as they put traditional management tools in place, did more forecasting, and moved toward a traditional-looking org chart.

I have seen this firsthand in dozens of amazing companies: when employees are subject to traditional organizational structures and incentives, certain specific bureaucratic behaviors result. It's an inevitable consequence of the way those systems are designed.

What these founders wanted to know was: Could we use Lean Startup techniques to prevent our organizations from becoming lethargic and bureaucratic as they scaled? Thanks to the work I'd been doing with larger organizations, I could tell them the answer was yes.

That's why, for the past five years, I've been living a double life. I've had plenty of days when I met with the leader of a mammoth, market-leading organization in the morning and then, in the afternoon, spent time with startups, from massive hyper-growth Silicon Valley success stories to tiny seed-stage hopefuls. The questions I'm asked are amazingly consistent:

How do I encourage the people who work for me to think more like entrepreneurs?

How can I build new products for new markets without losing my existing customers?

How do I hold people working in an entrepreneurial way accountable without putting my core business at risk?

How can I create a culture that will balance the needs of existing business with new sources of growth?

If you are reading this book, you have probably been asking these questions about your organization, too.

Learning from the companies I have been working with, I began to evolve a new body of work about principles that apply beyond the "getting started" phase, particularly in established and even large-scale enterprises.

- It's about how traditional management and what I call *entrepreneurial management* can work together.
- It's about what startups need to do beyond Lean Startup—when they have the problems that come with rapid growth and scale.
- It's about what an organizational transformation *process* should look like in order to move toward a leaner, more iterative way of working.

I've worked with thousands of managers and founders to test and refine this new approach. I've been in the trenches with them, launching new products, founding new companies, reinventing IT systems, auditing financial processes, rethinking HR practices and sales strategies—you name it. I've worked with leaders of every corporate function: from supply chain to legal to R&D. And I've worked in a crazy assortment of industries: deep-sea drilling, electronics, automotive, fashion, health care, the military, and education, to name just a few.

The new approach draws not just on my own direct work with companies, but on the wisdom of an entire movement of like-minded leaders. It is informed by case studies and wisdom from a variety of sources: iconic multinationals like GE and Toyota; established tech pioneers like Amazon, Intuit, and Facebook; the next generation of hypergrowth startups like Twilio, Dropbox, and Airbnb; and countless emerging startups you haven't heard of—yet. And, perhaps even more surprisingly, it draws on the work of innovators reforming some of the world's oldest and most bureaucratic institutions—including the U.S. federal government.

Visionary leaders across every kind of business are waking up to new possibilities, ones that blend the best of general management with the emerging discipline of entrepreneurial management.

Working with them, I have seen that entrepreneurship has the potential to revitalize management thinking in the twenty-first century. This is no longer just the way people work in one industry. It's the way people everywhere work—or want to work.

I call it the Startup Way.

THE FIVE PRINCIPLES BEHIND THE STARTUP WAY

The Startup Way combines the rigor of general management with the highly iterative nature of startups. It is a system that can be used in any organization that seeks to practice continuous innovation, regardless of size, age, or mission.

Think back to the definition of a startup I offered above. Because entrepreneurship is always about institution-building, it is, necessarily, about management. In the Startup Way, entrepreneurship is a management discipline, a new framework for organizing, evaluating, and allocating resources for the work of a company. It's a philosophy that replaces the old-fashioned template currently holding so many companies back, providing a new blueprint of how a modern company should work to create sustained growth through continuous innovation. In lieu of the current management system, which is bound by planning and forecasting, the Startup Way creates a system that embraces and even thrives on speed and uncertainty.

The five key principles behind the Startup Way philosophy are:

1. **CONTINUOUS INNOVATION:** Too many leaders are searching for that one key innovation. But long-term growth requires something different: a method for finding new breakthroughs repeatedly, drawing on the creativity and talent of every level of the organization.

2. **STARTUP AS ATOMIC UNIT OF WORK:** In order to create cycles of continuous innovation and unlock new sources of growth, companies need to have teams that can experiment to find them. These teams are internal startups, and they require a distinct organizational structure to support them.

3. **THE MISSING FUNCTION:** If you add startups to an organization's ecosystem, they must be managed in ways that confound traditional techniques. Most organizations are missing a core discipline—entrepreneurship—that is just as vital to their future success as marketing or finance.

4. **THE SECOND FOUNDING:** Making this kind of profound change

to an organization's structure is like founding the company all over again, whether it's five or a hundred years old.

5. **CONTINUOUS TRANSFORMATION:** All of this requires the development of a new organizational capability: the ability to rewrite the organization's DNA in response to new and diverse challenges. It would be a shame to transform only once. When a company has figured out how to transform, it can—and should—be prepared to do it many more times in the future.

It's important to note emphatically up front that committing the entire organization to this method of working does not mean that every single team is reorganized around startup principles. Nor does it mean that every employee magically starts acting like an entrepreneur. Instead, the goal is to *make it possible* for startup teams to operate reliably and give every employee the *opportunity* to act in an entrepreneurial way. This allows for the emergence of people who are naturally inclined to work this way—or could be inclined, given encouragement and permission. Accordingly, every manager in the company must become literate in the tools of entrepreneurial management, even managers who are not directly involved with startups. They need to understand why some people are working differently, be able to hold them accountable to new standards, and recognize when their own normal gatekeeper functions, such as HR, IT, legal, and compliance, are getting in the way.

THE BOOK

This is not a manifesto. We have enough of those already. Our world is awash with gurus and experts telling us all to move faster, be more innovative, and think outside the box. But we are short on specific details: How, exactly, do we attain these results? This book is an attempt to fill in the missing details. It offers proven techniques to rekindle an organization's entrepreneurial spirit—or prevent it from ever being lost in the first place.

If you are a leader—whether of a company or a team—this book will give you the blueprint for transforming your organization into one that is capable of finding new sources for growth over the long term. You'll learn how to create accountability structures that incentivize productive innovation—the kind that truly has value for a company. You'll learn how to structure work so that it's more fulfilling. You'll also get a new understanding of what your role is as a leader—a role that's quite different than what's still taught in many MBA programs or sought out by investors and board members. Scott Cook, co-founder of Intuit and now chairman of its executive committee, describes this change as one of perspective. It's the difference between "playing Caesar" (deciding which projects live or die), and "playing the scientist" (being perpetually open to search and discovery). It will make your work more interesting and more effective.

It is rooted in the experiences of actual living, breathing organizations that have successfully implemented these ideas across a wide array of sectors, industries, and scales. *The Startup Way* details a series of specific interventions that can help you invest in entrepreneurship as a core discipline, and walks you through how to change the mindset of senior leadership. Thanks to my work with GE, I have generously been granted extensive access to bring you "behind the scenes" of the FastWorks transformation, which will serve as a kind of extended case study to illustrate these concepts that have been implemented to make GE adaptable for the future. But I will also share detailed stories of many other organizations that have been through a similar journey.

In Part One, "The Modern Company," we'll uncover why

traditional management practices are no longer up to the task, and what about this particular historical moment has made the integration of entrepreneurial management so critical. We'll talk about the new capacities and ways of working needed now.

Part One defines how "the startup" is a new *atomic unit of work* for highly uncertain terrain, and it lays out the conditions required to build a portfolio of startups within an organization. We'll discuss how to lay the foundations of strong accountability for innovation projects, even in situations of high uncertainty, where planning and forecasting are difficult or impossible, and how to avoid the kinds of accountability measures that routinely kill worthwhile innovation projects. We'll also take a quick tour through the major points and processes detailed in *The Lean Startup*, such as *minimum viable products*, *pivots*, and the *build-measure-learn loop*.

In Part Two, "A Road Map for Transformation," we will dive into the "how" of the Startup Way. When teams are given the chance to organize in the Startup Way, they naturally gravitate to new and different processes than people are accustomed to. We will explore these unconventional techniques—some of which are based on concepts from *The Lean Startup*, and some of which are brand-new. We'll also talk about how to manage conflict between these new processes and legacy systems, including conflicts among the middle managers, who historically have been the assassins of progress.

For a modern company, the payoffs of continuous innovation are not only the breakthrough new products, services, internal systems, and commercial wins that it produces. Innovation also provides the opportunity to incubate a new culture, one that unleashes entrepreneurial creativity at every level of the organization. We'll explore how making the right accountability and process choices allows this new culture to thrive and grow.

We'll look at the personnel, hiring, and development needs

that are implied by this new way of working. We will address, head-on, the mistaken but widespread belief that working in an entrepreneurial way requires firing existing staff and going outside to look for fancy superstars. In every organization I have worked with—without exception and including some iconic Fortune 500 companies—I have found true entrepreneurs on the inside. We'll discuss how to bring those talented people out of the shadows, build a network of coaching and support, and ultimately help them succeed. We'll examine how the internal functions of a corporation, including HR, legal, finance, IT, and procurement, can be transformed in order to facilitate rather than block innovation. We'll look at the kinds of problems that uniquely arise during continuous innovation. Finally, we'll take a very close look at the process and mechanisms of *innovation accounting,* the financial structure that supports this new way of working.

In Part Three, "The Big Picture," we'll explore what happens once the transformation process is "complete." Or rather, the fact that it never really is. The ultimate goal of the Startup Way is for organizations to be in a state of continuous transformation, which will allow them to flourish in any circumstance. I believe this kind of flexibility can also be used far more broadly, so the final chapters are about the greater consequences of this new structure when applied to public policy and the problems we face as a society.

A PATH TO LONG-TERM THINKING

Continuing a theme from *The Lean Startup,* in this book I will return often to a central question: How can companies truly create *long-term* growth and results? Of all of the topics I discuss from day to day, this one is the most emotionally charged for today's managers and founders. Over and over again, I see people who desperately want to fulfill a long-term vision for the company, to leave a legacy of meaningful change behind. And yet they are continually frustrated by the short-term demands of our current business systems. All it takes is a few bad quarters for investors to demand change, and for the internal politics of a company to create massive upheaval, all the way to the top.

You might think an organization that measures its employees against strict quarterly deadlines, the way most companies currently do, would operate with a mindset that encourages rapid experimentation on an abbreviated schedule. But what actually happens is the opposite. Because of the short-term pressure, anything that can be done in one quarter has to be highly predictable in order to make future commitments based on its results. Instead of seeing the innovation opportunities that come with thinking in short cycles, companies become conservative and focus only on the projects they believe will maximize that quarter or fiscal year. That means they continue to do the same things, whether or not those things still work the way they used to. In addition, the company that demands predictability in the short term is also ill-equipped to hold teams working on longer projects accountable.

I believe the new framework described in this book provides concrete guidance for how to move beyond this dilemma to a new, more sustainable system for creating long-term growth and flexibility.

So now that you understand what we want to accomplish— changing the way the modern company operates—let's begin.

PART ONE

THE MODERN COMPANY

"HYPERGROWTH FOR A COMPANY ALSO REQUIRES HYPERGROWTH OF THE PEOPLE INSIDE IT."

In 2006, you probably never would have even thought of renting a stranger's apartment instead of checking in at the Hilton. As of this writing, more than 100 million people have,[1] thanks to Airbnb. At its core, the company is already experimental. If it weren't, it never would have uncovered a whole hidden market and grown in just ten years to a valuation of $30 billion. So what more could startup thinking possibly bring to a company that very recently found huge success by disrupting an entire market?

A few years after Airbnb launched, the company's original team started looking around for growth opportunities. They'd added new features to their existing product, including user verification and host insurance to increase confidence in the platform, and they'd formed a partnership with Concur Technologies to capture business travelers. But they knew that in order to keep growing, they needed to come up with something entirely different. "We said, 'What's next? Where is this going?'" recalls Joe Zadeh, one of the company's first employees and now its VP of product. As founder Brian Chesky said, in retrospect: "I had this sense of urgency or crisis. You can't stay the same."[2]

Zadeh and Chesky realized that in order to come up with something completely new, they needed to give themselves the time and space to experiment—something they'd had when they launched the company, purely because of circumstance, but hadn't been prioritiz-

ing as Airbnb grew. They created a small dedicated team within the company, led by Chesky, whose first mission was an afternoon at Fisherman's Wharf, a scenic spot overlooking San Francisco Bay, Alcatraz, and the Golden Gate Bridge, where out-of-towners flock and souvenir shops abound. The result, which came several years later, was the launch of Airbnb Trips, a trip-planning service that marks the company's first major expansion. In Chapter 8 you'll learn more about what came between that afternoon and the product launch, and about Airbnb's structure, which allows both for the maintenance of its core product and for experiments with new ideas, like Trips. It's the philosophy behind being able to make bets that may or may not pay off, rather than to simply refine a current success, that I want to highlight here. Zadeh sums it up: "Hypergrowth for a company also requires hypergrowth of the people inside it."

Airbnb is just one example of a startup structure that allows for experimentation. Throughout the book, we'll look at aspects of a variety of startups, including Dropbox, WordPress, and Emerald Cloud Lab, to see how they've done it.

Many startups, of course, are not yet at this point. But if they succeed, they'll reach it soon enough. Thinking about how to manage growth ahead of time, rather than when it's already happened and is creating a crisis, is critical. Understanding the tools that are available and the environment we're using them in is key to sustained, long-term success. As Palantir's Ari Gesher says, "Hypergrowth is painful—there's no way to do it gracefully. If it hurts, you're not doing it wrong, you're doing it right."[3]

In this part of the book, we'll talk about what it means to become a modern company, and the entrepreneurial structure required to survive and embody a long-term vision for the future. Implementing that vision takes patience and dedication—transformation is never a quick fix—but organizations that operate this way have the greatest chance at continued expansion. We'll walk through the elements of *startup culture and work that have made Silicon Valley and other startup hubs such dynamic places, as well as the lessons and theories from the past that form the foundation on which to build a new way of thinking about management. Finally, we'll synthesize these ideas into the Startup Way.*

## CHAPTER 1

RESPECT THE PAST, INVENT THE FUTURE: CREATING THE MODERN COMPANY

WHEN I FIRST began working with GE years ago, I sat down for a conversation with CEO Jeff Immelt. Something he said to me that day has stayed with me ever since: "Nobody wants to work at an old-fashioned company. Nobody wants to buy products from an old-fashioned company. And nobody wants to invest in an old-fashioned company."

What followed was an in-depth discussion of what makes a company truly modern. How do you know it when you see it?

I asked him to imagine the following: If I selected an employee of the company at random, from any level or function or region, and that employee had an absolutely brilliant idea that would unlock a dramatic new source of growth for the company, how would he or she get it implemented? Does the company have an automatic process for testing a new idea, to see if it is actually any good? And does the company have the management tools necessary to scale this idea up to maximum impact, even if it doesn't align with any of the company's current lines of business?

That's what a modern company does: harnesses the creativity and talent of every single one of its employees.

Jeff answered me directly: "That's what your next book should be about."

THE MARKETPLACE OF UNCERTAINTY

I think most business leaders recognize that the everyday challenges of executing their core business leave little time and energy for harnessing and testing new ideas. This stands to reason, as today's companies are operating in an environment quite different from their predecessors. I've had the privilege of meeting thousands of managers around the world in the past few years. Over and over again, I see their incredible anxiety about the unpredictability of the world they live in. The most common concerns I hear:

1. Globalization and the rise of new global competitors.
2. "Software eating the world"[1] and the way automation and IT seem to destroy the competitive "moats"[2] companies have been able to set up around their products and services in the past.
3. The increasing speed of technological change and consumer preference.
4. The ridiculous number of new potential high-growth startups that are entering every industry—even if most of them eventually flame out.[3]

And those are just examples of the *external* sources of uncertainty that face today's managers. Increasingly, today's managers are also under pressure to create more uncertainty themselves: by launching new, innovative products, seeking new sources of growth, or entering new markets.

TECHNOLOGY ADOPTION IS ACCELERATING

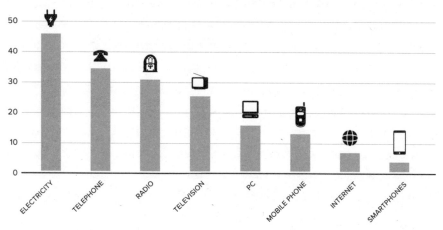

"Years Until a Technology Is Adopted by 25% of the U.S. Population" Source: U.S. Census, Wall Street Journal

The diffusion and adoption rates for new technologies have risen over the years. The graph shows the number of years it took technologies such as electricity, television, and the Internet to be adopted by at least 25 percent of the U.S. population.[4]

It's important to see this as the change it is. For most of the twentieth century, growth in most industries was constrained by capacity. It was considered completely obvious what a company would do if it had extra capacity: make more stuff and then sell it. "New products" meant mostly variations of what a company already made. "New growth" usually meant putting out more advertising to reach new audiences with existing products. The bases for competition were primarily price, quality, variety, and distribution. Barriers to entry were high, and if competitors did come on the scene, they entered and grew relatively slowly—by today's standards.

Today, global communications means that new products can be conceived and built anywhere, and customers can discover them at an unprecedented pace. What's more, individuals and small companies have unprecedented access to these new global systems, compared to a small number of owners of capital in the past.

This setup flips Karl Marx's old dictum on its head. What he called the *means of production* can now be rented. Entire global supply chains can be borrowed at little more than the marginal cost of the underlying products they produce. This dramatically lowers the initial capital costs required to try something new.

In addition, the basis of competition is shifting. Today's consumers have more choices and are more demanding. Technology trends reward businesses that have the broadest reach with near-monopoly-type power. The basis of competition is often design, brand, business model, or technology platform.

THE MANAGEMENT PORTFOLIO

This is the context in which a modern company operates. Plenty of companies still make commodity products. But more often, they require new sources of growth that can come only from innovation. This has very real effects for what I call the *management portfolio* of a company. Incremental improvements to existing products or new variations thereof are relatively predictable investments, as are process improvements to increase quality and margins. The tools of traditional management—from forecasting to typical performance objectives—work fine in these situations.

But for other parts of the management portfolio, where leaps of innovation are being attempted, the traditional management tools don't fit. Most companies don't have anything to replace them with—yet.

WHY TRADITIONAL MANAGEMENT TOOLS STRUGGLE WITH UNCERTAINTY

Some years ago, I picked up one of the classics of the management genre, Alfred Sloan's *My Years with General Motors* (1963). In it, he recounts the moment in 1921 when GM almost ran out of cash. The cause? Not some devastating catastrophe or embezzlement scandal. No, they simply dramatically overbought their inventory supplies, to the tune of several hundred million dollars (in 1920s dollars!), unaware that the general economy was slumping that year and demand would prove to be soft in 1920–21.

After saving the company through emergency measures, Sloan undertook a several-years-long journey to find a new management principle that could prevent this kind of problem from recurring. Eventually he made a breakthrough discovery, which he called "the key to co-ordinated control of decentralized operations."

The foundation of this system was the rigorous production of estimates, for each divisional manager, of the precise number of cars that GM should sell in an "ideal" year. Using these estimates in combination with a number of internal targets and external macroeconomic factors, the company would produce a forecast of how many cars each division was responsible for selling. Managers who exceeded this total were promoted, those who fell short were not. Once put into place, the system worked to prevent the kind of miscalculation and waste of resources that had previously occurred in the company.

The structure that Alfred Sloan pioneered became the basis for all of twentieth-century general management. You can't run a multiproduct, multidivision, multinational company and its attendant global supply chains without it. It is one of the true revolutionary ideas of the past one hundred years and is still widely in use today. Everyone knows the drill: beat your forecast, your stock goes up, you get promoted. Miss it and watch out.

But when I first read this story, what went through my head was: You're telling me that . . .

once upon a time . . .

people made forecasts . . .

and they *came true*?

And, not only that, the forecasts were so accurate that they could be used as a fair system for deciding who gets promoted and who doesn't? As an entrepreneur, I had never experienced such a thing.

The startups I had always worked on and got to know in Silicon Valley couldn't make accurate forecasts because they had no operating history at all. Because their product was unknown, their market was unknown—and in some cases, even the functionality of the technology itself was unknown—accurate forecasting was entirely impossible.[5]

Nevertheless, startups make forecasts, too—just not accurate ones.

Early in my career, I knew why *I* had always made a forecast for my businesses: you can't raise money for a startup without one. I assumed forecasting was a kind of *kabuki* ritual where entrepreneurs prove to investors how tough they are by showing how much spreadsheet pain they can endure. It was a fantasy exercise driven by our desire to show an outcome remotely plausible for an idea that was—usually, at that point—totally unproven.

Eventually, though, I found out that some investors actually *believed* the forecast. They would even try to use it as a tool of accountability—just like Alfred Sloan. If a startup failed to match the numbers in the original business plan, the investors would take this as a sign of poor execution. As an entrepreneur, I found this reaction baffling. Didn't they know that those numbers were entirely made up?

Later in my career, I befriended more managers in traditional corporate jobs who were trying to drive innovation. The more corporate innovators I met, the more I heard about how much faith their bosses put in forecasts as a tool for holding people accountable—even senior managers who (I thought) surely would know better. The "fantasy plan" of the original pitch is often far too optimistic to be used as a real forecast. But managers, lacking any other system to use, need something to hold on to. Without an alternative, they cling to the forecast—even if it's just made up.

You've probably started to sense the problem here: An older system of accountability, designed in a very different time and for a very different context, is still being used in situations where it doesn't work. Sometimes, failure to hit the forecast means a team executed poorly. But sometimes it means the forecast itself was a fantasy. How can we tell the difference?

HOW DO WE DEAL WITH FAILURE?

No doubt you've heard of Six Sigma, one of the most famous corporate transformations in management history. Introduced to GE in 1995 by CEO Jack Welch, Six Sigma is a process to develop and deliver near-perfect products. *Sigma* is a statistical term measuring how far a given process deviates from perfection. To achieve Six Sigma Quality, a process must produce no more than 3.4 defects per million opportunities, i.e., it must be defective less than 0.0000034 percent of the time. Welch introduced the process to GE with the goal of achieving Six Sigma Quality across the company within five years, stating, "Quality can truly change GE from one of the great companies to absolutely the greatest company in world business."[6]

As I traveled around GE training executives, a lot of questions arose, from both fans and skeptics of Six Sigma, as to whether FastWorks was to be GE's next "big thing." Did it render past Six Sigma training obsolete? If FastWorks was meant to work alongside Six Sigma, how would you know when to use which? Were there certifications and levels to Lean Startup knowledge akin to the colored belts of Six Sigma?

One day, as I was meeting with a Six Sigma black belt from one of GE's industrial businesses—who was quite skeptical— I found myself distracted by the mug on his desk, which read: FAILURE IS NOT AN OPTION. Nobody in the startup world could have such a mug, I mused; it would be ridiculous. My experience is full of situations where reality proved too unpredictable to avoid failure.

I thought of the best, most successful entrepreneurs I know. What would their mug say? I settled on: I EAT FAILURE FOR BREAKFAST.

The tension between those two slogans is a great starting point for understanding not only why startups have had such a hard time adopting traditional management methods, and vice versa—but also what connects them. There was a time when producing high-quality products on time, on budget, and at scale was one of the preeminent problems of the age. Understanding how to build quality into products from the inside out required mastering the new statistical science of variation, and then devising tools, methodologies, and training programs that could make doing so practical. Standardization, mass production, lean manufacturing, and Six Sigma are all fruits of this hard-won conceptual victory.

Baked into these methods is a presupposition that failure can be prevented through diligent preparation, planning, and execution. But the startup part of the management portfolio challenges this assumption. If some projects fail to meet their projections because the underlying uncertainty was extremely high, how do we hold those leaders accountable?

CHANGING HOW COMPANIES "GROW UP"

Aditya Agarwal, who worked at Facebook in the company's early years when it grew from ten people to about 2,500, is now VP of engineering at Dropbox. He sees the entrepreneurial dilemma this way:

> One of the reasons it's hard to build new things at larger companies is because people don't have the mental model of "My job is to actually learn new things." A lot of the mental model is you get really good at doing something and then you are supposed to keep on doing that. Yes, there's incremental learning, but it's more about perfecting your craft as opposed to bootstrapping your craft. Even companies that seem to have launched one good product won't easily know how to do it again.

You'd think that an innovative, hot startup like Dropbox, which was founded in 2007 and as of this writing has a $10 billion valuation, 500 million users, and roughly 1,500 employees worldwide,[7] would easily avoid the problem of replicating an old-fashioned structure, right? After all, it came into the marketplace with a product no one even knew they needed and blew up in a big way.

But it, too, has run into some of the problems we typically as-

sociate with traditional, more established companies. Why? Because over the course of its tremendous, and tremendously fast,
growth, the company was built to a familiar blueprint. It lost
some of the first principles of product thinking that made its
initial success possible. Its launches of two new flagship products,
Mailbox and Carousel, were, in Agarwal's words, "disappoint-
ing. There wasn't the massive scale we wanted and we ended up
having to sunset them."

The reasons for these failures were familiar. Says Agarwal,
"We did not get enough pertinent user feedback. We were building and building but not listening enough."

The difference between Dropbox and more established, legacy
companies, was that at the company's core, there remained the
original understanding of the best ways in which to test, market,
and grow ideas. "It was the most painful experience the company
has gone through," Agarwal says, "but also the most rewarding
and important one. It taught us so many things about what we
were doing wrong building new products. It's important that you
accept the pain and do all the postmortems and you learn from
it. And that's how you get better and stronger."

After adopting a series of changes, some of which I'll detail
in a later chapter, they released Dropbox Paper, a new feature for
communicating and collaborating on the platform that draws on
what they learned from previous attempts. It launched globally
and in twenty-one languages in January of 2017.

As Dropbox director of product Todd Jackson puts it, "It's a
different discipline to launch brand-new products." The aware-
ness of the need to both protect and grow an existing product
while also being able to experiment with new ones in this way is
critical to success in the twenty-first century, and a hallmark of a
modern company.

RESPECT THE PAST, INVENT THE FUTURE   31

THE LEADERS' ROLE

A few years ago, I was answering questions in a town hall–style meeting at a "unicorn"[8] startup—a private company valued at over $1 billion—that had quickly grown to over a thousand employees. Although the company was only a few years old and their technology cutting edge, their management practices were decidedly traditional. The town hall mostly focused on these basic questions: What happened to our startup DNA? Why have our velocity and agility dropped so much recently? And what can we do to get them back?

Afterward, the founder came to me with her frustrations and described her dilemma this way: A team had come to her with an idea they wanted to try out. Though she now sits at the helm of a large organization, she's an entrepreneur at heart. So she gave the team some funding, sent them on their way, and got back to the day-to-day work of managing the company. The new team updated her periodically, like every other team did, and all seemed to be going well. Six months later, she decided to walk over to take a look at what this team was working on, only to discover that they hadn't shipped anything. There were no customers yet, and the product was only half done and way more complicated than it was supposed to be.

The team had a million excuses about what had happened— lack of resources, the need to anticipate twelve other problems that might come up in the future and build the infrastructure that would support them, etc. It was a classic case of scope creep, as the team added more and more "essential" features to their product. The founder couldn't understand what had gone wrong. Why hadn't anyone said anything? Why didn't her team see this as a disaster? The answer was that they weren't being held accountable in a way that genuinely showed progress (or lack thereof).

This gave me the opportunity to ask the founder what her own early investors would have said if she'd made any of these same excuses. "Would they have flown, or would someone have said, 'That's great, but you don't have time to do twelve things. You have time to do one thing well. You don't have the resources to build all this extra stuff. You need to build what you actually need right now. You can make all these excuses about not having customers, but not having customers is like not having oxygen. You can't survive.'"

It was an odd moment. The CEO and founder was accustomed to thinking of herself as the plucky protagonist in the classic entrepreneurial story. Investors and advisors were just the supporting cast. But now she had to learn to see herself as an investor in the entrepreneurs that worked for her. She was the person in charge of building a program to support their efforts and give them the milestones and mechanisms to demonstrate the results of their work, and she hadn't done it. Looking at it from this new perspective, she realized that she had to reinterpret her role. Once she did, we had an exciting conversation about who the entrepreneurs in her company were and how she could empower them.

PROFITING FROM FAILURE AT AMAZON

Some companies, of course, are already working this way: They're the ones who are most successful in today's economy, and it's because they know how to think long-term even as they're acting rapidly and measuring results as they go. Think of the Amazon Fire phone. Over the course of four years, the project went from an idea detailed in an aspirational mocked-up press release to almost universal disappointment after its launch in the summer of 2014. Initially priced at $199, the Fire soon cost only $0.99, and by the following winter, the company took a $170 million write-down based mostly on unsold phones.[9] Where a more traditional company might have fired people and destroyed morale, Amazon used this opportunity to learn and reorganize. As Jeff Bezos said at the time:

> I've made billions of dollars of failures at Amazon.com. Literally. None of these things are fun, but they also don't matter. What matters is that companies that don't continue to experiment or embrace failure eventually get in the position where the only thing they can do is make a Hail Mary bet at the end of their corporate existence. I don't believe in bet-the-company bets.

Instead of shutting down Lab126 (the team that designed the Fire) and letting the people who'd created the Fire phone go, Amazon moved them to other projects: tablets, the Echo, the Alexa voice-activated assistant, and many things still to come.[10] At the same time, outside of the new-product space, the company was getting into food delivery, original television, and its own line of baby products. "There are many ways of thinking about this, but the reality is that Amazon is a collection of several businesses and initiatives," Bezos said that year. "It's kind of like we built this lemonade stand twenty years ago, and the lemonade stand has become very profitable over time, but we also decided to use our skills and the assets we've acquired to open a hamburger stand, a hot dog stand—we're investing in new initiatives."[11]

Even in situations where you can't forecast, you can still plan. Whatever the Fire's original business plan was, it surely didn't predict what happened. But the phone was built with an assumption of risk that created space for the company's reaction when it didn't play out as expected. It's that long-term vision—the understanding that the lemonade itself might end up not being a long-term bestseller, but instead some other bet might be—that allows the creation of a portfolio of experiments.

A FOCUS ON LEGACY

Most companies are struggling to come to grips with this new reality. Not because these organizations aren't filled with smart, ambitious people, but because they lack the tools to make proper use of them.

For most leaders in established companies this requires new skills. This is true even of leaders who themselves are accomplished entrepreneurs, because it involves embracing a new role. It's a surreal experience that involves unlearning habits and patterns that helped them earlier in their careers.

When I talk to leaders going through this transition, there is one concept I have found the most helpful: legacy. Most of us have inherited the organization where we work from a prior generation of leaders. This is true in governments and global companies like GE, but it's also true for almost anyone who is not the original founder of the organization where they work. So we have to ask ourselves: Do we want to leave behind an organization to the next generation of managers that is stronger than the one we inherited? What do we want our legacy to be?

Nor is this question just for older, established companies. One of my favorite stories about Sheryl Sandberg, Facebook's dynamic COO, comes from a company meeting in which employees were complaining about the "unfairness" of having their performance evaluated based on the success of the projects they had worked on, rather than just their individual contribution to those projects.

Sandberg acknowledged these concerns, but her reply has

stuck with me for years. She asked the employees to imagine a favorite company of theirs that had been disrupted. Kodak, say, or RIM. Imagine all the employees of that doomed company, in the months and years leading up to the disruption. Think of all the people who got positive reviews, got promoted, got paid bonuses for their excellent functional contribution—all while the company went down to ignoble defeat. Do you really want to be one of those managers?

The more senior the managers I speak to, the more resonant this question becomes. Many of them have already enjoyed a great deal of professional and financial success—that's how they became senior leaders in the first place. And although they still have drive and ambition to do more, they are also able to see their work through the longer-term lens of the organization's history.

The end goal of this process is to create a true synthesis: a new, modern way of thinking about organizations and leadership that can become the basis for twenty-first-century growth and innovation. In service to this goal, it would be crazy to throw away the hard-won managerial lessons of the past. It would be even crazier to allow ourselves to be trapped in rote conformance to past ideology in the face of change and disruption. Instead, it's time to start building on them.

THE MISSING SYSTEM

The first time I received a meeting invitation from Toyota, I have to admit, I was a little nervous. To someone who writes about lean processes, Toyota possesses near-mythical status, as that's where lean principles were first employed at scale. I called the theory I wrote about in 2011 "the Lean Startup" as a conscious homage to the intellectual debt I owe to Toyota and the previous generation of lean thinkers (a debt that continues through this volume, which owes its title to Jeffrey Liker's magisterial *The Toyota Way*). I hoped in *The Lean Startup* to show how lean ideas could be applied in a new domain—the entrepreneurial soil of extreme uncertainty—and find new relevance for a new generation of managers. (If you're not familiar with *The Lean Startup*, don't worry; we'll review its major conclusions in Chapter 4.)

Given Toyota's legendary status and business performance, it would have been perfectly understandable for them to reject *The Lean Startup* as something "not invented here." Certainly my lack of a manufacturing background or formal training in "the Toyota way" might have given them pause. But in the open culture at Toyota, these issues never came up. As we worked together, several early adopters within the company revealed why they thought Lean Startup could be beneficial when added to Toyota Production System (TPS).

Toyota has become world-leading in its ability to mass-produce high-quality products on time, on budget, and with industry-leading cost. The company has had some very successful innovations, like the Prius hybrid drive technology, but at the time of my meeting, they had not had the same level of success incorporating digital platform–style innovations into their products. As consumer preferences and autonomous vehicle technology both evolve, this threatens to become a company-defining vulnerability.

In getting the original project approved (you'll learn more about it in Chapter 6), I met with leaders up and down the corporate hierarchy, culminating in a sit-down with one of Toyota's most senior leaders, Shigeki Tomoyama (who at the time was the chief officer of the IT and ITS groups). Like many Toyota leaders, he spends much of his time on the road going to "see for himself" what is happening across the company's sprawling empire. I'm sure you can picture the scene when he came to meet with me. In the typical Japanese way, he traveled with a large entourage. I, and a few other Americans from the small branch office of the company who were my counterparts, sat across the table. I honestly didn't know how the meeting would go.

We spoke at great length and in great detail about *The Lean Startup* and about how it might apply at Toyota. Clearly, somebody in the entourage had read it—it had just been translated into Japanese. But Tomoyama-san himself did not speak at first; I couldn't read his body language to tell what he thought.

When he finally broke his silence, he said something I will never forget: "This is the missing half of the Toyota Production System. We have a system that is outstanding at producing what we specify, with high quality, but we don't have a corresponding system for discovering what to produce in the first place." He explained that Toyota had become so advanced in its ability to efficiently produce existing products that it had lost something of its early innovative spirit. Certainly the company had a method for discovering new ideas, but it was in need of improvement and integration with the company as a whole. To say I was honored by this comparison would be an understatement.

A modern company is one that has both halves, both systems. It has a capacity to produce products with great reliability and quality, but also to discover what new products to produce.

A TRULY MODERN COMPANY

So given all of this, how would you know a modern company if you saw it? And more important, what can we as leaders do to bring it about?

A modern company is one in which every employee has the opportunity to be an entrepreneur. It respects its employees and their ideas at a fundamental level.

A modern company is disciplined at the rigorous execution

of its core business—without discipline, no innovation is possible—but it also employs a complementary set of entrepreneurial management tools for dealing with situations of extreme uncertainty.

AN OLD-FASHIONED COMPANY is founded on steady growth through prescriptive management and controls, and is subject to tremendous pressure to perform in short-term intervals such as quarterly reports.
A MODERN COMPANY is founded on sustained impact via continuous innovation, and focused on long-term results.

———

AN OLD-FASHIONED COMPANY is made up of experts in specialized functional silos, between which work passes in a stage-gate or waterfall process that sends projects from function to function with specific milestones tied to each handover.
A MODERN COMPANY is made up of cross-functional teams that work together to serve customers through highly iterative and scientific processes.

———

AN OLD-FASHIONED COMPANY tends to operate huge programs.
A MODERN COMPANY operates rapid experiments.

———

AN OLD-FASHIONED COMPANY uses internal functions such as legal, IT, and finance to mitigate risk through compliance with detailed procedures.
A MODERN COMPANY uses internal functions to help its employees meet their goal of serving customers, sharing the responsibility to drive business results.

AN OLD-FASHIONED COMPANY prioritizes even highly uncertain projects based on ROI, traditional accounting, and market share. To measure success, project teams track and share numbers designed to look as good as possible ("vanity metrics")—but not necessarily to reveal the truth.

A MODERN COMPANY attempts to maximize the probability and scale of future *impact*. Project teams report and measure leading indicators using *innovation accounting*. In a for-profit context, this goal often follows Jeff Bezos's advice to "focus on long-term growth in free cash-flow per share" rather than traditional accounting measures.[12]

AN OLD-FASHIONED COMPANY is full of multitasking: meetings and deliberations where participants are only partly focused on the task at hand. There are lots of middle managers and experts in the room to give their input, even if they don't have direct responsibility for implementation. And most employees are dividing their creativity and focus across many different kinds of projects at the same time.

A MODERN COMPANY has a new tool in its arsenal: the internal startup, filled with a small number of passionate believers dedicated to one project at a time. Like Amazon's famous "two-pizza team"—no larger than you can feed with two pizzas—these small teams are able to experiment rapidly and scale their impact. Their ethos: "Think big. Start small. Scale fast."

AN OLD-FASHIONED COMPANY is composed of managers and their subordinates.

A MODERN COMPANY is composed of leaders and the entrepreneurs they empower.

———

AN OLD-FASHIONED COMPANY tends to pursue big projects that are expensive and slow to develop in order to make sure they're "right," using a system of *entitlement funding* that remains similar from year to year.

A MODERN COMPANY pursues a portfolio of smart experiments and contains the cost of failure by investing more in the ones that work, using a system of *metered funding* that increases as success is proved.

———

AN OLD-FASHIONED COMPANY is one in which efficiency means everyone is busy all the time, making it easy to "achieve failure" by efficiently building the wrong thing.

A MODERN COMPANY is one in which efficiency means figuring out the right thing to do for customers by whatever means necessary.

———

AN OLD-FASHIONED COMPANY believes that "failure is not an option," and managers are skilled at pretending it never happens by hiding it. They may pay lip service to the idea of "embracing failure," but their reward, promotion, and evaluation systems send a profoundly different message.

A MODERN COMPANY rewards *productive failures* that lead to smart changes in direction and provide useful information.

———

AN OLD-FASHIONED COMPANY is protected from competition via barriers to entry.

A MODERN COMPANY leaves competitors in the dust through continuous innovation.

If you study this list of differences, you will notice a number of paradoxes. Overall, even among old-fashioned companies that are focused on short-term results (such as quarterly reports), most initiatives are impossibly slow, are risk averse, and invest on an all-or-nothing basis. Modern management requires a long-term philosophy coupled with extremely rapid experimentation to discover which strategies will support a long-term vision.

## CHAPTER 2

ENTREPRENEURSHIP: THE MISSING FUNCTION

LET'S TRY A thought experiment. Imagine for a moment what companies must have been like before the advent of marketing as a recognized discipline. There were no chief marketing officers, no product marketing or brand managers as we recognize them. There was no way to get promoted on the strength of your marketing skills alone. Back then, everyone—and so, in truth, no one—was responsible for what we now call marketing: advertising, sales collateral, even product management.

There's a reason why marketing is now considered an essential component of virtually every organization. It demands excellence, and somebody needs to be in charge of it. The same goes for every other vital function: engineering, finance, IT, supply chain, HR, legal.

In the typical organizational structure, who's in charge of grappling with uncertainty, unlocking unexpected and dramatic new forms of growth and impact, translating research insights into viable products, and harnessing the forces of disruption in the organization? For small organizations, it is clearly the founders. But once an organization grows large enough, the honest answer usually is: nobody.

But even if there was somebody, what, exactly, would that person be in charge of? The lack of a system for acting on new ideas is a huge problem for existing corporations that have had decades—sometimes longer—to become encumbered by layers of bureaucracy or hampered by burdensome "this is how we've always done it" practices. But the problem is also not all that uncommon in hypergrowth startups. At the end of their incredible expansion, the original employees, who personally lived through the early stages of the company's development, are vastly outnumbered by the employees who did not—often by a factor of five or ten to one. Imagine where all those hundreds or thousands of new employees used to work. How many, do you think, were part of the extremely early stages of another successful startup? The law of large numbers says very few.

So by growing and hiring, successful startups inadvertently but inevitably transfuse an enormous amount of big company DNA into their company. Then comes the challenge of reorienting these people into a startup culture. And what tools do they have at their disposal? Training, compensation, team structure, physical environment—all the trappings of a traditional organization.

THE ENTREPRENEURIAL FUNCTION

When I meet with CEOs, I often ask them: Who in your organization is responsible right now for the following two things?

1. Overseeing high-potential growth initiatives that could one day become new divisions of the company.

2. Infusing everyday work across the organization with an entrepreneurial, experimental, iterative mindset.

Rarely do those responsibilities show up on the org chart. At best, they are a not-exactly-top-priority commitment of one of the existing functional managers (often engineering, marketing, or IT) or, even worse, they are "everybody's responsibility." Nobody is waking up every day determined to invest in the next generation of entrepreneurial leaders, fight off the forces of disruption or harness them for new growth, and ensure that every person in the organization is seen as a resource for potential new ideas.

So it's time to move beyond these half-hearted measures and to see entrepreneurship as a core discipline of a modern company. It has the singular role of being the overseer of the organization's "startup DNA"—infusing an entrepreneurial mindset and techniques into the whole organization in order to invest in the next generation of innovations on a continuous basis.

Many employees and managers of many functions are trained in the tools and procedures of, for example, finance—like basic budgeting or financial modeling. And finance has an important role in setting the standards that all teams must use to report progress or ask for resources. In most organizations, finance is not in charge of making resource-allocation decisions directly. That's left to the executives at corporate HQ. But the finance folks are responsible for determining how the process unfolds: what information is considered important, how progress is evaluated, and how resources are allocated.

One day entrepreneurship will operate similarly—as a dedicated function with its own career-path of *corporate entrepreneurs,* and also as a source of widespread basic knowledge, responsible for spreading entrepreneurial methods throughout the organization.

As we'll see, great entrepreneurs can (and should) come from anywhere and everywhere within the organization. Great ideas sometimes appear in unexpected places. So the entrepreneurial function has to be integrated into the fabric of the organization very carefully.

Modern companies need something more than just another innovation lab. They need something more than R&D and prototyping, something distinct from the secretive skunkworks projects of old. They need the ability to consistently and reliably make bets on high-risk, high-reward projects without having to bet the whole company. And they need to find, train, and retain the kinds of leaders who can pull this off. After witnessing and working with many companies, large and small, grappling with this, I believe we should simply call this function "entrepreneurship."

Startup as Atomic Unit of Work

The first responsibility of the entrepreneurship function is *to oversee the company's internal startups.* The company's leaders need to understand the startup as an *atomic unit of work,* distinct from other kinds of project teams that companies typically employ. Not everything a modern company does is best managed by a startup. It is, however, the organizational form that performs best in the context of extreme uncertainty. Because the types of projects that startups spearhead are best understood as experiments, internal startups must blend the scientific rigor of R&D, the customer-centered focus of sales and marketing, and the process discipline of engineering. Is it any wonder they don't have a logical home in the traditional org chart?

Not only that, but the entrepreneurs who lead these startups require a distinct career path with its own performance development standards of best practices and metrics for success, including mentorship in the high-impact techniques that accelerate growth. Figuring this out has been part of the secret sauce of Silicon Valley.[1]

Integrate Startups into the Parent Organization

The second responsibility of the entrepreneurial function is to *manage the problem of success*. Although I acknowledge the fact that most startups fail, the hardest part for most organizations is knowing what to do when they succeed. A startup within an established organization that is limping along is only moderately threatening to the established order. But a startup that is having real success is more dangerous. Whatever exceptions were made to allow the organization's existing middle managers to go along with the creation of this new experiment will come under tremendous strain during this process.

When I meet innovation lab directors, rarely do they have a plan for this scenario. And because the backlash can come swiftly (and fatally), it's not adequate to cross that bridge when we come to it. Establishing the metrics that define success, creating "islands of freedom" with appropriate (and scalable) liability constraints, and convincing senior leadership to adopt this new approach each involve difficult negotiations that require professional and full-time attention. Fundamentally, the question is: For any experiment that succeeds, how will it find a home in the organization? Will it be absorbed by an existing division or become an entirely new division? How is that decided? Whose decision is it? (Each of these topics will be covered in detail in Part Two.)

Here is one way of visualizing what is happening when a startup experiment is launched within a larger company. Every division needs a way to test, refine, and scale new ideas in order

IDEAS ARE VALIDATED, ADOPTED, AND SCALED

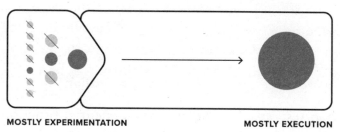

MOSTLY EXPERIMENTATION   **MOSTLY EXECUTION**

The path of one internal startup over time, within a division. It begins as part of a cohort of seed-stage experiments and, over time, grows. As many of its peers die for lack of traction, it continues. Over more time, the ratio of experimentation to execution shifts, until the startup is dominated by execution activities. Then and only then can the parent division take over full responsibility for managing it.

to innovate and grow. But ideas by themselves are worthless. They are valuable only when embedded within a dedicated team that can relentlessly pursue them, stay true to the vision of the experiment while being flexible enough to pivot when necessary (see Chapter 4), and ultimately discover their true full potential.

A number of thinkers have been beating the drum for a few years now that entrepreneurial management is distinct from general management.[2] But this leads to a common confusion: that these distinct forms of management can be kept in isolation from each other and operate separately. They cannot.

A tiny startup with a brand-new product is at one end of the experimentation-execution continuum. A mature division that is producing steady, quarter-over-quarter growth with an existing product is on the extreme other end.

But even a newly created startup has to execute. Even a startup with only ten customers has to start asking itself how much energy to invest in serving existing customers versus acquiring new ones. And the laws of corporate gravity still apply: The scarcity of resources most startups deal with argues for more, not less, financial discipline.

Similarly, even the stodgiest product team will be doing *some* experimentation and *some* innovation, a point the author of *The Innovator's Dilemma*, Clayton Christensen, has been trying to make for years. In most cases, good business practices will cause missed opportunities, because in order to serve existing customers well, companies don't want to do anything too radical. The team may be trapped by this dilemma and unable to produce something truly disruptive, but it is engaged in "sustaining innovations" that may still be quite radical in their own way.[3]

THE FLOW OF IDEAS IN THE MODERN COMPANY

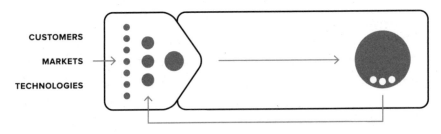

IDEAS FROM EXECUTING PRODUCT TEAMS

Thus, every organizational unit is more properly understood as a *portfolio* that contains some mix of experimentation and execution. As startups mature, the ratio between the two naturally changes. But it also changes when existing organizations reinvest in their own startup DNA. This has implications for the flow of ideas throughout the company, as well. Internal startups may well grow to become established lines of business or even entirely new divisions. But the innovation teams within established lines of business are also an important source of new ideas that can be tested. In this way, entrepreneurial management provides a systematic counterforce to the innovator's dilemma and other forms of corporate inertia.

But this hybrid portfolio within an existing company leads to a new problem, which is . . .

It Requires a New Leadership Style

Let's be honest. Entrepreneurs are not the easiest people in the world to manage. Even the best entrepreneurs I know struggle to create an environment that *other* entrepreneurs would want to join. And everyone struggles with the basic question of how to tell the difference between an entrepreneur and a renegade who simply lacks the discipline and commitment to follow rules.

Traditional management tools are focused on planning and forecasting, so we've developed outstanding measures for identifying managers who thrive in that environment. We have programs for high-potential managers. We have detailed training in leadership, product management, and sales. We have rotation programs for cross-training. And, increasingly, we are turning our attention to global challenges, valuing international exposure and experience in developing a well-rounded manager. *But how do we do all this for entrepreneurs?* How do we identify them? And how do we manage them?

Entrepreneurship Is Not Only for Products

It's natural, at this point, to think of an internal startup as being solely about creating new products, and of the "missing function" in companies as being strictly analogous to conventional functions such as engineering or marketing. That would give rise to an org chart that looks roughly like this:

This is a good place to start—but it's by no means the whole story. As we'll see throughout *The Startup Way*, there are a surprising number of other hidden startups tucked away within most organizations. (We'll revisit this org chart a few more times, in Chapter 5 and Chapter 10.) The org-chart diagrams throughout this book assume an organization that is managed as a matrix—with both separate functions and divisions operating simultaneously. But that is simply a convenient shorthand.

I've seen this approach work in organizations with a wide array of formal structures, including straight functional management (with no separate divisions or P&L responsibility) as well as true portfolio conglomerates, where corporate HQ is relatively small and each division owns its own functional structures. (And don't even get me started on the structure of the U.S. federal civil service.) The point is not the formal structure but that the responsibilities outlined in this chapter are located somewhere.

But this also points to another difficulty. The entrepreneurial function is not "just another function"—because it also impacts and supports the other functions in doing their work more effectively. It requires a level of integration with the company and its culture that is uniquely challenging even compared to other difficult corporate transformations. And this boundary-blurring behavior is just the beginning of the story, because . . .

Entrepreneurship Is Not Just for Entrepreneurs

I am an engineer by training, so, of course, I believe strongly in the importance of well-defined terms and their rigorous application. Still, it took me many years of struggle to accept this final point as something that is an essential part of entrepreneurial management. Every company that I have watched do this work begins by seeing entrepreneurship as something special that only certain people in the organization need to be concerned with. Perhaps it's only a few pilot product teams, as with FastWorks, or a few internal change initiatives, like the Presidential Innovation Fellows program created by the Obama administration to bring private-sector technologists and innovators into government for short periods of time, which I'll describe shortly. But, over time, the definition starts to expand. More varied kinds of projects are added. More functions get involved. And, eventually, everyone winds up realizing that part of the benefit of this new way of working is the impact it can have on the non-entrepreneurs in the organization.

Over my explicit (but, as it turned out, incorrect) objections, many of the companies I've worked with have insisted on using the same terminology to refer to two totally different things: first, the type of projects that embody the idea of the startup as "atomic unit of work" (as in FastWorks projects or other kinds of internal startups within a larger organization), and second, the idea that everyone in the company can act like an entrepreneur and use the tools of entrepreneurship to do their jobs more effectively (through initiatives like GE's FastWorks Everyday program, which you'll learn more about in Chapter 8). I even recounted the story in *The Lean Startup* about Intuit CEO Brad Smith telling the entire company: "This way of working applies to each and every one of us." Yet it has taken me some time to realize the implications of this statement.

Despite my initial resistance, I have come around to this way of thinking, having seen it work up close several times. Ultimately, the non-entrepreneurs are just as important customers of the entrepreneurial function as the entrepreneurs themselves, for three reasons:

1. Lean Startup–style tools are incredibly useful in a wide range of applications that don't have the *extreme* uncertainty of a new product but still have some uncertainty. I've heard dozens of stories from people who were tangentially involved in Lean Startup training who subsequently used some of the techniques on seemingly minor projects—sometimes as humble as creating a PowerPoint presentation for their boss—to great effect. Experimentation is just a generally useful tool.

2. Non-startup managers need to know what is going on. This

is critically important, because there is no way around the fact that entrepreneurs cause trouble! They foment conflict. Many internal startups are intentionally designed to challenge existing biases or sacred cows. This conflict will always—always!—wind up climbing the chain of command. Even if the startup's immediate manager has been trained in the Startup Way, what about all the other managers above her or him?

3. You never know who the entrepreneurs are going to be. We'll see this idea again in the next chapter, but startup-style meritocracy is a little different than what most people are used to. Even if you wanted to design a program that was only for entrepreneurs, it would be impossible to do so. What makes someone an entrepreneur is not that she or he got assigned that role by someone at corporate HQ. Good ideas come from unexpected places.

In fact, one of the lessons of the rise of startup accelerators like Y Combinator (YC) and Techstars is that they achieved their disproportionate impact on the world, in part, by bringing new people into the entrepreneurial ecosystem. This is one of the most striking things about reading the early YC applications in particular. Many of the founders of multibillion-dollar startups weren't sure they were cut out for entrepreneurship at all. By lowering the barriers to getting started, providing a low-risk way to try it out, and effective role modeling, YC has been able to bring unexpected talent into the ecosystem.[4]

In order for an organization to take advantage of the latent entrepreneurial talent within it, it has to invest in making the broad pool of its employee base aware of the possibilities of entrepreneurship as a career path. It needs to embrace the notion that meritocracy means that good ideas truly can originate at any level of the organization, not only among white-collar employees or people from certain backgrounds. I have seen evidence of it on the factory floor as well as in the executive suite. The organization must eradicate the many forms of bias that prevent people from bringing their ideas forward or from having their ideas taken seriously. It must invest in systems and processes so that employees know what to do the moment a brainstorm strikes. And, since most ideas are actually bad, it must give employees the platforms for experimentation to discover this on their own.

One of the key responsibilities of the entrepreneurial function is to weave startup thinking into the cultural fabric of the organization, taking in new recruits from all backgrounds and levels. It's because of this wide-ranging mandate that the Startup Way transformation inevitably winds up focusing on ways to make the company more meritocratic: eliminating bias, encouraging more scientific decision making, and inspiring better resource allocation and HR policies.

We'll return to these wide-ranging ideas of who is an entrepreneur in later chapters, especially Chapter 10. But, for now, I want to focus on the present reality facing most companies. Paradoxically, at the very moment in history when they critically need entrepreneurial talent, they are deeply confused about where to find it. Most organizations are replete with entrepreneurs already, but not only are they unable to recognize them, they inadvertently force them into hiding. Most companies are more likely to fire those who show entrepreneurial initiative than to promote them.

THE UNDERGROUND NETWORK

Every company has people who are willing to take risks to serve the customer better without regard for their own popularity. Rather than being rule breakers or lacking in regard for compliance, they're simply people who are prepared to figure out which of the company's policies really help serve the customer and to work around the ones that don't.

At GE, one of these people, Cory Nelson, was in charge of the very first FastWorks project we did, the Series X engine. Nelson was the GM for the Series X program for GE Distributed Power at the time, and he dove into the challenge with gusto. He didn't care at all that no one had gone before him—he just wanted to focus on what positive things might result. Or, as he puts it: "I'm attracted to shiny objects. I like new stuff, so I wouldn't have done this thing had I not."

Beth Comstock had known for years that people like Nelson existed. She just had no formal way of helping them thrive. "I think there are always people in the organization who just get it intuitively," she says. "They're just waiting to be unleashed. You don't know where they are, but once you give them the opportunity and the tools to focus them, they just are on fire." Another person in this category was Michael Mahan, a product manager in GE's appliances business.[5] He referred to his team, which was experimenting with 3-D printing and getting exceptions to standard protocols to test new refrigerators, as "the crazy kids in the corner." In Comstock's eyes, though, he was something much more valuable: "We had this Imagination Breakthrough program for the better part of a decade, and any time there was a good idea that bubbled up, he usually had some kind of fingerprint on it." The question was how to make his talents a regular part of the work he did at GE, rather than an occasional flash of brilliance that burned out quickly.

Even the federal government found it had similar creative people, and they were the foundation of a technological transformation that began when President Obama took office and is still going on. It included not only the rescue of HealthCare.gov, the site launched to facilitate the Affordable Care Act in 2013, which immediately melted down, but also the creation of new organizations within the government like the United States Digital Service and the Technology Transformation Service (all of which you'll read more about in later chapters).

These people exist in every organization—including yours. They're the people who are willing to say, "My peers think I'm nuts to be willing to get assigned to this project, but I believe in it." They're the employees that managers know to call when things look like they might go off the rails—or already have. On the outside, they look like everyone else, moving along the promotion chain and doing their jobs well. But they're also part of a kind of underground network that can be tapped for unusual projects from time to time. Frequently, when they do get the green light on a project, they wade in with little or no support from their peers or the organization as a whole.

Every manager I meet knows who to call if they get saddled with a high-risk, high-reward project. They know who's willing to risk career suicide to give it a shot. And so the question I ask them is: What if? What if we were to give these creative, energetic people a structure for working intelligently on the kinds of projects they want to work on, and then we reward them and recognize them for that skill? The promise of adding entrepreneurship as a function is the chance to create an environment where experimentation is encouraged, where ideas can be tested and then assimilated into the culture, where the passion to pursue the unexpected is not marginalized but systematized, not stymied but supported.

Without fail, enlightened managers see the potential in that idea. What they need to know is how to put it into practice.

THE MISSING ORGANIZATIONAL CAPABILITIES

To support this way of working, we must solve a series of puzzling challenges that require a new set of organizational capabilities.

1. How do we create space for experiments with appropriate liability constraints?

These preordained constraints create an "island of freedom" or "sandbox" in which to experiment without letting autonomous teams rack up unlimited liability. In Lean Startup, we call these limited-liability experiments *minimum viable products* (MVPs). We'll discuss the details of what makes a good MVP in Chapters 4 and 6. For now, I want to focus on the leadership challenge of giving teams the freedom to create experiments while still holding them to strong accountability standards.

When I talk to leaders (founders, especially) about islands of freedom, I ask them to recall how empowering it is for them to control a budget and make key decisions in their companies without asking for permission. Then I encourage them to ask themselves, "How do I pass that experience along? How can I become the curator of the entrepreneurial experience for other people?"

Entrepreneurs, contrary to the common caricature, aren't all reckless. The best entrepreneurs have the ability to work within constraints. In an early-stage company, where resources are scarce, constraints emerge naturally: only so many people or so much money or a certain number of months to get something done. In a bigger company, those constraints need to be created more consciously. Consider your typical product management meeting. There's really no substitute for being able to say: "Listen, we only have enough cash to stay in business for another six weeks. I know there are lot of things we'd love to be able to do, but if we don't make at least one of these things work before then, we're doomed."[6] It sounds stressful—and it is!—but it's also liberating. It's the highest-productivity way of working I've ever seen. It's one of the only environments in which there is a countervailing force constantly working against scope creep.

2. How do we fund projects without knowing the return on investment (ROI) in advance?

As we'll see repeatedly throughout this book, breakthrough projects almost always look like toys or downright bad ideas at first. But then again, so do most genuinely bad ideas! Learning to make investments on the basis of evidence, experimentation, and vision—without wasting money on vanity projects—is an extremely difficult yet profoundly important skill.

3. How do we create appropriate milestones for teams that are operating autonomously?

How do we define success and milestones if we are appropriately humble about our ability to predict the future? Without accurate forecasts, many of our traditional management tools no longer function. As we'll see in the next chapter, startup investors have long struggled with this curse. Ideally, investors would like to know, in advance, what they are going to get out of each round of financing. For example, after a traditional venture capital-backed "series A" investment, we'd like to know that a startup will have its new product launched, a million customers, and $10 million in recurring revenue.

But, in real life, this rarely happens. Usually, some—but not all—of the milestones are hit. Maybe the startup really does launch its product, but the customers it thought would gravitate to the first version weren't interested. Perhaps it has very passionate early adopters in a different market segment. Perhaps gross revenues are a lot lower than forecast, but revenue per customer is a lot higher than expected. In this ambiguous situation, what do we do?

Corporate finance professionals, generally speaking, have been trained to withdraw funding from teams that miss their accountability targets by even a few percentage points. Being a startup investor often requires doubling down on teams that miss their accountability targets by *orders of magnitude*. This requires creating a new kind of milestone that can work even in situations where we are unable to make an accurate forecast.

4. How do we provide professional development and coaching to help people get better at entrepreneurship as a skill?

For many leaders, this requires mentoring people with a distinctly different leadership style. Can you imagine trying to coach a young Steve Jobs? And yet most leaders claim that if "the next Steve Jobs" was working for them right now, they'd want that person to bring her or his vision and talent to bear for the organization's benefit, not to quit and start something new. But, in reality, people with a personality like Jobs's tend to get fired—and those who find a way to persist within a corporate environment know it's incredibly difficult to sustain a career with a track record of repeated failures on your résumé. Yet, those of us who have found success as entrepreneurs almost universally say that our failures were our best teachers. And most of us were lucky to have mentors and investors who coached us and helped us develop our entrepreneurial talents. As you'll see in the next chapter, Silicon Valley has an extensive network for those who pursue entrepreneurship as a career. Organizations that want to retain these kinds of employees will need to replicate these supports internally.

5. How do we provide networking and matchmaking in and out of the company, so people understand their new identity: "I'm a corporate entrepreneur."

There are no trade publications, no professional associations, and, in most organizations, no HR support for this emerging category of work. Together, as ambassadors of the Startup Way, we must create these supports if we expect this new function to thrive. Most people reading this book already have some kind of professional identity—as an engineer, a marketer, a developer, a salesperson. Think of how many kinds of support you can get for that role: from your functional colleagues in other divisions, from your functional direct or dotted-line managers, from peers at similar organizations, from trade shows and conferences. In most functions, you can even win awards for professional achievement and thought leadership. Some of these are available to venture-backed founders, but for entrepreneurial employees within organizations—even high-growth startup organizations!—there is almost no support available anywhere.

6. How do we put the right person on the right team?

"Nobody gets assigned to work at a startup," one corporate entrepreneur told me dismissively. And too many internal startups have teams that are indifferent to their success. Some managers have found ways around this, but identifying the perfect entrepreneur to lead the charge on a project or initiative shouldn't be done on the sly; it should be done through HR. Today, most managers are skilled at getting themselves assigned to projects that they think will help their careers. I often joke with senior managers that, as much as they think they do the assigning, their subordinates aren't stupid enough to let themselves get assigned to the wrong project, and they employ many tools for preventing it. All this politicking and maneuvering is a monumental waste of energy. Unloved, high-risk, uncertain projects need a separate and more rational way of attracting entrepreneurial personnel.

7. How do we create new incentive and advancement systems?

It takes skill to tell the difference between an individual who has black marks in his or her personnel file because of incompetence and someone who is circumventing the rules for good reason. It also takes skill to avoid falling for the fakery that some "fauxtrepreneurs" excel at, which can even include "putting on the black turtleneck" in hopes of association by wardrobe with Steve Jobs. (We have this problem in Silicon Valley, too, as some recent very public failures will attest.) A running joke at one famous venture capital firm in Silicon Valley is: "That guy [it's almost always a guy] has really let failure go to his head!" It refers to a type of person who's able to continually raise money for the same kind of startup over and over again, despite a lack of success. It's easy to laugh—until you remember that many of the most successful entrepreneurs in history had one or more failed startups under their belts before they found success.

.   .   .

If developing these new capabilities seems like a daunting amount of work or something that could never happen at your company, take heart. Precisely because our legacy management systems involve a high degree of waste, there is incredible latent energy available to be tapped.

Even venture-backed startups exist within a web of relationships and rules that constrain what founders can do. We take them so for granted that we often don't remark on them. But this can cause huge problems when startups "grow up" and forget these early lessons.

For that reason, we need to take a deeper look at the structures and systems of Silicon Valley, the subject of the next chapter.

## CHAPTER 3

A STARTUP STATE OF MIND

"THINK BIG. START SMALL. SCALE FAST."

Startup people are fractious. We disagree on a lot of things. But our factions and feuds belie a deeper truth: Everyone in the startup community universally adheres to a series of deeply held convictions. These convictions form the true foundation of the structures that allow Silicon Valley–style startups to achieve their unique blend of risk-taking and rapid growth.

What follows is not meant to be a comprehensive list of everything about how Silicon Valley works. Plenty of other books have covered this terrain, and I don't want to repeat the obvious points.[1] Rather, I want to talk about the distinctive management structures the startup movement has pioneered that—though rarely explicitly acknowledged—are key to its success.

Through many years of trial and error, we have worked out a novel system for managing risk, enhancing productivity, and finding new sources of hypergrowth. That system has, in turn, produced a culture supportive of long-term vision rather than immediate results.

Many find our solutions to common problems surprising. By studying these structures, we can find new tools that are valuable in a corporate context.

And although I refer throughout this chapter to "Silicon Valley" and "Silicon Valley–style startups," I am not referring literally to the roughly fifty square miles around my house. Increasingly, Silicon Valley is a state of mind, a shared set of beliefs and practices that have taken hold in dozens of startup hubs around the world. I use "Silicon Valley" only as a convenient shorthand for these beliefs. (For one example, see organizations like Rise of the Rest, founded by Steve Case, which works with entrepreneurs in emerging startup cities.[2])

So let's dive in. How does the startup movement work? What are our universal beliefs? How can its systems and structures be re-created in other organizations?

"IT'S ALL ABOUT THE TEAM."

The most commonly held belief in Silicon Valley is that "it's all about the team."[3] Beneath this catchphrase is a lot of deep thinking about how investors make decisions concerning which startups get funding and the chance to realize their founders' vision.

Most corporate managers are looking for good ideas, sound strategy, and a solid business plan. Once they determine *what* is to be done, they then try to find the right person or people within the organization to get it done. Personnel are evaluated by traditional criteria: past performance, résumé, and pedigree. (And, if we're being honest, a fair bit of politics.)

Silicon Valley investors, in contrast, make their investment decisions primarily based on the quality of the team: They look at the people first, *then* the idea. Of course, they believe that if a strong team has a solid idea and a seemingly sound strategy, the team is more likely to succeed—but not because the investors necessarily agree with the idea or strategy. In fact, most experienced investors believe that a team is likely to change its idea and strategy along the way. Rather, investors see the ability to formulate a good plan as a marker of future success even if the plan changes.

Similarly, a team that shows promising traction in terms of revenue, the reactions from its first groups of reference customers, and *validated learning* (insights based on real data) is more likely to prove a good investment. But again, not because of the traction itself but because of what the traction reveals about that team's ability to execute.

In *The Lean Startup,* I told a story about raising money for IMVU, a company I started in 2004, and a presentation we made in which our revenue was quite small, even though we had the classic hockey-stick growth pattern. We were embarrassed, but we shouldn't have been. The investor saw our presentation as a window into the way we thought—and the way we acted. We demonstrated fast cycle time, rigorous scientific decision making, product/design savvy, and good use of limited resources. He made a bet that if there was an opportunity in this space, we were the team to find it, and he turned out to be correct. This is the most prized attribute among professional startup investors: conviction, the ability to form independent judgments based on limited but revealing early information.

SMALL TEAMS BEAT BIG TEAMS

This is one of the startup movement's most cherished, universal beliefs. We believe in the power of small teams—whereas in traditional corporate structures, the size of the team equals the importance of the project. Or, as Mikey Dickerson, former head of the United States Digital Service, puts it, "If the government is doing a big, important system, by definition, it can't be that important if we don't have hundreds to thousands of people assigned to the project." By contrast, he points out, "Google tries super hard to have something the size of Google Web Search and run it with the very, very smallest number of people. If it is possible for ten to fifteen people to contain all of the knowledge necessary to debug Google Web Search, then that's how many there are. They push as hard as they can . . . and have the smallest number of people with the largest amount of responsibility that they can carry."

There's something uniquely powerful about a small, dedicated team trying to change the world. I speak from experience, of course, having had the privilege of being part of startup teams many times. There's a reason why everyone in the startup ecosystem venerates this special kind of team structure: We've seen it accomplish the impossible time and again.

So what gives a small startup team these seemingly magical powers? First, there's the intense bond and powerful communication that comes from being in proximity with true allies. Everyone who is there wants to be there, especially in the early years—many employees have taken considerable personal financial and career risk to join the team—and everyone simply does what needs to get done. The team also is extremely adaptable; it's almost impossible for bureaucracy to set in when every person is directly accountable to (and in communication with) everyone else. Many management problems that in a large organization make accountability difficult are solved by physical and emotional closeness, which is why startup teams are well suited to execute the Lean Startup concept of the *pivot*—a change in strategy without a change in vision (which we will explore in more detail in Chapter 4).

But there's another important factor: scarcity. If you passionately believe in a mission but lack the resources to make it unfurl in every possible way, you're absolutely forced to focus. There's simply no extra time and no extra money, and corporate death threatens at any moment.[4]

That's why, in the tech industry especially, small teams put a huge premium on reusing existing technology and assembling products out of preexisting components. More than at any other time in history, these components can be combined without requiring explicit permission or a business-development relationship. As reddit and Hipmunk co-founder Alexis Ohanian wrote in *Without Their Permission,* "The Internet is an open system: It works because you don't need to ask anyone's permission to be creative and because every address is equally accessible."[5] Imagine how Facebook would look if Mark Zuckerberg had needed to sign twenty partnership agreements before he was able to start experimenting with his idea on the Harvard campus.

There's an important paradox built into Silicon Valley's veneration of the power of small teams. Startups are distinct from small businesses; most startups resolutely do not want to stay small. Startup teams are like hunting parties, desperately searching for product/market fit. Once they find it, they must quickly reconfigure themselves into a full-on army. This metamorphosis brings with it new problems.

EVERY TEAM HAS A CROSS-FUNCTIONAL STRUCTURE AT ITS CORE

Startups are inherently cross-functional. Even if they begin with, say, a team of all engineers working on a hot new product, they inevitably face problems beyond engineering: financing, customer acquisition, marketing, customer service. Sometimes startups have enough success and funding to be able to hire experts in these other domains. Often, though, the founders and early team have to dive in and solve these problems themselves. (This cross-training sometimes yields unexpected results. Many of my own early experiences with techniques that would later become core to Lean Startup came about because I was forced to act as my startup's de facto head of marketing. Because I knew so little about marketing, I naturally brought an engineering mindset to the task.)

That's why Silicon Valley prioritizes cross-functional teams. The team may look different, depending on what the project is and which resources and people are available to it, but the organizing principle remains the same. For an industrial project, the team might bring together a product designer and someone on the manufacturing side who can determine what the customer truly values, along with a salesperson who has experience in the field. For an IT project, the team might consist of an engineer, a product person, a marketing person, and an accounts person. There are endless permutations, depending on what needs to get done.

EVERY PROJECT STARTS WITH THE CUSTOMER IN MIND

I can't tell you how many times I've worked with teams in traditional enterprises that literally don't know what problem they are trying to solve from the customer's point of view. I once worked with a group that planned to bring a copycat product into a commodity market that was already dominated by multiple competitors. When asked to present their problem statement, they said, "The problem is, our company doesn't have sufficient market share in this market." This is ludicrous: Customers don't care about our market share; they only care if we make their lives better.

For many internal projects—in IT, HR, and finance—as well as products sold via third-party distributors, people often don't know what the word *customer* even means. One IT team in a large enterprise I worked with refused to see the employees who used their product as customers. They insisted that employees had no choice and that IT could mandate the usage of any product. But the word *customer* always implies a choice in the matter, so rather than argue, we decided to go see for ourselves.

I asked the team to interview several existing users of the IT system within the firm to see what their rate of compliance was. The team was scandalized to learn that employees hated the software so much that they were using a wide array of work-arounds to avoid using it at all. Some employees were actually duplicating the system's calculations by hand on paper. Customers, even internal ones, always have a choice. No corporate mandate can ever hope to achieve 100 percent compliance unless employees buy in.

Amazon uses a method called "working backward" to make sure that discovering a true customer problem is the very first thing a team focuses on. It starts with one of the internal press releases I mentioned in the Amazon Fire phone story in Chapter 1. The audience for that document is the new or updated product's customers, internal or external, and it details not just the problem itself, but the current solutions and the ways in which the new solution will solve the problem better than anything before has.[6] Until the team can truly articulate the problem from the customer's point of view, nothing gets built. This hypothesis is crucial to keep the focus on learning.

The key word in this process is *better*. It's not enough just to solve the customer's problem. Silicon Valley–style companies aspire to *delight* customers by providing a solution that is dramatically better than anything they've seen before.

SILICON VALLEY STARTUPS HAVE A SPECIFIC FINANCIAL STRUCTURE

Despite all the talk of mission alignment and changing the world, startups are most often for-profit companies. However, this is not a requirement. I've worked over the years with what I lovingly refer to as "intentional not-for-profits." In Chapter 9, we'll explore the reasons why *impact* is a better way of evaluating startups, since the early years of almost every startup require working without profits. An essential part of Silicon Valley's way of working is to make sure that every employee has a *stake in the outcome*,[7] which, in for-profit and venture-backed startups, means that employees are offered equity ownership.

Startup equity is a complex financial derivative that powers the entire venture/startup ecosystem. It's not profit-sharing. It's not a union. But it is the greatest tool of employee empowerment I've ever seen. What is startup equity worth? This question bedevils outsiders and not a few insiders, too. Every time a startup raises money, investors and founders negotiate a valuation. Although this is expressed as a single number, it's really the product of two components. One is the asset value of what's been created so far: product, team and vendor relationships, and revenue. This is easy to assess. The more difficult part is the probability-weighted distribution of future outcomes: the experiment. A 1 percent chance to become a $100 billion company is worth $1 billion—right now![8] That's the part that is hardest for most people to wrap their minds around.

So what can make a startup more valuable?

1. Acquiring valuable assets, such as developing new products, hiring new people, and gaining more revenue.

2. Changing the probability of future success (the 1 percent that achieves $100 billion above).
3. Changing the magnitude of future success (the $100 billion above).

This helps explain why startups sometimes go through such dramatic changes in valuation, wildly out of proportion to their externally visible signs of progress. When they experiment, they both reveal how large the impact could be and also increase the probability of it happening—and often increase their asset value, too, by acquiring and serving real customers.[9] These factors sometimes—rarely—combine exponentially.

You can only see the asset value from the outside. But a rapidly growing startup is a double win from the investors' point of view: the asset value is increasing at the same time as what the startup is learning is clarifying the probability and magnitude of future success. The value of an innovation lies in the future impact it might have.

By giving employees access to equity, startups directly in-centivize learning in the most dramatic way. Equity ownership is not a cash bonus. It's a measurement of what the startup has learned about far future profits. It's a way to financialize learning.

Equity ownership allows for compensation, risk-taking, and investment in whatever is necessary. This means that during the early life of a startup, its management looks like that of a non-profit organization: it's all about impact and future impact.[10]

One other difference between startup equity ownership and a traditional small business has to do with the incentive to invest in the business. A sole proprietor struggles with the decision of what to do with earnings in a profitable year. Every dollar invested in growth is a dollar taken out of the proprietor's own pocket. It's a painful choice that must be made over and over again. Risky investments are especially painful because of the psychological phenomenon of loss aversion.

Because early-stage equity compensates every employee based on the company's long-term growth and success, it creates a much closer alignment between the financial incentives of employees and managers and the organization's long-term health. I don't claim that this bond is perfect in all cases, and, of course, most startups pay salaries as well as offer other kinds of bonus compensation.

Financial incentives aren't everything; research has shown that offering bonuses and other financial inducements to enhance productivity are often counterproductive.[11] Most people don't join a startup for the money, anyhow. They join because of their commitment to the mission and their desire to make an impact by fulfilling the startup's vision. Compared to other forms of compensation (sole proprietor, nonprofit, corporate bonuses, etc.), equity ownership is the least distortionary set of incentives. It allows employees' intrinsic creativity, commitment, and motivation to flourish.

WE FOCUS ON LEADING INDICATORS

Startups become more valuable when they learn important things about their future impact. Though different for every company, these metrics are specific and serve as guardrails at every stage to mitigate risk.

Implicit in this focus on metrics is a clear understanding of the difference between trailing indicators (such as gross revenue, profit, ROI, and market share) and *leading indicators* that might predict future success (such as customer engagement, satisfaction, unit economics, repeat usage, and conversion rates). Business plans tend to be made up of forecasts and predictions, always denominated in gross metrics (what we call in the Lean Startup movement *vanity metrics*). What Silicon Valley has learned the hard way over the past few decades is that "no business plan survives first contact with customers,"[12] as Steve Blank says (paraphrasing Prussian military strategist Helmuth von Moltke). Or, if you prefer General Eisenhower: "Plans are useless, but planning is indispensable."[13]

So what kind of metrics can we look at during the inevitable "flat part of the hockey stick," before the gross numbers tick up? In *The Lean Startup,* I give many examples from the software industry, including one of my own failures. I was celebrating the fact that, over a period of many months, the total number of customers our startup had attracted was going up, even though the conversion rate of customers from one stage of the sales funnel to the next remained the same. And yet, over this same period, we made many, many "improvements" to the product. It was only our board-level company dashboard that saved us from certain doom. It forced us to recognize that even though we thought the product was "improving," it wasn't changing customer behavior for the better. (We'll see more examples of this kind of metrics challenge in Chapter 9.)

Every modern startup possesses a metrics dashboard that the team and board revisit on a regular *cadence* (schedule). The even more recent trend is to post real-time versions of this dashboard up around the office, on large flat-screen monitors that are visible to everyone. This is part of the transparency that startups tend to favor and that many large enterprises find frightening. But as a coordinating device, it's extremely helpful. There can be no question about how well the company is doing when everyone shares the same set of facts.

METERED FUNDING STAGES RISK

I was once taking a team of large-company executives on a tour of Silicon Valley. We visited late-stage successes in big gleaming office complexes—cool, decked-out, exposed-brick spaces—and seed-stage startups, one of which was located in the rear of a converted warehouse in San Francisco's then-gritty South Park neighborhood; we accessed the offices via back stairs and a fire door.

Inside was the typical duality you'd expect of a tech startup: inexpensive secondhand furniture and floor-to-ceiling stacks of Costco snacks and quick calories alongside extremely high-end, sleekly designed computer hardware. It was quite a culture clash for the executives in suits.

As I facilitated a Q&A between the two groups, one particular question was asked again and again by the executives: How do your investors hold you accountable? How often do you report progress to them? And how do they make sure you don't go off the rails and do something stupid with their money?

The founder/CEO of the startup was baffled by these questions. As it happened, I was an investor in the company. The executives were aghast that I'd allow him to spend my money without explanation or oversight.

This was my chance to explain how we do risk mitigation in Silicon Valley, using something called *metered funding*. (This is the opposite of the typical corporate budgeting approach, which I call *entitlement funding* and discuss in Chapter 7.)

The seed-stage funding for this company was only a few hundred thousand dollars. Raising that initial money took time and energy on the part of the founding team—they probably pitched twenty or thirty investors over the course of several months. But once the fund-raising was over, the money was theirs. It was literally transferred to the team's bank account.

In Silicon Valley, the money you raise is yours. You can spend it on what you like with minimal oversight (especially in the early stages). But Lord help you if you try to raise more money and you haven't made any progress. (We'll talk about how this progress is measured, as *validated learning*, in Chapter 4.)

Seed-stage funding provides an excellent balance between risk mitigation and freedom to innovate. The structure of the startup limits the total liability of the team to the total money raised. And it strictly limits the amount of time and energy the team has to invest in acquiring and defending its budget. But at the same time, it creates a strong incentive to keep investors informed when there's something newsworthy to share so that they will want to continue investing and provide a positive reference to the next set of investors.

Not every startup has such an informal policy on investor updates. As startups grow and the stakes get larger, the frequency of board meetings tends to increase. This is one of those norms that is universally followed and yet rarely enforced via rules. The company is the one that schedules these meetings and sets the agenda. This is a stark reversal of roles compared to your typical corporate team, whose behavior is tightly overseen by managers.

BOARD/INVESTOR DYNAMICS ARE KEY

Every startup has a board of directors, and the company reports to them not on a fixed schedule but when the founders think it's time. The review is based on actual progress, not an artificial time line. Boards are designed to help the company think through strategic issues and whether or not to pivot. The process works because it's linked to *metered funding*.

Existing investors do not have day-to-day control of the company, and in most situations, they do not even have a majority of votes on the board. Their influence is created by the need to raise additional funding in the future. New investors will always want to hear a positive report from existing investors. And existing investors generally have every incentive to be honest, since startups exist in a reputation economy (and new investors are naturally skeptical). Every successful investor has to manage being on both sides of this negotiation many times over.[14]

The board also acts as a mechanism for updating the many other people who have an economic interest in the startup. Most venture firms are organized as partnerships, and generally only one partner sits on the board of each investment the firm makes. The other partners (to say nothing of the sometimes dozens of associates or other staff) are not free to pester the founders for updates. If they want an update, they speak to the partner on the board. Traditionally, these partnerships have weekly meetings (in the old days, always on a Monday) to share information about their various portfolio companies. There may be extensive discussion and analysis, but whatever work is required is borne by the venture firm, not the startup.

It's important to remember that most venture firms are not investing their own money. The partners represent the interests of sometimes hundreds of "limited partners," or LPs—wealthy individuals and institutions, such as family foundations, pension funds, and university endowments. Each of these LPs would like to know how its investments are performing. But they, too, are not free to pester the startups in the portfolio. They must seek information from the partner on the board. Traditionally, venture firms organize an annual meeting with their LPs, in which they give detailed updates on the performance of the startups in the portfolio.

Contrast this with the life of a typical corporate product manager. Most organizations subject their internal teams to an endless stream of meetings: formal reviews, budget updates, and a constant barrage of middle manager check-ins. I have spoken with many managers who report that simply keeping up with these (and their attendant politics) accounts for more than 50 percent of their time, day in and day out. It's an astonishing tax on their productivity. Instead, we in the startup movement favor a system that encourages the flow of information in a way that doesn't hinder progress, so that employees and managers can focus on producing results instead of just reporting them.

WE BELIEVE IN MERITOCRACY

This is one of the most widely held beliefs in the startup movement: Good ideas can come from anywhere, and people should be given resources and attention based on their talents, not their pedigree.

I use the word *meritocracy* cautiously, and I would be remiss if I did not make explicit the degree to which this point is bound up in controversy. I've written repeatedly about the flaws in Silicon Valley's view of meritocracy, as a result of which many deserving groups are disadvantaged unfairly in our funding and hiring practices.[15] And, to make matters worse, there is ample academic research showing that companies that believe themselves to be meritocracies are prone to more implicit bias than those that do not.[16]

Still, there is no way to understand Silicon Valley without this concept, because everyone who lives and works there wants it to be true. Although we often fall short of the goal, I've seen numerous occasions when this belief allows external pressure from activists, limited partners, and others to result in real change. I've also seen just how much harder it is to make these modifications in industries that do not value this concept.

What meritocracy actually means to Silicon Valley is that

your credentials or qualifications don't necessarily predict whether you'll be a good founder or not. This idea is implicitly connected to the importance of teams. You might wonder how Silicon Valley can be focused on high-quality founders and teams on the one hand, but also think of itself as a meritocracy that is open to misfits and people from nontraditional backgrounds on the other. The answer is that, instead of pedigree, we infer the quality of founders from the results they are able to deliver with limited resources, gambling on the chance that early success will be the hallmark of future greatness. Many investors believe that how a team runs the fund-raising process predicts how they'll run a company, and use it as a leading indicator.

There's a now-famous interview with Mark Zuckerberg, back when he was building what he called "TheFacebook.com," in which he's very passionate about his idea, but also not very clear about it. In a traditional business setting, people wouldn't have invested in his idea after listening to his description. He said, "I really just want to create a really cool college directory product that is very relevant for students. I don't know what that is."[17] But startup culture made it possible for investors to take him seriously, and it gave him a chance to experiment with his idea. The fact that he was inarticulate but had good early results is also important. One strong leading indicator is often enough to gain an investor's trust. Unlike in a corporate setting, where everything has to be right in order to proceed, a startup doesn't have to have everything figured out. Likewise, there's no one "right" leading indicator. Even the best investors vary in terms of what indicators they view as most important. But every early-stage professional investor has a point of view about what leading indicators matter most and is skilled at evaluating opportunities with insufficient information.

With the right structures in place, this kind of thing can happen as companies scale, too. Several years ago at Intuit, an executive administrative assistant in the company's TurboTax division attended a workshop as part of the company's Lean StartIN program with an idea for a "TurboTax Training Wheels" program to teach people how to do their taxes using TurboTax. She believed it would not only empower them but lead them to recommend the software to others. Within a few days in the workshop, through a series of experiments, her team proved their hypothesis was correct. They ran several larger-scale experiments and soon after, launched TurboTax Parties. The program started with 500 parties, had grown to 13,000 parties in just a few years, and is going strong.

Meritocracy is not an either/or concept. Meritocracies exist on a spectrum. All of us can get better and become more meritocratic. And yet how many organizations truly live up to this ideal?[18]

OUR CULTURE IS EXPERIMENTAL AND ITERATIVE

By establishing the structures outlined in this chapter, startups create experiments to try things out without causing financial ruin. This is key to inspiring a culture of trust. When a startup is set up properly, there's no incentive to cover up failure; the whole idea is to search for truth. This system is far from perfect—recent years have shown that loopholes remain where a charismatic founder can commit fraud all too easily. And, as we'll see in later chapters, it's easy for companies to lose this initial intensity, accountability, and experimental culture as they grow.

But it's important not to take for granted just how much experimentation this system allows. The combination of pulling good ideas from everywhere, having strict limits on funding (and, therefore, on liability), and creating a culture that tolerates failure allows the resulting ecosystem to pursue a diverse range of business ideas—most of which are terrible, but a few of which can be truly disruptive.

For those of us who work in Silicon Valley, it's a running joke that everyone has stories of the startups they didn't invest in or didn't go to work for that turned into megasuccesses. I personally have turned down opportunities to work at or invest in many major successes of the Internet era, including both Google and Facebook. (So don't let me give you investment advice!)

And I'm not alone. One of my favorite venture firms maintains an "anti-portfolio" comprising the companies that they declined to invest in when given the chance but continue to track and to publish their stellar performance.[19]

The point of these stories—and the reason they've become a cliché—is that you simply can't tell for sure ahead of time which experiments are going to pan out. Even the very best investors, the ones we laud for their "golden gut," get it wrong more often than they get it right.

The only way to win in this world is to take more shots on goal. Try more radical things. Pay close attention to what works and what doesn't. And double down on the winners.

A STARTUP IS MISSION—AND VISION—DRIVEN

Outside of Silicon Valley, Mark Zuckerberg's declaration that "We don't build services to make money; we make money to build better services"[20] was met with eye rolls. But in Silicon Valley, we really believe it.

Silicon Valley is obsessed with vision and the visionary founder who can uniquely execute it. This focus has been a source of some controversy as Lean Startup has become more popular. Because of our emphasis on science, metrics, and experimentation, it's a common (but misguided) criticism that Lean Startup seeks to replace vision or, in some ways, de-emphasize it. (I did my best to dispel this misunderstanding in *The Lean Startup*—starting on page 9! There's a reason why Part One of *The Lean Startup* was called "Vision.") No methodology or process can replace this essential element of a startup.

But why is vision so important? Some reasons are obvious: The vision makes plain what the startup hopes to accomplish. It is the primary coordination device as the team acts in decentralized fashion. As General Stanley McChrystal wrote in *Team of Teams,* "The key reason for the success of empowered execution lay in what had come *before* it: the foundation of shared consciousness."[21] Vision provides a profound sense of motivation and energy and an unparalleled recruiting advantage. Keep in mind that startups routinely hire people whom they can't remotely afford to pay market-rate salaries. In my career, I've frequently worked with people whose talent greatly exceeded my own, who were years older than I am, and who took a profound pay cut for the privilege of executing a promising mission. This is possible only in the presence of an inspiring vision.

However, there's another equally important reason for the primacy of vision and its role in a startup. And it's why the *startup as the atomic unit of work* is distinct from earlier management concepts such as the "cross-functional work cell" in lean or any number of functional team/committee "task force" structures that are common in corporate settings.

Without a vision you cannot pivot.

The accuracy of that statement is baked into the very definition of *pivot*: A pivot is *a change in strategy without a change in vision*. The vision is the part of the team's mission that is nonnegotiable. It's what you'd rather go out of business for than compromise on. It's the essential resistance against which teams can push in order to find unusual breakthrough strategies. (We'll go over this in more detail in Chapter 4.)

As Jeff Lawson, the CEO of cloud communications company Twilio, says, "You're not going to get anywhere if you have a big vision but you're not solving the customer's problem. If you're not solving a problem, you're never going to be given the ability to implement that grand vision." And the way to solve problems is to uncover them as you go and then pivot to meet them.

Vision is often discovered through the process of building a startup. As the process unfolds and the visionary is forced to confront difficult choices about what to change and what to stick with, she actually comes to realize which aspects of the original vision are expendable and which are essential.

Vision is often the reason that startup teams are able to pivot in a way that traditional product teams seldom can. The structure of the startup team forces it to confront reality in all its unpleasant particularities, but the vision always remains a beacon.

WE BELIEVE IN ENTREPRENEURSHIP AS A CAREER PATH

It's important to understand that the entrepreneurial way of thinking about vision applies across the board, to far more people than just the CEO and the original founders of a company. Silicon Valley has a deep appreciation for the "founder mentality" that entrepreneurial employees develop through their careers in startups. Early employees at a successful startup are given many opportunities to gain new responsibilities at a much faster rate than is typical in other types of organizations. This rapid change doesn't agree with everyone, but those who thrive in such an environment quickly develop reputations as more than just good engineers, marketers, or managers. They become known as key lieutenants who can make things happen in the highly uncertain domain where startups live. And, of course, they are seen as high-potential future founders themselves.

The ability to both work in and lead these kinds of high-performance teams requires particular skills. They do not come naturally to everyone, and are absolutely distinct from most other business skills that lead to success in a corporate environment. (An active debate exists about whether these skills are innate or can be learned. I think Lean Startup has demonstrated that they are teachable to an extent not previously realized.)

Entrepreneurship is not a linear career path. I've worked for people who have, subsequently, worked for me. I've hired former founders into key executive roles and personally encouraged former employees of mine to become founders themselves. And, of course, most successful people in Silicon Valley become angel investors, even if on a small scale. So the roles get deeply intertwined. It's a reciprocal web of trust, expertise, and reputation that is an important part of why startup hubs drive so much entrepreneurial success.

This career path has only recently become something widely available in contemporary economies. But I think this is just the tip of the iceberg in terms of how this professional identity will evolve in the coming years and decades. Genius is widely distributed, but as of yet, opportunity is not. As more and more people are given the chance to try their hand at entrepreneurship, the world will never be the same.

· · ·

This tour of startup practices is not meant to paint our industry as infallible, nor is it meant to suggest that naïvely aping these practices will make other industries more innovative. Rather, it's meant to serve as a common language for talking about these practices as they inform and influence the management system presented in this book.

One of the main lessons I learned from writing *The Lean Startup* is that formalizing practices into a rational system, complete with a common vocabulary, allows more people to use that system than the old apprenticeship method. This has paid dividends in spreading ideas, as well as in improving practices within Silicon Valley itself. In fact, I routinely meet new graduates coming out of Stanford and Berkeley who consider concepts such as *minimum viable product* so obvious, they can't believe that anyone had to write a book about them! (And you should see the look on their faces when they find out it was published in 2011, not 1981.)

A clear understanding of the tools of the Lean Startup is necessary before diving further into the Startup Way. The next chapter is a look at the methods that make up the Lean Startup way of working, complete with tools and examples. For newcomers, this chapter will provide an introduction to the foundational concepts of the Lean Startup. For those familiar with it, I've tried to focus on seeing the concepts through a new lens: how, as leaders, we can help our teams live these principles every day.

## CHAPTER 4

LESSONS FROM THE LEAN STARTUP

THERE'S A REASON why the Startup Way has emerged out of the Lean Startup movement. There have always been leaders seeking to work more innovatively. What has been missing is a comprehensive framework that helps startups—whether internal or external—figure out what to do and how to do it every day. How do they measure progress to be sure they are getting closer to their goals? How do they maximize the talent they already have? How do they discover the truth through experimentation? That's what Lean Startup provides.

So, before we go any further, let's take a look at its basic principles.

HOW THE LEAN STARTUP WORKS

Here is an overview of the basics of the Lean Startup method. We'll get into each one, and each specialized term, in greater detail.

1. Identify the beliefs about what must be true in order for the startup to succeed. We call these *leap-of-faith assumptions.*
2. Create an experiment to test those assumptions as quickly and inexpensively as possible. We call this initial effort a *minimum viable product.*
3. Think like a scientist. Treat each experiment as an opportunity to learn what's working and what's not. We call this "unit of progress" for startups *validated learning.*
4. Take the learning from each experiment and start the loop over again. This cycle of iteration is called the *build-measure-learn feedback loop.*
5. On a regular schedule (*cadence*), make a decision about whether to make a change in strategy (*pivot*) or stay the course (*persevere*).

As we discussed in Chapter 3, every startup is first and foremost about vision. The goal of Lean Startup is to find the fastest possible path to realizing this vision. The specifics of how to arrive at the answers will, of course, look different for each project but will follow the same basic steps, employing the scientific method to systematically break down the plan into its component parts through rapid experimentation.

LEAN STARTUP AT THE DEPARTMENT OF EDUCATION

In August of 2013, President Obama announced that he was in search of a better way to hold colleges and universities accountable for their performance in serving students. If you are the parent of a college-age or near-college-age kid, you've probably looked at a few lists—the best colleges in your state or the best ones for the majors your child is interested in. In many of these college rating guides, however, the criteria used to evaluate schools don't correlate to how good the schools actually are at educating students and preparing them for the workforce. Investing in new buildings or raising a lot of money from their alumni count as much as overall graduation rates, graduation rates by income bracket, how much debt a student might incur by attending school, and how much students stand to earn after graduation. Lisa Gelobter, the chief digital service officer of the Department of Education, who led the project, recalls, "Using metrics having to do with access, affordability, and outcomes, the president wanted to change the conversation about what defines a school's value."

Everyone in Gelobter's department had ideas about how to figure out which criteria to include in the search tool they wanted to build. Should people be able to look not just at the "sticker price" of a school, but how much one might pay as a low-income student with financial aid? How could the team explain that a school with a graduation rate of 15 percent was probably not a good bet to a person who was unfamiliar with looking at data? The number of factors to consider and possible ways of approaching the project were overwhelming.

Then the team decided to hit the pause button. "We took a step back and asked, 'Hold on. What is the problem we're trying to solve?'" Gelobter remembers. "What we wanted to do is change the conversation about what makes for a good school, then enable consumers to make informed decisions and vote with their feet." In thinking about the project in a customer-centric way, Gelobter's team realized that they needed to get into the field and start experimenting.

To figure out what they really needed to test, they began by immersing themselves with real customers. "We identified who we wanted to talk to: students and parents and guidance counselors. If we wanted to help students figure out what college to go to, we should talk to some of them." This was practically unheard of in government. Or, as Gelobter puts it, "It was a little bit unusual."

So many projects like this get bogged down in months- or years-long market research and "analysis paralysis." This team deliberately kept it simple. They went down to the Washington Mall and began seeking out high school juniors and seniors in order to ask them about their experiences in the college application process. They visited the Mall at least once a week, asking the students six simple questions and using the answers to refine their hypotheses about the features they thought customers wanted.

It didn't take long before they were turning these ideas into tangible experiments. Instead of reaching for expensive software tools, they made cardboard phones with sliding panels to replicate the experience of using an app they planned to design, and they brought the pretend phones with them to the Mall. "It was great," says Gelobter. "People would use their thumb to slide through."

The team tested everything, discovering what information people actually searched for and what features they ignored. "We originally had a feature where in your search results you could add schools to a compare list," Gelobter remembers. "Then you could compare them side by side. Not a single person had any interest in doing that. No one asked about it. No one clicked on it."

Each cardboard prototype worked a little better than the last. Once the team had confidence in its new design, they started building the consumer tool, as well as an API (application programming interface) version so that the data could be accessed beyond the Department of Education's website.

THE TOOLS AND PROCESSES OF LEAN STARTUP

These are the methods that allowed the College Scorecard team to create a standout product in so little time.

1. Leap-of-Faith Assumptions (LOFA)

Recall from Chapter 1 that Lean Startup is designed to operate in situations where we face such extreme uncertainty that we can't make an accurate forecast for what might happen. In such a circumstance, the best we can do is form a set of hypotheses—in the scientific sense—about what we'd like to see happen. These hypotheses are called *leap-of-faith assumptions.* In a traditional business plan, they embody the company's current guess at how its strategy will lead to the realization of its vision. Lean Startup requires making these assumptions explicit, so that we can find out as soon as possible which are true and which are not. The College Scorecard team, for example, was sure that people would want to compare colleges. Only by testing that feature (even before it was programmed) did they learn it was of no interest at all.

When testing leap-of-faith assumptions, it's tempting to ask customers directly what they want, either through individual customer interviews, a focus group, or a survey. Many of us were taught to do this kind of market research. But there's a problem with this approach: people often think they know what they want, but it turns out that they're wrong.[1]

That's why the College Scorecard team went out to the Washington Mall not with a survey but with a prototype product. They could observe what customers actually did with it. The reason to run experiments is to discover customers' revealed preferences through their behavior. In other words, don't ask customers what they want. Design experiments that allow you to observe it.[2]

"WAIT A MINUTE"
A few years ago, I did a daylong workshop with a group of software teams within a huge corporation. Though they worked in a

high-tech industry, they were still working in the classic waterfall style, marked by stage-gate deliverables and milestones.

As we started discussing their assumptions about the projects they were working on, someone suddenly said: "Wait a minute. I'm starting to realize that we've been working on this project for two years, and we're not actually sure if there are any customers for it." They had been taking it on faith that the projections in their business plan were going to play out once the product was done.

When I asked them whose job it was to figure that out and why it still hadn't happened after two years, each member of the team had a different excuse. One said, "I'm the project manager. My job is to make sure the project is done on time." Someone else said, "I'm the engineering manager. My job is to make sure the software and hardware work the way they are supposed to—according to the specification document." The product manager conceived her job as ensuring the product met the predetermined requirements from the business plan. And on and on.

At the end, after the project manager had said, "I was told to build this project, so it's my job to make sure it gets built," they realized that it was no one's job to make sure there were actual customers for the product. They had been operating with one very large leap-of-faith assumption—that people wanted this product—and had never acknowledged it as an assumption or tested it.

ARTICULATING ASSUMPTIONS

Of course, making assumptions is something we all do naturally. Every vision for a business is based on assumptions about what is possible to build, what customers want, what kind of customers want it, what distribution channels are available, and so on. Every part of a business plan contains assumptions.

But it's crucial that teams, managers, and leaders take an honest look at the company's plans and accept that they are filled with technical assumptions about product features and specifications as well as commercial assumptions about marketing and sales strategies. We need to put those assumptions to the test through experimentation, measure what has been learned, and then move to the next action step: either staying the course with whatever modifications are called for—or shifting the strategy altogether.

Articulate assumptions before getting too far into the building process. Luckily, it doesn't have to be complicated. A simple way to do it is to make it a habit to write down expectations about interactions with a customer or colleague. "I believe the customer will be willing to participate in a follow-up call," or "I believe this software feature will be important and appealing to the finance department at my company," or "I believe the hospital will be interested in purchasing the medical device I'm developing."

Then ask these kinds of questions:

- What assumptions would have to be true in order for the project to succeed? Are they assumptions about customers? Partners? Competitors?
- How much do we really know about customers' habits, preferences, and need for solutions like ours?
- What evidence is there that customers *really* have the problem being solved for them and strongly desire (and are willing to pay for) a solution to it?
- What is *really* known about what customers want in that solution?

By writing down what they think will happen ahead of time, team members are reminded that they won't always be right—which is fine. The goal is to learn.

KEEP IT SIMPLE

Here's what an entrepreneur named Pedro Miguel, a member of the online community connected to my Kickstarter book, *The Leader's Guide,*[3] has to say about the process of asking questions as the first step in creating a new product or process:

> Validating ideas by talking to people is hard but crucial to understand if people really have the problem you are trying to solve. One way that works for me is to build a simple three-question survey that validates key assumptions:
>
> 1. Do people really have the problem you think they do?
> 2. How do they approach the problem today?
> 3. Is your concept a better alternative for them?
>
>   Only after I have tested with customers do I start building.

Don't overdo it. As tempting as it may be to list every possible leap-of-faith assumption that comes up in team meetings, try to limit the analysis to the ones that fit the true definition of the term: Leap-of-faith assumptions are the claims in a business plan that will have the *greatest impact* on its success or failure.

Avoid analysis paralysis at all costs, and usually that means focusing on fewer rather than more assumptions (one team I worked with identified well over a hundred of them for a single project). A good method for pruning the list is to identify the riskiest parts of the plan and focus on those initially. Some teams also tend to be overly focused on assumptions about the distant future—industry trends, oil prices, or what the commercial road map will look like several years hence. There's nothing wrong with documenting these assumptions, but it's far more important to focus on the ones that are a little closer to now.

Why? Because we all tend to gravitate toward the comfortable—the areas we know most about that feel the safest. When we go where we are least comfortable, it's usually the area in which we don't know as much as is necessary in order to find success, and the learning gained from testing those assumptions is all the more important.

This is a simple form of risk mitigation: Focus on actions that present the greatest opportunities for learning. For the College Scorecard team, the riskiest assumptions were about what features customers wanted, so they chose to focus their early tests on those.

PRIORITIZING LEAP-OF-FAITH ASSUMPTIONS

"Hypergrowth Lemonade Stand (HLS)"

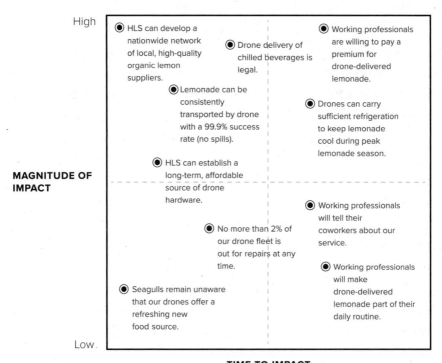

DETERMINE THE VALUE HYPOTHESIS
AND GROWTH HYPOTHESIS

Among its leap-of-faith assumptions, a startup has two that are fundamental: the *value hypothesis,*[4] which tests whether a product or service really delights customers once they begin using it; and the *growth hypothesis,* which tests how, given some customers, it's possible to get more. (See chart, opposite.)

I generally recommend that teams start by determining their value hypothesis before moving on to the growth hypothesis. It makes sense to ensure that a small number of customers want what's on offer before thinking about how to scale up your efforts.

For the College Scorecard, for example, the value hypothesis was that the team could create a tool that would provide students with good metrics to help them understand the value a school provided and help them make an informed choice about what college to attend. The growth hypothesis was that once the team had the data they needed, they would be able to share it through an API that anyone could access (as Gelobter says, "Not everyone is going to come to an ed.gov website to research schools") in order to reach communities and customers that might not access it through the app.

BUT WHAT IF MY LOFA ANALYSIS IS WRONG?

One thing I see teams worry about is that their LOFA prioritization will be off and that this will lead them astray. In fact, we know for sure that it *will* be wrong, as I discussed back in Chapter 1. This is why we call the kinds of experiments we do in Lean Startup *minimum viable products.* They are not just academic exercises, as we'll see in a moment. They are real-life products, no matter how limited, that create maximum opportunity for us to be surprised by customer behavior. These surprises often upend

DETERMINING VALUE AND GROWTH HYPOTHESES

	DEFINITION	EXAMPLES	QUESTIONS TO ASK
VALUE HYPOTHESIS	Tests whether the new product or service will create value for the customer	**Example 1** Customers desire high-quality, artisanal lemonade. **Example 2** Customers will pay a premium to experience drone delivery.	1. Is this a valuable proposition for my target customers? 2. Will customers be willing to pay for it? 3. Will customers return?
GROWTH HYPOTHESIS	Tests how new customers will adopt the product or process	**Example 1** We believe customers will become HLS evangelists by spreading the word among their colleagues and peers. **Example 2** We believe customers will purchase at least two lemonades per order to share with colleagues or serve at meetings.	1. Once the project has piloted and shown value, what mechanism will we use to grow it? 2. How will we know if learnings from the pilot region apply across multiple geographies? 3. How can we encourage and reward word-of-mouth evangelism?

our entire LOFA framework. That's yet another reason why the LOFA analysis process should be kept as simple as possible. As Mark Zuckerberg says in his famous manifesto (in Facebook's S-1 filing): "Try to build the best services over the long term by quickly releasing and learning from smaller iterations rather than [by] trying to get everything right all at once. . . . We have the words *Done is better than perfect* painted on our walls to remind ourselves to always keep shipping."[5]

2. Minimum Viable Product (MVP)

Once we've gathered predictions and assumptions and articulated value and growth hypotheses, the next step is to build an experiment called a *minimum viable product* or *MVP*.

An MVP is an early version of a new product that allows a team to collect the maximum amount of *validated learning* (learning based on real data gathering rather than guesses about the future) about customers. Ideally, this learning will maximize the number of LOFAs tested while minimizing cost, time, and effort.

In today's marketplace of uncertainty, whoever learns fastest wins. The lean manufacturing concept of "fundamental cycle time" is defined by the time elapsed between receiving an order from the customer and delivering a high-quality product at a good price. For a startup "innovation factory," the fundamental cycle time is defined by how much time elapses between having an idea and validating whether that idea is brilliant or crazy. Teams that drive down the validation cycle time are much more likely to find product/market fit,[6] because it increases (not guarantees, of course) the probability of success.

A minimum viable product quickly turns an idea into something real—even if imperfect—in order to begin the process of iterating and retesting. Although individual MVPs may be imperfect, the goal is to ultimately create the most successful process or product possible with the least waste.

You read about College Scorecard's initial MVP. Rather than launching their software to the public, they used cardboard mockups and observed customer interactions. In that way, they were able to experiment with the product immediately, change it quickly, and test again.

Most of us don't leap to do work this way. It's uncomfortable to put an imperfect, messy product out there, especially when we are enthralled with the big vision for our project, as most entrepreneurs are.

"The thing about Minimum Viable Products is that while you decide what's Minimum, the customer decides if it's Viable," writes David Bland, a consultant and early Lean Startup evangelist. "You'll need to lead your team out of the trough of sorrow after they experience this despair for the first time. Minimum Viable Products are optimized for learning, not for scaling. This is one of the hardest things to convey to people who've spent their lives building to build, not building to learn."[7]

TYPES OF MVPs

MVPs come in all sizes and flavors. It all depends on what you're trying to learn. Every company needs to develop its own guidelines for how to talk about rapid experimentation, how to train employees to use these techniques, and how to hold them accountable for what they've learned.

At Intuit, they describe the process this way: "The goal of rapid experiments is to learn as fast as possible from real customers, based on real behaviors, before investing additional resources in a given idea or course of action." To see a number of types and examples of MVPs, go to Appendix 2 (page 359), where I'm delighted to be able to share Intuit's internal MVP catalog and guidelines—with their permission, of course.

MVP IS A STATE OF MIND

One internal startup team that came to one of my workshops had a "hidden in plain sight" MVP story. They were building a consumer product that traditionally would have taken three to five years to design and ship. In the course of the workshop, we started to explore ways that they could use new technologies, like 3-D printing, to bring this cycle time down. But the team remained stubbornly focused on only the manufacturing side of cycle time. I kept trying to get them to focus on how to learn more quickly.

This being a hardware product, I figured the hard part would be finding a way to build a functional prototype that customers could see. But, the team explained, they'd already done that! They'd had to build a functioning prototype in order to get their safety certifications. It was already sitting in their office.

So then I assumed the problem must be that they didn't have easy access to customers. Perhaps they needed to find a local retailer and work out a special arrangement to get access to their customers. Wrong again. "We already have a model store in our facility, where customers can come and see our latest and greatest products." So, I figured, it must be a problem of corporate politics. Did they know the manager of the model store? "Sure, he's always asking us for new things to show off."

So what was the problem? Was the store really far away from their office? No, it was in the same building. Was the prototype really heavy? Did they need a special dolly to lug it over there?

As it turned out, there was absolutely no physical, organizational, political, or regulatory barrier to doing an experiment that very day. The only impediment was the ingrained force of habit that led this team to overlook this simple solution. As you'll see in the next few chapters, this is incredibly common. The problem isn't that the engineers can't figure out how to build an MVP; it's that they've never considered it worth doing. When the mental landscape is shaped by management habits, it's hard to have a breakthrough. Lean Startup is designed to remove that psychological obstacle.

MVP SCORING CHART

There are no set instructions as to what to build as an MVP, as long as it's something that maximizes learning.

What's most important, though, is to always brainstorm *multiple* MVPs for any given project. At Intuit, one of the core pillars of their Design for Delight program (their version of a Lean Startup program, similar to FastWorks) is "Go Broad to Go Narrow."[8]

It's human nature to prematurely anchor to one solution. I can't tell you how many teams I've worked with over the years that are convinced that their original plan is the only MVP they could possibly build.

It's important to help teams consider radically different alternatives. In my more basic workshops, I will often ask teams to pick a single assumption from their plan and then brainstorm three different MVPs. We start with the easy one: the thing they already want to do. Then we do a fun one: one that is *dramatically more expensive* (the ultimate, gold-plated version). Finally, I ask teams to try to create a third possibility—one that is as distant in complexity and cost from their original design as the gold-plated MVP *but* in the direction of simplicity. That is, something so stupid and simple, they're almost embarrassed to admit they thought of it.

TESTING A HYPOTHESIS WITH MVPS

Most critical leap of faith assumption

Customers desire artisanal lemonade.

Hypothesis statement

If high-quality artisanal lemonade is available for on-demand delivery, customers will increase their lemonade consumption.

Brainstorm a series of potential MVPs.

ASK YOURSELF
• Who is this new product/process being built for?
• What is the simplest product/process that can be built to begin learning?

MVP 1   Street corner lemonade stand with tables, chairs, and basic signage.

MVP 2   Landing page enabling on-demand ordering and delivery by humans.

MVP 3   Website and app enabling on-demand ordering and delivery by drone in the SoMa neighborhood of San Francisco.

MVP 4   Website and app enabling on-demand ordering and delivery by a fleet of drones anywhere in the state of California.

This kind of brainstorming is not just for workshops. Intuit's Scott Cook once explained to me a technique he used in a staff meeting. It took only fifteen minutes total. He asked each person to consider the project she or he was working on at that moment and to spend five minutes writing down leap-of-faith assumptions. Then he asked each person to pick *just one* LOFA and spend five minutes brainstorming different metrics that he or she could use to measure whether the LOFA was true. Finally, he

asked each person to pick *one single metric* and brainstorm different MVPs that could generate that data. Even after only fifteen
minutes, he found that his team was able to consider much more
varied and interesting proposals.

For teams that are ready for a more advanced technique, here's
a chart I've used with a number of clients to help them decide
which MVP is worth pursuing. This creates a common scorecard for evaluating the prospects of the brainstormed MVPs. (See
chart on page 102.)

First, this chart helps us recognize that not every MVP will
bear directly on every LOFA. That's okay. Sometimes the right
answer is simply to pick one that's good enough to get started.
At other times, it makes sense to work on several different MVPs
in a parallel fashion in order to get a more comprehensive set of
tests going.[9]

But what constantly surprises me when doing this exercise
with teams is how often startups are considering multiple MVPs
that test exactly the same assumptions and yet cost dramatically
different amounts of money. In these cases, we can almost always
eliminate the more expensive MVPs from consideration, even if
doing so feels uncomfortable.

3. Validated Learning

In *The Lean Startup*, I told an embarrassing story about the time
I spent six months building a piece of software that, as it turned
out, customers didn't even want to download. A single web page
offering that product would have revealed the same information
in a single day—instead of six months of backbreaking labor.
These are the kinds of dramatic efficiencies Lean Startup makes
possible. Not figuring out how to achieve the specification with
slightly less effort, but figuring out how to achieve the same
learning value with a dramatically simpler specification.

MVP SCORING CHART

Determine which experiments to run, and in what order. Mark which MVP
tests which assumptions, and estimate the cost of each experiment and the
amount of time it will take. Some experiments may be unnecessary because
their assumptions can be tested with a cheaper and/or faster MVP.

LEAP-OF-FAITH ASSUMPTION	MVP 1 Street corner lemonade stand/ table and chairs	MVP 2 Simple landing page with order button	MVP 3 Drone prototype with delivery service	MVP 4 Drone delivery service
Customers desire artisanal lemonade.	✓	✓	✓	✓
Customers will pay a premium for organic, locally-sourced lemonade ingredients.	✓	✓		
On-demand ordering increases customers' lemonade consumption.		✓	✓	✓
Customers are willing to pay a premium for drone delivery.			✓	✓
Customers are in drone-accessible locations.				✓
Customers prefer to pay with bitcoin.		✓	✓	✓

Estimate of the cost of each experiment and how much time each will take.

	MVP 1	MVP 2	MVP 3	MVP 4
COST	$250	$2,500	$25,000	$1.5m
TIME	1 week	1 month	6 months	18 months

The information I could have gained with that simple web
page—but didn't—is what we call *validated learning*. It's what
any MVP provides: understanding what people actually want,
not what we think they want. The goal of a sequence of MVPs
is traction: to show that each experiment is driving superior customer behavior compared to the one before.

Over time, it wasn't necessarily that we had more customers, but that each cohort of customers liked what we were offering better. That was our leading indicator, but every company and team has to determine what to measure in order to learn what they want to know.

Most startups think the right metric for them is obvious. An e-commerce company will insist that what matters is customer purchases and their attendant conversion rates. Consumer products, from apps to toys, require a product that customers love and use regularly. There is not one universally correct behavior that is most important to measure.

However, what all of these behaviors have in common is an *exchange of value*. Value can be anything scarce a potential customer is willing to give up in exchange for access to the product: sometimes that's money, but it can also be things like time, energy, reputation, or detailed feedback. Just as the College Scorecard team knew they were on to something when they discovered no one wanted to compare colleges, they could also see they were making progress when the people who tried out their cardboard phones spent more and more time with them.

Validated learning is the scientific inference we can make from improvements in this exchange of value from one experiment to the next. (We'll talk more about metrics in Chapters 6 and 9.) For metrics to support a valid inference, they must follow the three A's: *actionable, accessible,* and *auditable.*

ACTIONABLE. For a report to be considered actionable, the data must demonstrate clear cause and effect and be related to changes in the product itself. Otherwise, it's merely a vanity metric. The fact that a website has seen an uptick in visitors doesn't necessarily mean the product is improving. What does it mean? Why are visitors there? What are they doing? What product changes drove this result?

ACCESSIBLE. Everyone involved in the project should be able to see these reports and understand them, or there is no way they can be put to use. Many organizations use public screens to follow data. *The Washington Post* is a recent example; under Jeff Bezos's ownership, the company created a technology platform called Arc that aims to translate Amazon's understanding of the customer experience to the newspaper business. Arc tracks readers' interaction with the website and apps and integrates targeted marketing based on the user experience. The company now offers Arc as a service to other newspapers around the world.[10]

AUDITABLE. The data has to be credible. Often when projects are killed because of poor metrics, a team or an individual will challenge that decision. What's it based on? The numbers and the analysis must be clear and sound, not complicated and not wishy-washy.

Dan Smith, a product manager who shared his ideas in *The Leader's Guide* community, says:

> All else being equal (which it never is), I like to look at whatever my "one metric that matters" is; i.e., paid conversions, purchases, shares, uploads, etc., and see if I am hitting a certain velocity. Ideally, and this depends on what the churn rate and unit of time in a model looks like, I want to see sustained exponential weekly or monthly growth. Borrowing a retail analogy, if I can't keep enough of the widgets in stock, I know I have something. I'm a big believer in looking at everything through the function of time and cohorts. I've found it highlights potential faults in the model as well as opportunities to accelerate growth. This assumes, of course, I've already validated my customer.

Often the hardest part of running a startup is simply getting everyone on the team to agree on the same set of facts. Only then can we figure out if we are making progress.

4. Build-Measure-Learn

Building an MVP is not meant to be a one-time event. After measuring and analyzing it, it's possible to see where the idea has traction and where it doesn't. Then build another MVP and launch it to keep learning.

BUILD-MEASURE-LEARN LOOP

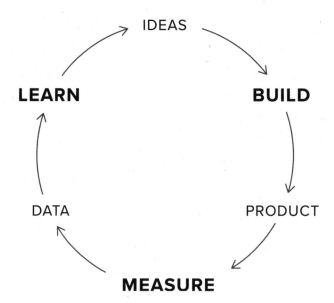

For example, as they tested their MVP with potential customers, the College Scorecard team learned what websites people went to when they searched for colleges and why. They learned that people automatically assumed public college would cost less. They learned that most people came into their search for a college already knowing what they wanted to major in. Then they incorporated features that took people's actual concerns into account and went out for more testing. They continued to move through this build-measure-learn feedback loop until they had created an MVP that customers clearly loved and were excited about.

Paradoxically, when the quest for perfection is replaced with a willingness to experiment with and adapt the original idea, the ultimate result is a more perfect product. The key is to always drive down the total time through this loop.

TWILIO'S BUILD-MEASURE-LEARN LOOP

When the cloud communications platform company Twilio, which has a current market cap of $2.56 billion and a recent successful IPO, first started in 2008, it began with small teams of engineers. The methods they used to identify opportunities have remained in place through the company's rapid growth. Managers start by asking each team to experiment with an opportunity—for example, testing the theory that Twilio could be used for call centers. Rather than be told what to build, the team is asked to figure out why customers haven't already built the call centers themselves. The process starts with an exercise called PRFAQ, a technique used to test an idea through contact with customers to get the answer to that initial question.

In the PRFAQ, the team writes a press release (similar to the Amazon process) and FAQ document for the customer, including information like the product launch date and cost (or at least a good estimate). Then the team sits down with customers who've been given the release to get feedback. "We try and get as much information as we can from the customer on the final product before we've spent any time building it," says Patrick Malatack, vice president of product management. Sometimes customers—internal as well as external—will say they aren't at all interested in an idea. Other times, they'll say they can't wait to start using it, at which point the team will dig deeper. And sometimes, the response includes requests for features that the team hadn't even considered.

Once all this information is gathered, the team decides whether or not to move forward. If the answer is yes, they build a "very, very, very basic" product that they can start iterating immediately (recent efforts include adding video chat or MMS messages on top of their regular voice or text services). There's no set time line for following these steps. It looks different for every team. But each team is held accountable by the same measures of learning. "Each independent team is building a sense of ownership," says former COO Roy Ng. "The one rule you want to apply is to get customer feedback, and you need to try to get it as early as possible," says Malatack. "And then you need to experiment and iterate by coming up with a hypothesis and testing that as you do each iteration. That's the one thing we've drilled test teams on, but beyond that it's not one size fits all."

5. Pivot or Persevere

The goal of all this experimentation is to learn enough to have a pivot-or-persevere meeting to evaluate whether the current strategy is working. If each experiment seems more productive than the last—there's a lot of learning *and* data that supports at least some leap-of-faith assumptions—the next step is to *persevere,* do another MVP that is a refinement of the previous one, and continue through the build-measure-learn cycle.

If not, and the same negative feedback (or indifference) is

coming from customers over and over even though the product is "better," or if the data convincingly invalidates a key assumption, it's time to *pivot*. This is perhaps Lean Startup's most famous (or infamous, depending on your point of view) bit of jargon: the pivot, *a change in strategy without a change in vision.*

THE PIVOT

A change in strategy without a change in vision

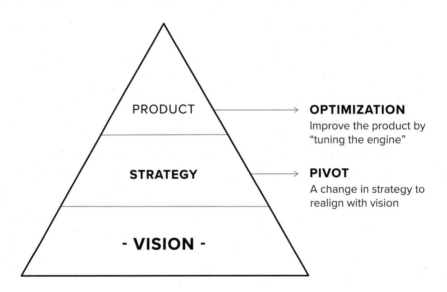

PRODUCT → **OPTIMIZATION**
Improve the product by "tuning the engine"

STRATEGY → **PIVOT**
A change in strategy to realign with vision

- VISION -

Founders always have a vision. To achieve their goals and reach that vision, they need to define a strategy. There's no reason why that strategy should forever remain the same, but the vision certainly can—and almost always will. In a pivot, the target market for, or feature set of, the product might change without changing the overall vision for the problem. Each pivot creates a new series of hypotheses, and the process begins again.

Startup history is filled with legendary pivot stories. Among them are PayPal, which went from a money transfer mechanism for Palm Pilots only to the web-based version we now have; Netflix, which moved from mailing DVDs to customers to streaming; and some of the companies whose stories I told in *The Lean Startup,* such as Wealthfront (which began as the online gaming business KaChing) and Groupon.

But pivots aren't just for startups. An executive at one major publishing house recently told me the company has lately been "disrupting the way we do everything in the typical publication process."

They've been testing cover designs, content, and titles, mostly within a given author's existing audience but also with groups unfamiliar with the author and the content.

In the past, the publisher didn't seek out much of any feedback from test groups or from author communities. "Beforehand we kind of just trusted ourselves," explained the executive. "We trusted our individual biases and the hubris that we actually knew more than the consumer."

But as the publishing market has shifted, from one that mostly relied on foot traffic coming and going from bookstores to a dominant online market, the company has had to pivot to adapt to the buyer's habits. "We, as an industry, realized we needed to figure out how we're getting to the consumer directly."

In one case, the publisher tested an entire manuscript. The book was in production already, but the executive and her team were interested to find out more about how potential readers would respond to the book, even though they didn't anticipate making any significant changes to the manuscript.

As they started getting feedback and compiling data, they were quite surprised to learn that the thirty-five- to sixty-year-old demographic the publisher anticipated targeting wasn't at all the core audience. Instead, the book was resonating with millennials. That was when they pivoted in order to maximize their success. "We scrapped our entire marketing and publicity campaign directed toward that older demographic and skewed it toward millennials," the executive said. Their vision for the book hadn't changed, only the audience for it.

WHEN TO PIVOT

If you've ever been in a real-life pivot situation, you know how stressful it can be. Often, we wait until far too late to consider a pivot. The roof is on fire. The walls are caving in. There's a board meeting tomorrow morning. We're about to run out of money. This is not really an environment conducive to rational decision making.

There are perfectly good reasons we delay pivoting. Simply raising the question "Is our strategy working?" can seem like a criticism of the team's current direction. It risks morale. It's rare for everyone on the team to agree about how well the current strategy is working, so pivoting may be a source of conflict. And there's the eternal optimism of the startup mind: that maybe, if we give it just one more try, growth will materialize.

So, one last suggestion on the topic of pivot-or-persevere meetings: Nearly every great startup success had to pivot along the way. It's a universal consequence of the conditions of extreme uncertainty that startups live in. But if we know for sure that we are going to have to pivot, why wait until the very last minute to think about it? My suggestion is: *Schedule the pivot-or-persevere meeting in advance.* Put it on the calendar. Make it a routine part of everyday life.

Find the right cadence for the startup in question. I usually recommend about once every six weeks—certainly not more often than once a month or less frequently than once a quarter. Have the meeting, and let it be no big deal. It's not an existential crisis. It's not an admission that we don't know what we are doing. It's just a chance to ask ourselves: What evidence do we have that our current strategy is taking us closer to our vision?

Not only is this a calmer environment than a crisis in which to make these decisions, but there is another benefit, too. A previously scheduled pivot-or-persevere meeting also acts as a focusing device for everyone on the team. In the early days especially, all the team members can be asking themselves between meetings: Is the thing I'm working on *right now* going to help us six weeks from now at our next pivot-or-persevere meeting? This can eliminate massive sources of waste, such as making elaborate plans for what to do after the product launch, adding features that customers don't yet need, trying to serve mainstream customers when the product doesn't even have early adopters, staffing up customer service in anticipation of future demand, and (my favorite) prematurely investing in scalable infrastructure.

THE PIVOT TO OBLIVION

Sometimes, one pivot leads to another pivot, and then another, until the team runs out of pivots and realizes that their vision, great as it might have seemed, cannot find successful footing. That's exactly what happened to one of GE's Turbomachinery Solutions teams, that nevertheless counts the cancellation of their project as a good outcome.

The team's plan was to develop a new component to increase the efficiency and production of large natural gas plants. The Flash Liquid Expander (FLE) would increase gas liquefaction capacity from the plants and create additional revenue streams for the company. The new process would also provide a side benefit: recovered energy that could be used for other purposes in the same plant, increasing overall efficiency.

As Silvio Sferruzza, NPI (new-product introduction) excellence leader and FastWorks program manager at GE Oil & Gas, puts it, the team knew that "From a technology viewpoint, the project was absolutely feasible. If we understood how to go to market, there was no question that the FLE could be built." The team had created an impressive business case for the project based on the large number of existing plants in which the new equipment would ultimately be installed, and on the assumption that, given the anticipated benefit for the potential customers (up to $100 million per year), the operators of the majority of the existing plants would want to carry out the retrofit. They also believed that the new equipment would become a popular option for new plants as they were built.

"The business case on paper was great," Sferruzza remembers. It directly addressed the team's customer problem statement: "The customer will want to increase plant efficiency without any impact on availability. The increased production would generate additional revenues." But the business case was also built entirely on assumptions. As Sferruzza puts it, "We are a technology company. Our approach has been to focus on how to do things, to look at technical challenges. Everybody is happy to work on that."

The question for the team, which included sales, engineering, commercial operations, and a FastWorks coach, was not whether they *could* build the Flash Liquid Expander (FLE), but whether they *should* build it. Would customers like this new product enough to pay for it? "In the past, before we adopted the Fast-Works approach, we would have worked on this project from start to finish without questioning customer assumptions too much," Sferruzza says. "We would have gone through the process of development looking mainly at technical risks."

These were their commercial leap-of-faith assumptions:

- No competitor was earlier in the market with this idea.
- The Liquified Natural Gas process licensor (the company with the patent for the natural gas liquefaction process that reviews and approves new technology to make sure it meets the required standards) was willing to open a discussion with GE about the new process (i.e., there were no preexisting barriers, such as an exclusive relationship with another company).
- The LNG process licensor would be willing to adopt GE's new solution, making it the new standard in the field.
- The technology would be scalable to other applications in other markets.
- Customers would be engaged partners in the process of iterating and rapidly prototyping the new product.

Working closely with the sales team, the Turbomachinery Solutions team connected with clients with whom they had good relationships. In this early stage, their MVP was just a presentation about how the new component worked. As FastWorks coach Giulio Canegallo explains it, the "exchange of value was mainly about information—to share and collect information about the process with the different customers."

This one MVP allowed them to test many of their leap-of-faith assumptions. They very quickly learned that a few of their key ideas about how to go to market were wrong.

With this feedback in hand, the team went back to the drawing board to see if there was another market they might tap into for the FLE in order to pivot. They'd learned from one of their customers that they might be able to supply the new component to the cryogenic market (industrial refrigeration applications), as well, thereby adding to the product's potential.

After two and a half months and a few thousand dollars testing the cryogenic market, the team came to the conclusion that it wasn't big enough to merit the kind of investment necessary to develop and build the FLE, even as an MVP. At that point, at the team's final pivot-or-persevere meeting, they decided to kill the project.

The meeting where they presented their findings was uncomfortable for many of the team members, who were understandably disappointed that their project failed. But there was a huge upside, as well. As Canegallo sums it up:

> It was a mix of feelings. On one side, the team was sad because an exciting, potentially great product turned out to be not as great as it initially seemed. On the other side, they were happy and proud to have discovered that much earlier and more cheaply than they would have after developing it. They recognized that they had saved the company's money and people's time, which have since been invested in more profitable activities.

And, of course, the team members were also personally grateful not to have put years of their time and energy into a product that ultimately would not have created value for customers and would have been a failure for the company. In the end, the team spent $30,000 and seven months testing their assumptions, rather than millions of dollars and years of time and effort, only to watch their project fail. And the internal board that was overseeing their funding—called a *growth board*[11]—not only saw that but applauded it. "They recognized the effort put into testing the assumptions, valued the learning achieved, and congratulated the team for their courage to recognize and admit they were wrong. All the team members have been rewarded because of that," Canegallo adds. Incentivizing learning in this case saved the company from wasting time and money. "We celebrate the team's attitude as a best practice within Turbomachinery Solutions."

LEAN STARTUP FOR LEADERS

In the Lean Startup methodology, one of the most important things a leader has to do is ask questions of the people doing the build-measure-learn work. The most important questions for the leaders to ask are:

1. What did you learn?
2. How do you know?

As we'll see again and again throughout this book, so much of this change in management approach comes down to culture, mindset, and habits. One of the hardest assumptions to dispel is the idea that the leader is the supreme expert: The leader makes the plan, and subordinates execute it. When there is uncertainty, the leader provides definitive answers. And if any subordinate fails to deliver, the leader metes out appropriate punishment—because failure to execute the plan is a sign of incompetence.

By now I hope you see how many situations in the modern world defy this older paradigm. Many failures are caused not by incompetent execution but by reality failing to live up to the assumptions built into the plan. If only customers would read the business plan, then they would know how to behave!

Therefore, part of the new leadership paradigm is changing this older paradigm to a learning orientation. Scott Cook calls it "setting the grand challenge" and creating the platforms for experimentation that teams need to get the answers for themselves. By asking about learning—rather than yelling about failure— leaders create more and better opportunities to experiment.

For those people leading startup teams, this is obviously beneficial. But the change in mindset can carry over into all kinds of non-startup contexts, too. One executive I worked closely with told me a story that stuck with me. He had been through Lean Startup training and was acting as executive sponsor to a corporate internal startup. He met with this team regularly.

One day he was wrapping up with his innovation team after they had agreed to a new pivot. As is true for most executives, that was only one meeting of many that day. He dutifully attended the next: a call with a regional sales manager reporting on quarterly results in his sales territory in central Europe. The sales manager was calling with bad news: Their go-to-market strategy for a new product had come in well under quota.

The executive knew just what to do, he told me. He had years of practice at "taking this guy's head off." He was about to upbraid his subordinate when he had a thought. What would happen if he treated this call like the pivot-or-persevere meeting he'd had moments before? Instead of grilling the subordinate, he started asking questions: What did you learn? How do you know?

The regional sales manager was so surprised he almost dropped the phone. It turned out that the go-to-market strategy had revealed some unexpected facts. This region had special requirements that were different from those in the United States. (Why are American companies always surprised to learn this?) Indigenous competitors had decent products already in the market. And the parent company's brand wasn't very strong in this region, so distribution was more difficult than expected. In other words, although neither realized it, this go-to-market plan had been an experiment all along. It had seemed like a low-risk, high-certainty initiative and, therefore, amenable to classic management techniques. But real life had intervened.

After probing a bit to make sure what he was hearing was the truth and not just a bunch of excuses, the executive made a much better plan to go to market in that region with great success. He realized that just by asking a different set of questions, he had achieved a business result his older training would have overlooked.

This is just one story of a leader who was able to find new results by changing his own behavior and mindset. There are many more such stories to come in later chapters. What they all have in common is the synthesis of the tools of the Lean Startup with management practices that enable continuous innovation. In the next chapter, I'll describe what that new systemic approach looks like in practice.

## CHAPTER 5

A MANAGEMENT SYSTEM FOR INNOVATION AT SCALE

MY WORK WITH companies has taken me to many exotic locales, but one of the trips that most made an impression on me was decidedly less glamorous: I was in America's rust belt, walking the factory floor of an old-school manufacturing plant that had been in continuous operation for decades, churning out thousands of common household appliances. The company was in the midst of a lean transformation and had been making tremendous strides toward eliminating waste in inventory while at the same time improving product quality and plant safety.

One of the company's product managers took me on a tour so I could see firsthand the progress they had made. For all my years studying and talking about lean manufacturing, I rarely get to take the most important lean advice: *genchi gembutsu*—go see for yourself.[1] On this tour, I came to profoundly appreciate how much craft and skill goes into the production of even the most humble appliance. Every little button is hand-wired by a human being to the circuit boards behind it, thousands upon thousands of times every day. Even in this age of automation, a simply awesome amount of skilled labor goes into nearly every product you buy.

As I was discussing this with the leadership of the company, I couldn't stop thinking about my own kitchen, where I have an inexpensive microwave. It has twenty-nine buttons on the front panel (I counted). Even being very generous, I think I have only ever pressed five of them. The other twenty-four serve no purpose for me. I asked the company's leaders: On average, how many of the buttons that are lovingly and skillfully handcrafted into your appliances are never pressed by even a single customer? What percentage are completely useless?

They didn't know. And, in another era, I suppose this would have been unremarkable. Collecting this kind of data from the field is challenging—or, at least, it used to be.

But this is the twenty-first century. Service technicians routinely download usage data from appliances. Many appliances are themselves connected to the Internet. And it's easier than ever to directly survey customers or ask them to record their own usage. When I asked the leaders about this, they admitted to me that yes, the data exists. They just hadn't looked at it.

Why do you think they covered their eyes, all the while knowing that this information was available? I think, deep down, they knew that the data would be depressing. Visualize, if you can, the incredible number of hours of skilled labor that go into painstakingly wiring up thousands upon thousands of buttons that are *never pressed by anyone*. If you take that vision seriously, you should find it painful. What a dreadful waste of human energy and potential.

Why is it happening? Is it the the fault of the individual factory worker? Certainly not—each of them is carrying out his or her assignment superbly.

How about the factory foreman? Of course not. With skill and dedication, he or she is overseeing the implementation of a system designed for quality and efficiency.

What about the many lean experts who are looking to drive waste out of this factory? Not their problem. The buttons are not part of the "work in process inventory" that they are currently eliminating.[2] And because the buttons are part of the existing product specifications, they're not empowered to remove them, anyway.

Surely, then, the blame lies with the product managers? When asked, they, too, vigorously deny responsibility. "We're simply responding to what the customer wants!"

How could consumers want extra buttons that they don't push? I can't remember the last time I heard someone bemoaning the fact that a user interface was "too simple—if only it had more buttons!"

It turns out that when the product managers told me the customers wanted more buttons, they weren't actually talking about the consumer, because the consumer is not *their* customer. "The customer is the category buyer at the big-box retail stores where we sell most of our appliances," they explained. "Our sales team spends extensive time with the customer to find out what they want us to build."

So . . . it's the sales team's fault? Not really. If you talk to them, you'll find out that they are honestly and clearly representing what the customer is asking for. That, after all, is their job.

It must be the category buyer's fault? Nope, her needs are completely rational, too. Microwaves are a commodity product. She has to somehow organize giant shelves full of them. The easiest way? Make sure that the more expensive ones have more bells and whistles (or, in this case, buttons). Then line them up by number of buttons to make it easy for consumers to navigate the choices.

In this entire "value chain," no one has taken the responsibility for answering this simple question: What is the evidence that more buttons make customers more likely to buy this appliance, then buy from this company again and again over the long term?

Every function is doing its job. Everyone is making money. Leaders are being promoted and rewarded. So nobody is to blame.

Yet this kind of thing happens. Every. Single. Day. Thousands of skilled craftspeople wire up thousands upon thousands of buttons that are never pushed by anyone. Now, multiply this waste by thousands of similar products being produced all over the world.

This is not some dystopian-future novel; this is happening right now. There has to be a better way.

WHAT IS TO BE DONE?

When established organizations first started asking me to work as a consultant, I thought my primary task would be to bring the "Silicon Valley way of working" to them. And, to some extent, I have. But the biggest surprise has been the extent to which my Silicon Valley colleagues have been interested in learning from my war stories of working to implement Lean Startup techniques in corporate settings. It's what led to my realization that the Startup Way requires reforms and changes on both sides of the traditional "startup" and "enterprise" divide.

A modern company isn't about working just one way—the Silicon Valley way—or the other—the current corporate management way. If it were, we'd just recommend that every big company that needs innovation buy some startups. Or, if the way established corporations and organizations were working now was the answer, we could simply have them teach their management principles to the next generation.

But the truth is that each of these systems has its own set of unique problems. In established companies, an incredible amount of talent and energy gets wasted because innovation is blocked by the archaic, inflexible structures and protocols in place.

On the other side of the divide, Silicon Valley startups have a problem that is caused by their own successes: scale. No startup wants to structure itself, as it grows, along the lines of a gigantic company with functions so siloed that they don't even come into contact with one another. Yet that's often what happens when startups get too large to be managed as a single team. The systems that work so well for small companies don't translate into the larger ecosystem that a growing company needs, so the company eventually stalls.

ACCOUNTABILITY IS THE FOUNDATION OF MANAGEMENT

Entrepreneurial management is a leadership framework designed specifically for twenty-first-century uncertainty. It's not a replacement for traditional management. It's a discipline designed to help leaders become as rigorous in the entrepreneurial part of their management portfolio as they are in the general management part. Just because innovation is decentralized and unpredictable doesn't mean it can't be managed. It just requires different tools and different safeguards than the ones we're accustomed to seeing in traditional management settings. The power of the Startup Way lies in the fact that it combines the strengths of two different ways of working.

In *The Lean Startup,* I included my first attempt to articulate "the startup way" of working with this simple diagram (inspired by a famous diagram in *The Toyota Way*)[3]:

THE STARTUP WAY

The foundation of the Startup Way is made up of these same elements, beginning with **ACCOUNTABILITY**: the systems, rewards, and incentives that drive employees' behavior and focus their attention. What are people compensated for, promoted for, celebrated for, or fired for in the organization? What performance objectives really matter for employees' careers at the end of the day? Accountability systems must be aligned with the goals—both long- and short-term—that the company wants to achieve.

PROCESS concerns the tools and tactics that employees habitually use every day to get work done, such as project planning, management, team coordination, and collaboration. Process flows out of accountability, because every company's accountability systems constrain its choices. Most teams, given the right incentives (or, more specifically, the absence of harmful incentives), can self-organize around new tools and tactics. If, for example, an accountability system punishes any kind of failure, it's going to be impossible to implement processes for rapid experimentation and iteration (which always involve a whole lot of failing).

Over time, these habits and ways of working congeal into **CULTURE**: the shared, often unstated, beliefs that determine what employees believe to be possible, because "that's just the way things are around here." Culture is the institutional muscle memory, based not on how the organization aspires to operate but on how it really has in the past. You cannot change culture by simply putting up posters that exhort employees to "Be more innovative!" or "Think outside the box!" Not even Facebook's famous "Move fast and break things!" spray-painted on your walls will have any effect. Culture is formed over time, the residue leftover from the process and accountability choices of the company's past.

Every culture attracts certain kinds of **PEOPLE**: the ultimate corporate resource. A toxic or old-fashioned culture repels innovative talent. Ultimately, the success of any organization depends on the caliber of the people it is able to attract and retain. Think back to Jeff Immelt's dramatic statement from Chapter 1 about how no company wants to be perceived as "old-fashioned," since that label makes it harder to hire great people. Or the stories we all know so well of entrepreneurial people who suffered "organ rejection" despite their incredible talents.

To incubate a new culture requires individual teams to self-organize. New cultures come from the *lived experience of seeing a new way succeed*. These teams can become the seeds of a new company-wide culture if carefully nurtured. In fact, in many successful transformations I have witnessed, future leaders who became instrumental change agents began as ordinary employees working on early pilot projects. Once they saw what was possible, they made the choice to dedicate their careers to bringing those benefits to others in the company.

As I mentioned in Chapter 1, this new way stands on the shoulders of revolutions past: scientific management, mass production, lean manufacturing, Six Sigma, agile software development, customer development, maneuver warfare, design thinking, and more. Even within a single organization, entrepreneurial principles and general management principles share common foundations—especially the importance of long-term thinking—and common values—a need for rigor and discipline in execution. I have attempted to summarize these commonalities and differences between the two sets of principles in a "house" diagram, shown on page 126.

A NEW ORGANIZATIONAL FORM

Even as the tools of entrepreneurial management are used throughout the organization for projects that require innovation or that operate in contexts of uncertainty, entrepreneurship also needs its own dedicated home within the organization. Once we acknowledge that entrepreneurship requires a specialized set of skills and its own distinctive best practices, we can give it its own home in the org chart, as a peer function to engineering, marketing, sales, IT, HR, finance, etc. (See org chart on page 127.)

As we'll see in more detail in Part Two, the entrepreneurial function changes how other functions operate by introducing entrepreneurial techniques into purely internal projects and processes. It even offers the possibility of incubating whole new company divisions and functions, as we'll see in Part Three.

RESULTS

Sustainable Growth · Team Morale

Continuous Innovation · Continuous Transformation

SHARED VALUES

Commitment to Truth

Discipline

THE STARTUP WAY

Excellence

Continuous Improvement

PEOPLE

Cross-functional teams · Two-pizza teams
Entrepreneurs · Founder's mindset

CULTURE

"I eat failure for breakfast" · Productive failures
"Black swan" farming · Innovation as a verb

PROCESS

Highly iterative, scientific process
Build, measure, learn · Economies of speed
Portfolio of rapid experiments

ACCOUNTABILITY

Innovation Accounting · Leading Indicators
Future absolute cash flow · Metered funding

FOUNDATION

Vision · Purpose · Investment in People · Long-Term Thinking

RESULTS

PEOPLE

Experts · Optimizers · Consistent
Managers · Specialists

CULTURE

"Failure is not an option" · Risk mitigation
Innovation as a noun · Compliance
Predictability

PROCESS

Functional hand-offs · Huge programs
Quality through reduction of variability
Economies of scale · Statistical process control

ACCOUNTABILITY

ROI · Cost reduction · Market share
Margins · Incremental growth
Entitlement funding

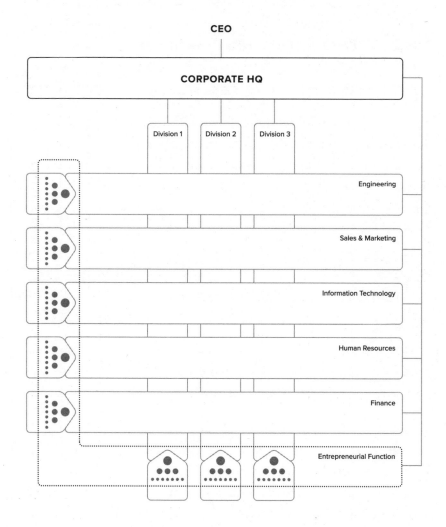

"Wait a minute," you might say. "If this requires changing the org chart, the other functions, the culture of the company, who we hire and promote—that sounds very difficult." That's right, it is. I don't want to sugarcoat this. It requires building a new kind of organization in response to a new blueprint, and doing so is especially hard because everyone involved has muscle memory and habits formed in the old order.[4]

But I believe the benefits are worth the pain.

THE OUTCOMES OF TRANSFORMATION

1. It provides many more opportunities for leadership

One of the challenges of today's hierarchies is that there are actually only a few true general manager jobs with full P&L responsibility. And in companies that create smaller leadership positions, the positions often don't count as real leadership roles precisely because they are small. In most organizations, small is seen as irrelevant. Internal startups provide the best of both worlds: real, honest-to-God opportunity but small, well-contained liability. Someone with the knack for turning those seeds into real impact has the opportunity to prove herself a true leader even if her background makes her seem too risky to give mature P&L responsibility.

2. It helps keep innovative people in the company instead of incentivizing them to leave

When talented people leave to form their own company, this is—on average—a good thing for the overall economy.[5] But to their former company, it's a loss.

When a company buys a successful startup, it is thought of as a corporate development victory. But I would argue that when the founders of the startup are ex-employees of the parent company, this is not a corp-dev victory but an HR failure. The founders never should have been allowed to walk out the door to begin with; they were forced out by the old-fashioned bureaucracy.

3. It reduces wasted time and energy

"How do you know that the work you do every day creates value for somebody else?" A huge percentage of people can't answer that question. Think of the workers hand-wiring the twenty-nine buttons on the microwave.

Lean manufacturing theory identifies seven kinds of waste: transportation, inventory, motion, waiting, overprocessing, over-production, and defects. Recently, the lean community has been thinking beyond traditional categories of waste. We need to recognize that doing something efficiently that nobody wants once it's done is another foundational form of waste. This problem plagues companies of every size, startups and established organizations alike: *We pour time and energy into building the wrong product.*[6]

The Startup Way focuses management effort on figuring out the right things to build in the first place.

4. It's a much better way to kill projects

Most people whose projects get killed in corporate America feel that someone had it in for them: "I had a good idea, but so-and-so shut it down." This thinking, true or not, is terrible for morale and also causes internecine strife. In addition, it prevents people from voicing dissent, because that can set off a chain of dangerous events; it's much easier to let a project continue to limp along like a zombie. Canceling a project often has significant political consequences. As a result, companies don't do it nearly often enough. Once a project starts to gather political momentum, it becomes hard for a stage-gate process to stop it.[7] Middle managers are forced to act like executioners—when they do have to kill a project, it's usually quite painful.

In fact, I've sat in on a lot of corporate reviews over the years. Most companies use a "green, yellow, red" evaluation system to determine where a team is in terms of hitting necessary milestones. Generally speaking, if there are ten criteria for conducting the evaluation, every team always seems to present seven greens, two yellows, and one red. It's like magic—they're always the same!

Why? Every manager knows that if you show too many greens, you won't sound credible. On the other hand, too many problems could get your project canceled. Managers are perfectly calibrating their status updates to what is needed to pass through the gates. The amount of behind-the-scenes time and energy spent on constructing this narrative, which often has little connection to how the project is actually progressing, is huge.[8]

Startups, on the other hand, fail all the time. The immediate proximate cause is always the same: They run out of money before they become profitable and cannot raise more. While some founders may grumble about the investors who didn't back them, the general culture accepts that failure of the enterprise is caused by its leaders and their decisions. That doesn't mean we end their careers—trust me, I've been the cause of startup failure myself—but we expect them to take responsibility. If they can't raise additional money, it is because the results they generated weren't compelling enough to advance to the next stage.

Most corporate projects lack this level of accountability. Our goal as leaders should be: If a project fails, it's on the project founder. The *entrepreneur* didn't deliver the results. *He or she allowed it to die*—not some higher-up manager. Taking responsibility for that failure is harder in the short term, but failing with honor is a skill.[9] And it takes advantage of the most important lesson of the scientific method: If you can't fail, you can't learn. Experimenting rapidly, teams learn for themselves what's important, and the lessons teams learn—about customers, about the market, about themselves—are much more profound than they would be otherwise. And many failed projects—think back to Amazon's Fire phone from Chapter 1—lay the foundation for future successes.

5. The ability to solve heterogeneous problems with speed and agility

There are certain problems that, when they arise, require the whole organization to reinvent itself to solve them, like a massive product recall or some other highly visible crisis.

But what about urgent problems that, for whatever reason (real or political), don't rise to the CEO's personal attention? What about the problems that require collaboration between one function or division that feels the acute pain and another that does not? And what about the frustrating, everyday problems that afflict "only" ordinary workers? Today's management system struggles to bring attention and resources to bear in these situations. A more entrepreneurial approach offers a better answer: Put a startup on it. Run an experiment. Measure the results. Scale it up—maybe even bring it to the attention of senior leadership—if and when the results merit this treatment. Take advantage of the fact that the vast majority of experiments fail, and so they don't need to take up senior management bandwidth (nor do they necessarily benefit from senior management meddling). By the time the organization needs to have a strategy conversation about whether to double down on the new idea, it can have a rational discussion—complete with actual customer data.

And while we're talking about problems, how about the kind that could be solved more efficiently and potentially change and even save lives? That's what the founders of Emerald Cloud Lab (ECL), a web-based life sciences lab, believe working in this new way can do. "Biotech is the farthest from lean you can get," says co-founder Brian Frezza.[10] The cure for cancer, the answer to Alzheimer's, a more effective drug for depression; these potential medical breakthroughs all originate in labs. And each of the labs costs at least $10 million—sometimes twice that amount—just to spend years running tests and trials. It makes biotech a complicated and expensive field. To get a new drug to market can often take eleven years.

Typically, labs are structured as follows: There is one principal to whom many scientists report, who in turn manages many researchers, while all research slowly filters back up to the principal. Some of it never gets there, and much of it takes years. "The people making instrumental decisions have to guess at what people want at the higher levels," explains Frezza. "A lot of it gets filtered out because you only want to give your boss the best results."

All the while, health spending is increasing. In fact, life sciences spend more than any other industry in R&D expenditures per person.

It can also take six to twelve months to get experiments set up and another six to twelve months of actual testing. And that's assuming everything is going smoothly. If there's an error or the lab runs into a problem, you can count on another six to twelve months before things start up again. "Imagine if you were a software developer and your administrator came to you and said, 'We expect to be back online next year,'" says Frezza.

ECL does things very differently. It allows customers to specify complete experiments electronically. It then uses its technology platform to carry them out.

Every day there is a team of operators who are cross-trained with the equipment. No one specializes so each person can work on a variety of experiments, depending on the requests and clients. Requests come through an online system through a server, data is generated and put back on the server, and investigators can look at it and move on to the next step. This system allows the industry, and particularly the data, to grow exponentially. Every time a problem is solved, it's solved in code and exists for the next generation. It doesn't need to be redone every time a new lab is set up.

6. . . . Profit?[11]

By addressing uncertainty and helping companies build more new products, the Startup Way of working allows managers to be more adaptive and agile in the marketplace.

I once brought a group of finance executives from public companies to visit Intuit to learn about their Lean Startup transformation. Intuit's culture is very open and friendly, very Silicon Valley, very customer- and design-centric. There was quite a culture clash in this meeting. As the Intuit team was presenting their Design for Delight approach, I could see the increasing skepticism on the finance folks' faces. Eventually, they started to press: What are the metrics you use to gauge success? How do you know these improvements are really driven by this change in culture and process? To their shock, the Intuit team pulled up the live company dashboard right there in front of them. They showed the company's top-level innovation goals, as well as how they broke down by division and team. The finance folks were astounded—where were the financial metrics? Almost everything was customer-centric and product-centric.

At this point, I think the finance execs were pretty confident they were going to cut Intuit and its newfangled way of operating down to size. A company that doesn't tend to its finances is probably in trouble. So they started to ask their toughest financial questions: How is Intuit stock doing? How are the multiples and P/E ratios changing as a result? The Intuit team was totally honest in admitting they didn't know. They were focused on customers, not finances, and trusted that good products would eventually lead to good outcomes.

Finally, one of the finance execs decided to answer his own question. He pulled out his laptop and began to look at the company's public filings. He was shocked again: The stock price was up over the period covered by the transformation. But not only up in raw terms; the P/E ratio was up, too. Now we had the finance executives' attention.

After the meeting, the financial executives discussed with me their main takeaways. This is what stood out for them: "Our stock price is stuck at the low end of the range because we can't get the markets to give us credit for future growth. Even if we have a good year, or an individual breakthrough product, it's hard to convince analysts that it was anything more than a fluke. They think our innovation story is—frankly—bullshit. What Intuit has done has not just changed their growth trajectory but proved to the markets that this growth is driven by a comprehensible process. That means that, over time, they've been able to convince the markets that their growth is no fluke."

I believe this is the promise of working in a new way: new sources of growth and a system for continually finding them that can be explained to investors, employees, and the outside world.

. . .

We've seen how the current siloed function structure makes a problem like the microwave button issue hard to solve. These little wastes are just as important as the big breakthroughs. A modern company can eradicate them by having an experimental system available at all levels and all times. Not only that, such a system delivers not only waste reduction and better morale but the possibility of an extra bonus return. Sometimes by fixing a small problem you stumble on an amazing opportunity.

How would a company steeped in the Startup Way resolve the question of the many useless microwave buttons? By now, I hope the answer is clear: put a small "two-pizza team" on the problem and treat them as an internal startup. Have the startup build some minimum viable products and attempt to sell them to customers. One of my manufacturing clients actually did this, taking each MVP to a different local retailer and measuring the differences in both customer interest and conversion rates to real orders. This method will quickly determine whether more or fewer buttons are really key to driving the right customer behaviors. Maybe these experiments would reveal a dramatically different strategy for the whole product line, in which case the team would double down and scale this new solution. But maybe the experiment would prove that the current method of designing and stocking microwaves is the right one.

Either way, this knowledge is immensely valuable: either to pursue a new business opportunity or to give the people working on the product true certainty that their work matters to customers.

The point is that in the grand scheme of things, this is a problem too small to rise to the level of the CEO or senior leaders. In order to solve it, the ability to experiment and pivot and learn has to be embedded in the fabric of a company. It has to be available to every employee.

And yet, to most managers I meet, this new way of working sounds like science fiction. We take the wastes of our current paradigm for granted. If we are going to change, how on earth do we get from here to there? This is the topic of Part Two.

## PART TWO

A ROAD MAP FOR TRANSFORMATION

"WHO IS TALKING, AND WHAT ARE WE TALKING ABOUT?"

When people tell me they don't think these methods will work in their organizations, I like to tell them the story of HealthCare.gov. I mean, sure, your organization may be political and bureaucratic. But compared to the Department of Health and Human Services (roughly 80,000 employees and counting[1])? The political maelstrom of Obamacare? Is your situation really more challenging than that?

In October of 2013 Mikey Dickerson, a site reliability engineer at Google, made a phone call that changed not only his life but the lives of millions of Americans. He had worked on President Barack Obama's 2012 reelection campaign and had been watching in horror the recent news about HealthCare.gov, the technological centerpiece of the Affordable Care Act, which the Obama administration had launched on October 1. The online marketplace, built at a cost of $800 million over three years by a collection of fifty-five different contractors,[2] had immediately crashed. At the end of its first day, only six people had managed to sign up for insurance. By the end of the second day, the number was up—to an equally unimpressive 248.[3] HealthCare.gov, the crowning achievement of decades of tough policy work, was not only a disaster, it was a very public disaster. The site's failure made headline news on every program, website, and social media channel, nearly destroying a cornerstone of Obama's legacy.

When a friend from Dickerson's campaigning days passed him a phone number and asked him to call it on a specific Friday morning, Dickerson thought he was going to learn more about the problems the site was having. Punching in the numbers in the early-morning darkness—it was 5:30 a.m. in California—he settled in for what he thought would be a routine conference call.

What he got was something else entirely. He'd apparently joined a meeting that was already in progress, in which "people were talking about what they were going to do and how this team was going to work on HealthCare.gov," he recalls. "I eventually had to interrupt and say, 'Who is talking, and what are we talking about? I don't understand what's going on.'"

That was when Todd Park, then the chief technology officer of the United States, whom Dickerson had never even heard of, much less met, introduced himself and all the others present, including Dickerson, who was busy looking up each name on Wikipedia and trying to verify whether the call was real. "This wasn't really a conference call with a plan and an agenda to talk about how we're going to attack this problem, what we're looking for, and are you interested," he realized. Instead, he had been thrust into a conversation with a handful of people from inside and outside government who had been handpicked to form a team to work on the website. "This was just a very confusing and weird experience to be having at five thirty in the morning sitting on a beanbag chair in my living room," Dickerson recounted. Nevertheless, three days later, he was on a plane for Washington, D.C.

Upon his arrival, Dickerson, along with the tiny team of technologists Todd Park had pulled together, dove into the problem, which, initially, had very little to do with tech at all. To begin with, it involved dozens of contractors from different companies working on the project from multiple locations, with no coordination mechanism. This was, Dickerson soon discovered, in no way atypical for government. But it was anathema to everything he knew from the private sector. "We spent three or four weeks when the only visible thing we were doing was making everybody come to one place," he recalls. "When things went wrong, we just went and found the person who was responsible."

In addition, the site architecture was so bad that the slightest problem had the potential to knock the whole thing out. There was no way to track issues, and none of the fault tolerance or resistance that such a massive system should have had in place, as a matter of course, existed.

Faced with this quagmire, the team asked a single question: "Why is the site not working on October 22?" Then they worked backward, applying the management and technological practices that by now should sound familiar: small teams, rapid iteration, accountability metrics, and a culture of transparency without fear of recrimination. This last matter was particularly intractable. Dickerson held two stand-up meetings per day, at 10:00 a.m. and 6:30 p.m., and issued three rules about how the recovery process would be undertaken, which were posted on the door of what came to be called the "war room":

RULE 1: *The war room and the meetings are for solving problems. There are plenty of other venues where people can devote their creative energies to shifting blame.*

RULE 2: *The ones who should be doing the talking are the people who know the most about an issue, not the ones with the highest rank. If anyone finds themselves sitting passively while managers and executives talk over them with less accurate information, we have gone off the rails, and I would like to know about it.*

RULE 3: *We need to stay focused on the most urgent issues, like things that will hurt us in the next 24–48 hours.*[4]

In other words, Dickerson helped guide the teams in the ways he knew to be the most useful from his work at Google—methods that should sound familiar from earlier chapters. He got people into the same room, he made them work together, he prioritized, he enforced a culture of meritocracy, and he asked for honesty. Two months later, four out of five people who wanted to sign up for insurance could do so, and the site was improving daily. According to The Washington Post, *"The turnaround was fostered mainly by an abrupt culture shift in which government workers, contractors, and the tech imports worked hand in hand."*[5]

Thanks, in part, to Dickerson's leadership, by December 1, the system was able to handle 50,000 users at a time, more than 400 bugs had been fixed, and uptimes had gone from 43 percent at the beginning of November to 95 percent.[6]

THE "HOW" BEHIND THE STARTUP WAY

As exciting as the HealthCare.gov rescue story is, it's only a small part of the much bigger story of a massive, ongoing change in the way the federal government implements and manages its digital dimension. The other parts of the story, which, like at GE, include early efforts that uncovered change agents and then a period of growth, are just one example of what this section of the book is about. Part Two tackles the real and difficult details of how to move an organization to a more effective, entrepreneurial way of working, and it answers three fundamental questions:

1. *What, exactly, are the systems and structures we need to implement?*
2. *How, exactly, do we convince managers and employees alike to try something different than what they've known their whole careers? (Remember, even in a hypergrowth startup, most employees were not present for the founding of the company.)*
3. *When, exactly, is a company ready to make this transformation happen?*

THE THREE PHASES

Part Two is structured around three common phases of transformations I've observed. **Phase One** *is about laying the foundation through experimentation, adaptation, and translation. It is about preparing for the moment when decisive change becomes possible by building a critical mass of success stories and demonstrating that the new way of working is not only viable but preferable. In the government, a committed group of technologists was already in place, making this first phase work, collecting data, and preparing for a bigger role.*

Once that moment arrives, the organization shifts into **Phase Two**, *which is for rapid scaling and deployment. All the resisters and objectors come out of the woodwork. The transformation either develops its own political heft or it dies. When Mikey Dickerson took the phone call, he actually entered the middle of the government's transformation story.*

If these early efforts succeed, they will eventually have the power to tackle **Phase Three:** *dealing with the deep systems of the corporation. Here, finally, it becomes possible to address the structures that cause people, again and again, to return to the old ways. For Dickerson and the government, that meant the establishment of the United States Digital Service and, later, the Technology Transformation Service. If we neglect them, any change will only be temporary. But if we attempt to touch these "third rails" too early, we'll lack the power to overhaul them.*

In Chapters 6 through 8, we'll talk about how to move an organization through each phase of the transformation, and you'll read the surprising stories and lessons learned from people who have done this work in their own organizations.

While I will walk you through how I've seen these transforma-

tions play out, starting simply and gradually getting more complex, do not treat these chapters as a step-by-step guide to everything you must do. Rather, use these stories and tools to prepare for the specific challenges that will inevitably arise. Every organization is different, and in fact many of the techniques you'll see are about how to experiment to learn what works best in any specific context. Pay attention to the way these entrepreneurs think, and how they devised experiments that revealed the right path forward, rather than making any attempt to slavishly copy their stories.

This chart (opposite) provides an overview of how the three phases tend to play out across the different scales of an organization. It's a kind of summary or rough map of the terrain we're entering.

Each of the topics in this chart (opposite) will be addressed in detail as we move ahead. Then, at the end of Part Two, we'll do a deep dive into the workings of the financial mechanisms and structures that support the Startup Way.

PHASES AND SCALES

	PHASE ONE: CRITICAL MASS	PHASE TWO: SCALING UP	PHASE THREE: DEEP SYSTEMS
TEAM LEVEL	Start small, figure out what works and doesn't for our company, touch a variety of divisions/functions/regions.	Scale up the number of teams, build programs and accelerators as needed. Include all divisions/functions/regions.	This is "the way we work," tools and training widely available to all kinds of teams. Not limited to high-uncertainty projects.
DIVISION LEVEL	Enlist a small number of senior leaders as "champions" to make exceptions to company policies as needed.	Train all senior leaders, even those who are not directly responsible for innovation, so they have literacy in the new way.	Establish growth boards, innovation accounting, and strict accountability for all senior leaders to allocate resources to the change.
ENTERPRISE LEVEL	Get agreement with the most senior leaders about what success looks like (cycle time, morale, productivity). Focus on leading indicators. Establish criteria to move to Phase Two. As word of successes starts to spread throughout the organization, recruit early adopters at all levels.	Build a transformation organization with heft. Develop coaches, a company-specific playbook, new finance and accountability tools like growth boards.	Tackle the hardest deep systems of the company: compensation and promotion, finance, resource allocation, supply chain, legal.
OVERALL GOAL	Build critical mass to get senior leadership bought into rolling this out company-wide. Translate the Startup Way into company-specific culture.	Build organizational clout to have the political capital necessary to tackle the thorny issues of Phase Three.	Build an organizational capability for continuous transformation.

## CHAPTER 6

PHASE ONE: CRITICAL MASS

EVERY AUGUST, GE has its annual officers' meeting in Crotonville, New York, at the company's executive training facility. It was at that meeting, in 2012, that I spoke to the company's highest-level executives about *The Lean Startup* at Beth Comstock and Jeff Immelt's invitation. The talk was followed in the second half of the day by a workshop with the Series X team—and a few dozen GE officers in the back of the room "just to observe." These were pivotal meetings, in which I pleaded utter ignorance of diesel engines (and they were kind enough to listen to me anyway), as I described in the Introduction. They turned out to be the beginning of GE's transformation journey.

I made my presentation on the ground level of an auditorium-style lecture hall. Rising above me in stadium seating were roughly two hundred executives—all skeptics. As Beth Comstock, who shared the stage with me that day, describes them: "A lot of these people were engineers and finance people. They run regions. They're functional leaders. They crossed their arms.

They shifted. You could just see the thought bubble over their heads, like, 'Okay smarty-pants software dude. You can change a software order fifty times in a day, but try that in a jet engine.'"

It was no accident that Series X had been picked as the first project to test; a huge multiplatform engine is about as far away from software as you can get. The thinking was that if we could get this project operating in a new way, there would be no limit to Lean Startup applications company-wide, which aligned perfectly with the company's desire to simplify its way of working across its many businesses.

SERIES X: "RAISE YOUR HAND IF YOU BELIEVE THIS FORECAST."

Hours after addressing the officers, I found myself in a business school–type classroom elsewhere in the building along with engineers representing the businesses involved in the Series X engine development, the CEOs of each of those businesses, plus a small cross-functional group of top-level executives who'd orchestrated my visit that day. And don't forget the GE officers there "just to observe."

We had gathered to try to answer one of Jeff Immelt's most persistent questions: "Why is it taking me five years to get a Series X engine?"

I kicked off the workshop by asking the Series X team to walk us all through their five-year business plan. Cory Nelson, the GM for the Series X program at the time,[1] describes the scene far better than I can: "I tell people it was like free falling." My role was to ask questions about what the team actually knew versus what they had guessed. What do we know about how this product will work? Who are the customers, and how do we know they will want it? What aspects of the timeline are determined by the laws of physics versus GE's internal processes? (From our discussion in Chapter 4, you'll recognize these as leap-of-faith assumptions.)

The team proceeded to present the currently approved business case for the Series X, including a revenue forecast with graph bars going up and to the right with such velocity that the chart showed this as-yet-unbuilt engine making literally billions of dollars a year for GE as far into the future as thirty years hence. Beth Comstock recalls: "It was like all the business plans we see, with a hockey stick that is going to grow to the moon in five years, and everything is going to be perfect."

I remember thinking to myself, "I may not know very much about diesel engines, but this business plan looks awfully familiar—it's like every startup's ludicrous fantasy plan. Step into my office!" So I made a simple request of the room: "Raise your hand if you believe this forecast."

I am not making this up: Everybody in the room raised a hand! And, to be honest, they seemed a little irritated at the question, and at having to explain to the software guy who knew nothing about engines that they never would have invested millions of dollars in this plan if they didn't believe in it. After all, this team had already spent months collecting requirements. The best and brightest minds in the company had already thoroughly vetted this project and approved it. You can see why they saw my question as an insult to their intelligence.

But I kept going, this time pointing to one specific bar on the chart: "Seriously, who *really* believes that in the year 2028, you're going to make exactly this many billion dollars from this engine?"

This time, no one raised a hand.

Everyone knows you can't predict the future with that kind of accuracy. And yet many of the talented executives in the room had forged successful careers by doing precisely that.

After a prolonged moment of discomfort, we moved on. The team told me that their main competitor in this space had a long history of market domination with a product that was technically inferior to what the Series X could be. GE planned to build something that was 20 to 30 percent more energy efficient and use this superiority to convince customers to switch.

Buried in a footnote to the appendix of their business plan was a tiny detail: The key to the competitor's success was its network of local franchises, which meant it had in place a huge support system that fostered customer relationships. Obviously this was a serious competitive advantage, so I asked the team what their plan was for distribution. "We're going to go build our own distribution network," they told me. "Do you know how to do that?" I asked. "Have you done it before?" And, most important, "*When* are you going to do it?" The answer to this last question was most telling of all. "After the product is done."

What that meant was that the team would spend five years building a product and then another chunk of time setting up a distribution network, all for a product that by then might have been designed nearly a decade earlier.

Still, the question loomed over the room. Why does it take so long to build this engine?

I don't want to undersell the technical challenges that led to the original five-year plan. The specifications required an audacious engineering effort that combined a difficult set of design parameters with the need for a new mass-production facility and global supply chain. A lot of brilliant people had done real, hard work to ensure that the plan was feasible and technically viable.

But a large part of the technical difficulty of this project was driven by the specifications themselves. Remember that this product had to support five distinct uses in very different physical terrains (visualize how different the circumstances are at sea, in stationary drilling, on a train, for power generation, and in mobile fracking). The uses for the engine were based on a series of assumptions about the size of the market, competitors' offerings, and the financial gains to be had by supporting so many different customers all at once.

These "requirements" had been gathered using traditional market-research techniques. But surveys and focus groups are not experiments. Customers don't always know what they want, though they are often more than happy to tell you anyway. The incentives that govern most customer research promote more rather than fewer requirements (especially when you use a third party).

And just because we *can* serve multiple customer segments with the same product doesn't mean we have to. (In fact, this is a typical source of scope creep. In order to create a more alluring fantasy plan, we increase the degree of difficulty for the engineers.) If we could find a way to make the technical requirements easier, maybe we could find a way to shorten the cycle time.

There were also many questions about the plan's commercial assumptions. One of the executives present, Steve Liguori, then GE's executive director of global innovation and new models, recalled, "We had a whole list of these leap-of-faith assumptions around the marketplace and the customer. What percentage gains is the customer looking for? Are you going to sell it with a direct sales force or an indirect sales force? Are you going to sell it or lease it or rent it? Are you going to pay for distribution? We had about two dozen of these questions, and it turns out that when we asked the team how many of them they thought they could answer, it was only two of the twenty-four." Liguori recalls this as the "aha moment." The company had been so focused on the technical risks—*Can this product be built?*—that it hadn't focused on the marketing and sales-related risks—*Should this product be built?*

Since the best way to test market assumptions is to get something out to customers, I made what was, to the room, a really radical suggestion: an MVP diesel engine. This team was trying to design a piece of equipment that would work in multiple contexts. As a result of this complexity, not only did it not have a specific target customer, it was caught up in the budgeting and political constraints that accompany such a multifaceted project. What would happen if we decided to target only one use case at first and make the engineering problem easier?

The room went a little wild. The engineers said it couldn't be done. Then one of them made a joke: "It's not literally impossible, though. I mean, I could do it by going to our competitor, buying one of their engines, painting over the logo, and putting ours on." Cue the nervous chuckles in the room.

Of course, they never would have actually done this, but the joke led to a conversation about which of the five uses was the easiest to build. The marine application had to be waterproof. The mobile fracking application needed wheels. Ultimately, the team arrived at a stationary power generator as the simplest technical prospect. One of the engineers thought this could cut their cycle time from five years to two.

"Five years to two is a pretty good improvement," I said. "But let's keep going. In this new time line, how long would it take to build that first engine?" This question seemed to once again cause some irritation in the room. The participants started to painstakingly explain to me the economics of mass production. It's the same amount of work to set up a factory and supply chain no matter how many engines you subsequently produce.

I apologized once again. "Forgive my ignorance, but I'm not asking about one *line* of engines. How long would it take you to produce just one single unit? You must have a testing process, right?" They did, and it required that the first working prototype be done and tested within the first year. When I asked if anyone in the room had a customer who might be interested in buying the first prototype, one of the VPs present suddenly said, "I've got someone who comes into my office every month asking for that. I'm pretty sure they'd buy it."

Now the energy in the room was starting to shift. We'd gone from five years to one year for putting a real product into the hands of a real customer. But the team kept going. "You know, if you just want to sell one engine, to that one specific customer," said one engineer, "we don't even need to build anything new. We could modify one of our existing products." Everyone in the room stared in disbelief. It turned out that there was an engine called the 616 that, with a few adjustments, would meet the specs for just the power generation use. (Of course, the 616 wouldn't be nearly as profitable as the proposed Series X, as it had the wrong weight and cost profile. But since we were literally talking about a single engine, I asked, could we afford to sell the modified 616 at the lower Series X price—just to test demand? The GE balance sheet could take the hit.)

This new MVP was literally an order of magnitude faster than the original plan: from more than five years to fewer than six months.

In the course of just a few hours—by asking a few deceptively simple questions—we'd dramatically cut the project's cycle time and found a way for this team to learn quickly. And, if they decided to pursue this course, we could potentially be on track to save the company millions of dollars. What if it turned out that that first customer didn't want to buy the MVP? What if the lack of a service and support network was a deal killer? Wouldn't you want to know that now rather than five years from now?

I'll be honest: I was getting pretty excited. It seemed like a perfect ending.

Or was it? As the workshop wound to its conclusion, one of the executives in the back of the room couldn't stand it anymore.

He had been mostly silent so far, but finally he decided to speak up: "What is the point," he asked, "of selling just one engine to one customer?" From his point of view, we had just gone from talking about a project potentially worth billions to one worth practically nothing.

His objections continued. Even putting aside the futility of selling only one engine, targeting only one customer use effectively lowered the target market for this product by 80 percent. What would that do to the ROI profile of this investment?

I'll never forget what happened next. "You're right," I said. "If we don't need to learn anything, if you believe in this plan and its attendant forecast that we looked at a few minutes ago, then what I'm describing is a waste of time. Testing is a distraction from the real work of executing to plan." I kid you not—this executive looked satisfied.

And that would have been the end of my time at GE, except for the fact that several of his peers objected. Hadn't we just admitted a few minutes ago that we weren't entirely sure that this forecast was accurate? The executives themselves started to brainstorm all the things that could go wrong that might be revealed by this MVP: What if the customer's requirements are different? What if the service and support needs are more difficult than we anticipate? What if the customer's physical environment is more demanding? What if the customer doesn't trust our brand in this new market segment?

When the conversation shifted from "What does this outsider think?" to "What do we, ourselves, think?" it was a whole new ball game.

Even the most senior technical leader in the entire company at the time, Mark Little, who was then senior vice president and chief technology officer of GE Global Research, had a change of heart. He was the person the engineers in the room most looked up to, and whose skepticism—voiced quite clearly earlier in the day—had them most worried. He ended our workshop by saying something that stunned the room: "I get it now. I am the problem." He truly understood that for the company to move faster in the way that Jeff Immelt wanted, he, along with every other leader, had to adapt. The standard processes were holding back growth, and he, as a guardian of process, had to make a change.

"What was really important and interesting to me was that the workshop changed the attitude of the team from one of being really scared about making a mistake to being engaged and thoughtful and willing to take a risk and try stuff, and it got the management team to think more about testing assumptions than creating failures," he recalled. "That was very liberating."

This was not the end of the story, as you'll see. The Series X team turned into one of the many pilot projects for the program we came to call FastWorks. The team got the test engine to market dramatically sooner and immediately got an order for five engines. During the time they would have been doing stealth R&D in the conventional process, waiting for what Mark Little calls "the big bang," they were gaining market insights and earning revenue from their MVP.

We'll come back to the role of coaches in helping teams learn these methods in the next chapter. But for a moment, I want to dwell on an important fact. During this workshop—and the months of coaching that followed—no one had to tell these engineers what to do. Not me, not Beth Comstock, not Mark Little, not even Jeff Immelt. Once presented with the right framework for rethinking their assumptions, the engineers came up with the new plan through their own analysis and their own insights. It became obvious to everyone in the room that this method had worked and that the team had arrived at an outcome that the company would not have been able to get to any other way.

"The Lean Startup just simplified it," Cory Nelson recounts. "We were trying to drag around so much complexity and so much overhead. The Lean Startup said, 'Don't make it so hard. Take it a step at a time.' Let's get an engine out there, let's go learn some things, then let's pivot when we need to. There may be some intermediate stops along the way. It's not going to be a straight line to get there, but it's having the faith that you're going to figure out a *way* to get there."

PHASE ONE: COMMON PATTERNS

At GE, the transformation began with the single project I just told you about: the Series X engine. Of course, not every company has a multiplatform engine on tap, so the way the company launched their efforts to change was, in that sense, unique. But in many ways, the project was absolutely typical of the start of a transformation process. No matter what size or kind of company, the earliest stages of implementing this new way of working are local, ad hoc, and chaotic. Early adopters experiment with new approaches, sometimes an external or internal coach may help a handful of individual teams. The beginning of a Startup Way transformation is very grassroots. It makes progress, one project at a time, in service of proving a larger thesis, both to management (top-down) and to the teams doing the testing (bottom-up). It looks different depending on the organization, but I've noticed certain common patterns that recur in many different kinds of organizations:

• Start with a limited number of projects and build from there in order to create a comprehensive set of cases, stories, and results to show how the new method works in this particular organization.

- Create dedicated, cross-functional teams to undertake the pilot projects in order to embed functional diversity from the start.
- Create a growth board–type system that allows executives to make swift, clear decisions about the projects presented to them.
- Teach early teams how to design Lean Startup–type experiments that help them plot a course through uncertain terrain.
- Use the right startup-style metrics to measure the results of those experiments.
- Build a network of leaders in the organization who can help resolve problems that come up as the new way of working comes into conflict with entrenched methods. Work by exception at the start in order to move forward quickly and to defer deep changes to organizational structures until later phases.
- Translate the new concepts into company-specific language and tools.

THE ENERGY FOR TRANSFORMATION

The steps above are, obviously, no small amount of work to undertake. Where do organizations get the motivation to embark on a Startup Way type of transformation? I have seen three distinct driving forces behind this kind of change:

1. **CRISIS:** Sometimes, a crisis forces change. Earlier I recounted the story of how the very public meltdown of HealthCare .gov—a crisis of the highest order—was the catalyst for real change at numerous agencies across the federal government, beginning with an epic lesson in what can happen if you rely on traditional "safe" management methods.

2. **STRATEGY:** Other times, a new organizational strategy clearly necessitates a new way of working. At GE and Intuit, change was driven from the very top by a recognition that new strategic imperatives required a dramatic overhaul. This can work only when the most senior leaders in the company have bought into the new approach and are determined to see it through. It is also not the kind of decision that can be made lightly, which is why it becomes critical, after the first stages, to demonstrate how the new methods function and to lay the groundwork for full mobilization across the entire organization.

3. **HYPERGROWTH:** Success can be its own form of crisis. When a startup achieves product/market fit, it can be forced to grow extremely rapidly. As legendary Silicon Valley investor Marc Andreessen, also founder of Netscape and general partner of the VC firm Andreessen Horowitz, put it (in one of the startup movement's most famous pieces of writing):

> In a great market—a market with lots of real potential customers—the market pulls product out of the startup. . . . And you can always feel product/market fit when it's happening. The customers are buying the product just as fast as you can make it—or usage is growing just as fast as you can add more servers. Money from customers is piling up in your company checking account. You're hiring sales and customer support staff as fast as you can. Reporters are calling because they've heard about your hot new thing and they want to talk to you about it. You start getting entrepreneur of the year awards from Harvard Business School. Investment bankers are staking out your house.[2]

What all three of those scenarios have in common is that they unleash a tremendous amount of energy. Like breaking the nuclear bonds of an atom, this discharge must be carefully managed. The kind of energy released in each scenario is different, but once it's unlocked, what happens next follows the same pattern. If the bonds are broken randomly, without the apparatus to manage the energy, the process can be tremendously destructive. Those who have a way to turn that energy into productive change are at a decisive advantage.

HOW THE SUCCESS OF SERIES X INFLUENCED GE

The Series X workshop kicked off a transformation process. After its success, we continued to coach new teams until we had a critical mass that touched every combination of function, region, and business unit in the entire company. The early participants were not chosen at random. Nor was the work they did an end in itself—although it was real, important work. Rather, these initial proofs of concept were designed to demonstrate to senior management that this new way of working would be viable across the organization.

GE made an early key decision that was a big driver of Fast-Works's later success. The CEO appointed a cross-functional team of senior executives to oversee the initiative. Comprising the top executives across each of the core disciplines of engineering, marketing, HR, IT, and finance,[3] this team served as a kind of steering committee. (Later we would formally organize it as a growth board.) Appointing the right people to be in charge of the effort is critical.

Jeff Immelt immediately recognized that they were on to something important, and not just for new products. Beth Comstock recalled his excitement after the Series X report. "Jeff said, 'You see, we can do something here. Can we go beyond product scope? Can we use this to go after bureaucracy?'" As Viv Goldstein remembers, "That was the entire intent with the Series X engine—to get a single proof point on the board that said, 'Can it work in a very complicated, very difficult environment?' And if it could, then what do we do?"

What we did was start training more teams. First, one team at a time. Then four at a time, and then batches of eight, including both new products and new process projects. There were teams focused around refrigerators and engines and neonatal incubators, along with a corporate process redesign team, an enterprise resource planning (ERP) project for manufacturing supply chains, an IT project, and an HR hiring project. Each of these projects was chosen intentionally.

The goal was to test as many kinds of teams and functions as possible to show that the FastWorks methodology could work company-wide on a broad cross-section of lines of business, functions, and geographic regions. This critical mass eventually set off a chain reaction of change throughout the company, sparked and driven by the confident buy-in of senior management.

. . .

1. Start Small

This first phase is about looking at the results of early projects and asking what went well and what went poorly. Which behaviors and practices support experimentation and entrepreneurial behavior? Which employees have proven to be change agents who will help to scale these efforts?

At GE the scale of the program was determined by how many people the company wanted to train at each stage. The total number of people affected in the early teams that we coached was a tiny fraction of GE's 300,000-plus workforce. At a startup, the scale of the program is determined by the size of the company.

The fact is, there is no such thing as a sixty-person company.

There's only a sixty-person company on its way to becoming a sixty-five-person company, then a hundred-person company, then six hundred, then six thousand, depending on the rate of growth. That is why it's important to gradually weave what worked well for a young company into the overall management process—to be integrative rather than retroactive. As Patrick Malatack of Twilio puts it: "The failure pattern is: as you scale your business, you stop applying what you had to do out of necessity when you were smaller. You stop experimenting the way you had to experiment because you didn't have enough resources to go do a three-year project that goes nowhere. As you grow your organization, you need to make sure that you are able to still continue to experiment and try new things." As Twilio has grown from thirty-five people to six hundred and fifty, they've worked hard to keep the early structures in place. "It's strange how the size of your organization creates this failure pattern for you if you're not careful," Malatack says.

TRANSFORMING THE FEDERAL GOVERNMENT

The story I told you about HealthCare.gov and Mikey Dickerson may sound like the beginning of the government's transformation story, but it's actually the middle. Long before HealthCare .gov, innovative pilot projects and teams were being tested by Todd Park and others, along with a group of young technologists from President Obama's transition team. They were trying to find ways to implement desperately needed tech reform. Among them was Haley Van Dyck, who had arrived in Washington after working on the presidential campaign as part of the technology team developing and deploying the campaign's mobile and text messaging platforms, the first of their kind in politics. Now she and many of her colleagues were in D.C. with "a very similar mandate of using technology to connect citizens to the government, instead of voters to the campaign."

On his first full day in office, President Obama signed the Memorandum on Transparency and Open Government. A few months later, he appointed Aneesh Chopra, then the secretary of technology for the state of Virginia, to the newly created post of chief technology officer of the United States. Together with Vivek Kundra, America's first chief information officer, and later Jeffrey Zients, the new chief performance officer, Chopra would be responsible for "promot[ing] technological innovation to help achieve our most urgent priorities." It would be done within a sprawling, interconnected organization made up of dozens of agencies employing 2.8 million people using computer systems dating back to the 1950s: the federal government.[4]

Teams were parachuted into a few agencies under the name "New Media" offices. A team was also set up within the White House to improve digital communication and civic engagement with the public, building on the campaign's great success.

These were wild, experimental days and, as is typical of Phase One, quite chaotic. There was little to no organization or coordination among teams, no consistent structure in terms of who was reporting to whom or even agreement over what people's individual missions were.

But these pioneers also learned that there was a real place for technology and startup talent within government. It was the first time anyone was able to gather real evidence for this idea at scale. (A previous lean version of HealthCare.gov built before the failed launch of the official site barely saw the light of day—it was too small to matter!) Van Dyck herself became part of a successful team at the Federal Communications Commission (FCC). As is almost always the case, her team discovered plenty of people inside the agency who were ready for change. They just had had no system for supporting it. If it had not been for these early efforts, there could not have been an effective HealthCare.gov rescue.

The Presidential Innovation Fellows Program

After several early successes, Todd Park, who had been promoted to federal CTO after Aneesh Chopra stepped down, proposed a program called the Presidential Innovation Fellows (PIFs), in which leaders from the tech industry would do "tours of duty," in partnership with civil servants inside the agencies, to tackle specific problems in government that seemed intractable. The idea was to combine the experience and expertise of inside stakeholders with the skills and talents of outside entrepreneurs, designers, and engineers, just as Park would himself do during the HealthCare .gov meltdown and rescue. "What we said was," Park explained, "what are you trying to do? What kinds of capabilities and skills do you want to bring in from the outside to help you? Let's form a team that has your best people on it and bring people in from the outside who have the skills you want, and then have that team execute [operations] in a Lean Startup mode to do more than either could do separately and deliver successfully against that mission."[5]

The program itself was an experiment. No one knew if it would even be possible to get Silicon Valley people into government, so that became the team's first hypothesis. To test it, Park got on a plane and announced the new program at TechCrunch Disrupt, a gathering of entrepreneurs, investors, hackers, and tech fans.

The response was overwhelming—nearly seven hundred people applied.[6] Park ended up selecting eighteen fellows for that first class and "just throwing them into a small number of projects, and [we] were off to the races to see the kind of results it delivered," says Van Dyck. As of 2017, 112 fellows had been through the program, more than half of whom had stayed on in the federal government to continue their work.[7]

The PIF program was the government's version of the Fast-Works pilot projects we did at GE. It was created not only to do important work, but to continue gathering evidence that this new way of working could take hold in a wide variety of agencies and across a huge range of projects.

2. Build Dedicated, Cross-Functional Teams

The goal of building cross-functional teams is to harness and share collaborative energy from various disciplines within the organization, allowing functional diversity to grow over time. Chances are, the initial teams won't have the ideal mix of functions, but it's important to assemble as many necessary functions as possible. Sometimes this means including people who aren't officially on the team but are willing to volunteer their time and expertise.

On one team I worked with at a large corporation, the leader wanted an industrial designer on the team full-time. But this team didn't have the budget or political capital to get someone with the right skills assigned to it. Design was considered a separate function from product in this company, so there was a lot of resistance to assigning someone from a rival function. Convincing leaders not only to build truly cross-functional teams but to make them fully dedicated is one of the most significant challenges I typically face when I work with companies of any size. This was a perfect example.

However, the leader of this team knew a designer who believed in his vision, so he approached that person and asked if she would move her desk to the room where the team had set up. This designer wasn't working for the team or officially assigned to it. She was not being paid out of the team's budget. She was just a committed volunteer sitting nearby so that when questions arose, team members could consult her. This team was also working on physical prototypes, and her proximity to the process allowed her to intervene if she saw something she knew wouldn't work.

Of course, not every team needs an industrial designer, just as some won't need IT or legal support but might need engineering, marketing, or sales. The key is to identify which functions each team requires to make progress.

Susana Jurado Apruzzese, head of the innovation portfolio at Telefónica, says that one of the biggest challenges her company faces is the transfer of knowledge in innovation projects from the innovation area to the business unit for commercialization. To take the success of a project to the next step—namely, to market—the project must be transferred to sales and marketing. Jurado Apruzzese finds that including the business side on her team early on makes getting their buy-in much easier. It's also an ideal way to make sure that sales and marketing are well versed in the knowledge around the product so that they fully understand what it is they're selling when the time comes.

"We have realized that unless you are involving the business unit in terms of being a sponsor or a stakeholder from the very beginning, it's not going to work as well, because they don't feel like the product is theirs," says Jurado Apruzzese.

WHAT TO DO IF A FUNCTION ISN'T REPRESENTED

Most organizations are resistant to working cross-functionally. The politics and budgeting issues alone can derail the initiative. But in the early days, these kinds of failures can turn into valuable learning opportunities for the organization.

During my first months at GE, I worked with a health care team in the company's Life Sciences business that was developing a very advanced product that they planned to commercialize over several years at a cost of $35 million. This complex, FDA-regulated, technologically intensive device had been in serious R&D for many years, and the company finally felt the technology was mature enough for commercialization.

After going through the FastWorks process, the team decided

to build an MVP that they could show a specific customer within a few weeks—instead of waiting for years. They built the prototype, which was nonfunctional but showed how the device would both look and work, and set up a meeting with their customer.

The night before the big reveal, I got an urgent phone call from the team. "Legal said no to our experiment," they fretted. This team, naturally, did not have a lawyer on board, so they relied on the company's legal function for approvals.

Because of the nature of their work, they'd known they'd eventually have to consult legal for approval, but they hadn't planned ahead. Imagine if they had enlisted legal expertise from the start from someone who knew all along that there was no real risk to a patient or anyone else in this MVP—that there was no liability involved until the customer actually said yes to the product and then, eighteen months later, paid money for it. Eighteen months is a long time to resolve any liability issues. They got their project approved, but it required a last-minute exception that added a lot of tension to the process.

FUNCTIONAL AMBASSADORS

I want to highlight one additional critical aspect of cross-functionality. Functional team members serve not only as the team's conscience in their particular area of expertise, but also as enthusiastic *ambassadors*. As the Startup Way of working starts to spread, it's important to have people on board who can go back to their colleagues in each function and tell them about the new method.

Ambassadors also act as *translators* who can explain their role in terms others on the team can understand. I experienced this firsthand with a team at a major manufacturer. An engineer was brought in to ensure that the rigor of the process wasn't lost as the team transitioned to experimenting and making MVPs. He understood the principles so organically that he was able to translate them into very technical, mechanical engineering terms that were foreign to me but easily understood by the team. We would often have him meet with teams, who said, "We'd love to do this, but we can't compromise our new-product development process." His response? "I helped write that process for our division. Here's how to rethink it to ensure that safety and compliance standards are met, even as we change the mechanics of how we work."

3. Wield the Golden Sword

At GE, we held "report out" sessions at the end of every three-day training for the teams in Phase One. The second part of the presentation was like a corporate version of the TV show *Deal or No Deal*. We would explain what was required in order to make the new plan succeed. I encouraged every team to be honest and ask for what was *really* needed, not the usual corporate-speak padded estimates.

To the surprise of senior leaders, teams rarely asked for more funding. What they usually requested was air cover and clearing away of bureaucratic obstacles. One team needed its team reduced—from a twenty-five-person committee of part-timers to a five-person dedicated team. Other teams needed experts from other functions assigned on a full-time basis. And many of them simply needed senior leadership's assurance that if they worked in this new way they wouldn't be eaten alive by middle managers. Using this process, they generally got what they asked for in an extremely efficient manner.

Over the years, I've been repeatedly amazed at how many "impossible" problems could be solved by using the simple process I call the "Golden Sword" because it cuts through bureaucracy in one swift stroke. It comes into play during meetings between teams and executives, and it goes like this. The team presents an offer to the senior leaders, saying here is what you get: faster cycle time, more insight into what's happening on the ground, and a promise to solve the problem fully and control spending along the way. And here is what it will cost you: air cover, secure funding, and cross-functional collaborators. From the point of view of most executives, that's a true bargain. Greater accountability, greater confidence that the team will deliver real results, and all for the low, low cost of some political maneuvering, which is one thing they excel at.

Of course, getting what they want doesn't mean a team will automatically succeed. When we launched the first cohort of projects at one company, I had a conversation with executives in which I explained, with all due respect, it would be a triumph if even one team succeeded. True to corporate form there was a lot of pressure to ensure a 100 percent success rate. This kind of thinking, of course, is incompatible with startup thinking, which understands failure and experimentation as part of the methodology. Wielding the Golden Sword helps leadership become a part of that process.

TRANSPARENCY AND A BACKUP POWER SYSTEM

One GE team I worked with was working on a next-generation uninterruptible power supply (UPS)—a system that gets sold to big data centers and ensures that if there's a utility outage the system has power until a second generator is available. The team believed they could build a more efficient system using a higher-voltage architecture. Their plan, when they came into the workshop, was to spend three years and roughly $10 million, followed by a huge public launch.

This was one of the first GE teams to organize an internal board. They would have regular pivot-or-persevere meetings in which they would assess the latest MVP they were considering, and the board would make funding decisions based on asking them questions about what they'd learned and how.

Following our initial workshop, the team agreed to build an MVP in three months instead of three years. The team spent a few weeks on electrical diagrams to ensure they could build the product. Then came the moment of truth: A customer requested a proposal, saw the diagrams, and instantly rejected them. The team tried again with another customer, then another. When the rejections piled up, they knew their plan was fundamentally off.

It was no small thing to admit this to their executive sponsor. But, luckily, the Golden Sword process made it easier to keep the conversation focused on what the team had learned following each customer visit. Once they got up the courage to admit this, the team was able to pivot several times and ultimately come up with a new system that turned out to be a winner—and bore only a tangential relationship to their original product specifications.[8]

4. Design a Good Experiment

In order for an experiment to tell us what we need to know, i.e., whether it's worth continuing, it needs to have certain features. Teams don't do experiments just to see what might happen (if they did, they'd always be successful because something will always happen!). They do them to gain knowledge by measuring customer actions, not just what customers say. Every experiment should have:

- *A clear falsifiable hypothesis.* Without a clear vision of what is supposed to happen, we can't judge success or failure. And if you cannot fail, you cannot learn.
- *An obvious next action.* Build-measure-learn is a cycle, which means every experiment should lead directly to a follow-on action. One experiment is never enough to draw the necessary

conclusions. Only a series of experiments can reveal the truth.

- *Strict risk containment.* What's the worst that can happen? is usually a question we ask flippantly. But here we really need to know the answer—and make sure we can live with it. The goal isn't to prevent anything bad from happening. It's to make sure, by modifying the experiment, that whatever that bad thing is isn't disastrous. Risk containment strategies include restricting the number of customers who are exposed; not putting the corporate brand on the MVP; not compromising safety or compliance (even better, having a compliance expert on the team); giving the customer a more-than-money-back guarantee; offering to pay extra penalties for non-performance. Commit to always making it right for the customer, no matter the cost (remember, you won't have very many customers at first).

- *A tie between what is measured and at least one LOFA.* If we're not using an experiment to test an assumption, it's not giving us useful information.

THE CONNECTED CAR

After the meeting with Toyota executives I described in Chapter 1 took place, Matt Kresse, a researcher at the company's innovation hub, the InfoTechnology Center (ITC), and those same executives agreed to the idea of a Lean Startup project. In March of 2013, Kresse and Vinuth Rai, director of the Toyota InfoTechnology Center, began a series of experiments designed to discover and develop state-of-the-art technology for an Internet-connected car.

Their first step was to test an assumption: They ran an ad on Craigslist under the heading "Do you hate your commute?," inviting people to come into the research center and complain about their current driving experience. Within an hour, three hundred people had responded. "It was an immediate and very overwhelming response," Kresse remembers. "We didn't build anything until we heard the main pain points customers were expressing. It was, I think, the first time we were getting this raw data from users. It felt so good, because we had been operating mostly in a lablike environment where the setting is very sterile. That's not very conducive for someone to give you an honest response, so this was pretty refreshing."

The team offered five of the thirty people they brought in for interviews a prototype device to put in their cars for a month and told them that if they liked it they could keep it; if not, they'd receive $100 for their participation. This MVP was nothing more than an Android tablet with a very basic navigation system connected to an inexpensive microcontroller that was wired into the ignition and steering controls and packaged with a Toyota faceplate. "You've got to get stuff in front of people, get feedback from people early on," Kresse remembers thinking.

It was the first time Kresse's group was able to test their ideas with real consumers. They tracked which applications drivers were using in real time. They then met with people periodically to find out what each individual liked and didn't. "We were in this process of rapidly reiterating the applications," says Kresse. When the month was up, 60 percent of the people who tried the prototype navigation system wanted to keep it, and 40 percent of them said they'd recommend it to another person.

This kind of data got the attention of Toyota executives. Again, there was very little risk involved—the key to a smart MVP. Kresse and Rai weren't launching anything outside of the incubator-style ITC. But once their work was recognized, they got the go-ahead to start working with the company's product groups.

In November of 2016, Toyota launched its new connected "Mobility Service Platform" (MSPF) within its Toyota Connected business, of which Shigeki Tomoyama is president. They've come a long way from a humble Craigslist post seeking frustrated drivers.

BUSINESS MODEL EXPERIMENTS

One of the early teams I worked with at GE was designing a new gas turbine for a combined cycle power plant. Their goal was to build something that would be 5 percent more efficient than anything else on the market. They predicted it would take about four years to produce and would require the creation of a new supply chain. As they were getting into the planning, a team member said: "Hold on. Four years from now, the competitors' efficiency will have improved, so let's make sure that we extrapolate out the new efficiency target and be 5 percent better than that." Fair enough. But then they had to reestimate and required six years until launch, at which point someone else added, "Wait a minute—in six years, won't the efficiency need to be even greater?" Before anything had actually happened, the team was already trying to anticipate how they'd know whether they'd have market-leading efficiency by the time the engine was done. It was a downward spiral into near-infinite scope creep.

Their solution was to come up with a new business model. In the old model, GE's main job was to sell equipment. If and when customers came back for maintenance, try to sell them new efficiencies and upgrades. The team imagined a new model: include upgrades up front and commit to future improvements. There was also a clause that stipulated that GE would be responsible for damages related to any missed deadlines.

As one team member summarized the value proposition, "What if we approached the customer and said, 'Instead of waiting ten years for a turbine that's 5 percent more efficient, what if we sold you one right now that is pretty good, the added value being that every year from now on, we'll offer you an upgrade to replace the blades and fans, and tune the turbine to increase efficiency,'" the team brainstormed. "'You'll have the option, once a year, for us to install these parts, and we'll have a pre-existing contract that says we get paid for every point of efficiency we drive with each new upgrade.'"

We took this plan to the executives, who were excited about it. It offered a dramatically faster cycle-to-market time, and every iteration would provide greater efficiency. The customer is able to buy a turbine with best-in-class efficiency in perpetuity. Then someone asked the fatal question: "Is the revenue that we make each year from installing the upgraded parts product revenue or service revenue?"

Naïvely, I said, "Who cares? Revenue is revenue." But the answer mattered to them—a lot. It represented a turf war within the company that couldn't be resolved at the time. Still, the team kept at it, and the customer feedback remained positive. Ultimately, the executives came around to understanding that they needed to think about what was right for the customer rather than relying on traditional paradigms. Guy DeLeonardo, gas turbine product manager for GE Power, recalls, "It took the threat of losing a one-billion-dollar deal with a major utility company and valued customer for the two division leaders (the turf owners) to find a way to resolve this. You have to understand, this is how we had worked for the past thirty-plus years."

With the new model in place, the team launched the 7HA.02 Gas Turbine, which is now an industry leader for product efficiency and had $2 billion in sales in 2016. The team can add new innovations annually, knowing that customers want and will pay for them because the commercial terms have been agreed on in advance. "It doesn't matter where the revenue goes to the customer," says DeLeonardo. "We got out of our own way to do what's right for the customer."

. . .

When experimenting with business models,[9] here are a few things to keep in mind:

- Whose balance sheet should the product be on? Does it really make sense to force a small business or a consumer to pay cash up front?
- Why make a distinction between product and service? If products are designed to require periodic maintenance, why not take responsibility for providing it?
- Should a company profit from a product that may not actually fulfill the customer's needs? By charging only when the product performs—per-use or performance-based compensation—the company stays fully aligned with the customer's needs.
- Cycle times are faster when the company controls every aspect of service delivery. Can we take responsibility for intermediate steps in order to bring new innovations to market faster?
- When a company puts itself on the customer's side of the transaction (we profit only when they profit), we are able to discover more ways to add value.
- Are new competitive dynamics available to gain market share? For example, in GE's commercial lighting division, they have building-maintenance contracts that charge per socket rather than per bulb. GE is responsible for keeping the socket filled and operational. Every socket covered by a long-term agreement of this type effectively shrinks the total available market that is eligible for old-fashioned competitors to pursue.

In Lean Startup terms, we understand cycle time as build-measure-learn, which means that sometimes nontechnical parts of the cycle can be collapsed through business model changes. One product team I worked with kept running into a problem. After their product was designed and built, it took a year or more for customers to be given the chance to buy the new model. Why? Because distributors had to purchase the new product and revamp their showrooms in order to display it. Many distributors found this expensive and had little incentive to do it frequently. In markets with few distributors, there was little pressure on distributors to have the latest models on display. Nobody on either side of the divide found this arrangement strange—it was simply how the industry had always operated. And in terms of the long-term profitability of each product, it probably made little difference. Still, from a learning and cycle-time point of view, this setup is quite expensive. Compared to the cost of developing a new product, the cost of helping the distributor is quite modest. Why not move showroom costs onto our balance sheet?

5. Create New Ways to Measure Success

In this first phase of transformation, the organization is setting up cross-functional teams and doing experiments. But how do the teams know if they're succeeding? Through the use of *leading indicators* that measure *validated learning*.

LEADING INDICATORS

Leading indicators come in many forms. Their purpose is to track signs that the process is working at the team level. The goal is to show that the probability of something good happening is increasing. For example, one executive I worked with was very focused on cycle time as a leading indicator for success. He was happy if his product teams achieved an order-of-magnitude improvement in cycle time, even if they didn't produce other tangible benefits immediately. He was convinced that just getting to market faster and learning from customers sooner would eventually produce better commercial outcomes. More often than not, he was right. And this conviction allowed his teams to become more bold in their thinking.

Another good early indicator is customer satisfaction and engagement. As Todd Jackson, VP of product at Dropbox, learned, "Having early passionate users who advocate for your product means they will also tell other users. The number one best form of marketing is word of mouth."

The customer of one GE team was annoyed to learn that a perfect product would take another five or ten years to deliver. After going through FastWorks and coming up with a new plan, the team went back to this customer and said, "Instead of bringing you perfection, how about we bring you something that is still significantly better than what you have now but is just a start? We can bring it to you next year instead of in five years if you would help us by becoming an engaged part of the process." The customer was excited enough by this idea to want to start collaborating immediately, an experience the team had never had before. They hadn't done anything yet except have a conversation, but already their relationship with the customer had changed fundamentally. They knew they were on the right track.

The excitement at making new connections with real customers and seeing the potential there ties in to another important leading indicator: team morale. Change is hard, but it can also be contagious. Enthusiasm for a new way of working can make a huge impression on other people. Often one exposure to a truly engaged team is enough to get people saying things like, "I want my whole team to work like that," or even, "I wish my whole division thought and acted that way." Morale is powerful.

Notice a universal pattern in all of these stories: In every case, senior leadership has a point of view—and conviction—that the leading indicators the change agents are working toward point to good things ahead. Without this agreement, all the experimentation in the world in Phase One is for naught. Of course, a lot of work happens in later phases to confirm that these leading indicators do, in fact, signal positive business outcomes. But without leadership conviction, there's no way to get to those later phases.

METRICS

A little farther along on the path of experimentation, it's important to create metrics to measure the success of entrepreneurial projects. This entails replacing traditional metrics—often ROI—with *validated learning*: scientifically gathered information based on frequent experiments. For example, when the Dropbox team was building Paper, in order not to repeat the mistakes of Carousel and Mailbox, they looked at two critical behaviors: "We were disciplined about signing up first users who were representative of our entire customer and user base," Aditya Agarwal explains. "We made sure we weren't siloing ourselves."

Dropbox's two basic metrics were:

1. *Virality.* "We did not want Paper to become a single-user tool. If someone was using Paper to replace [to-do list software] Evernote, we weren't interested in that. We needed it to spread and be collaborative."
2. *Week-two retention.* "We invited someone, they tried it. Did they come back in week two?"

Metrics need not be complicated. Jeff Smith was hired into the role of CIO at IBM in 2014 to lead an agile transformation in the IT division. He says, "We used to measure too many damn things that did not have anything to do with the actual business value created." Now they have a list of four: (1) how fast a team can get a new task done; (2) how many tasks a team can complete in the course of one regular work cycle (however long that is); (3) how long it takes for a task pulled out of the backlog lineup to get into production; and (4) how long a task has been sitting in the backlog, which includes pruning projects that have been made irrelevant by the passage of time.

"The simpler your metrics, the simpler your goals," Smith says. "If everyone can understand it without a manual, people start getting better at a faster rate."

This is true no matter what the context. As Brian Lefler, a software engineer who transitioned into government IT, says, "Software companies have plenty of parts of their company that don't make obvious, clear money. At Google, when I worked in Ads it was very clear—I knew how much money we brought in divided by the number of people on my engineering team. But it wasn't that way when I worked in Amazon Ordering, which was a cost center. We were either costing our salaries or we were costing our salaries plus all sales missed, because we were broken. We figured out how to measure the success of teams so we had a proxy for market interactions."

When Lefler is working on a project for the federal government, partnering with an agency, these are some of the metrics he likes to use at the outset instead of just asking, "How did this week go?":

- How many bugs were there?
- How often was the system up?
- How many minutes did it take someone to process his or her form?
- How many cards (in the case of an immigration project involving green cards) did we print today?

Metrics are critical, Lefler says, because "when leadership can't measure results, the common response is to require all decisions to go up to their level. The first-order effect of better measurements is better decision making. The second-order effect is that leadership gives high-performing teams the autonomy to act faster and focus their attention on the right things."

6. Work by Exception

Every team that's working in the Startup Way needs to have someone in company leadership they can call upon, when needed, to resolve the toughest problems they face when interacting with the wider organization. The lack of such a person can be fatal to an internal startup at worst and cause a huge waste of time at best. Without such a sponsor, the team will have to spend precious resources explaining, navigating, and apologizing for their methods to others in the organization.

These executive sponsors fall into two different categories. One is the executive sponsor for the company's change agents. At GE those change agents were Viv Goldstein and Janice Semper, who on a daily basis drove the larger project to get the company to change its ways. The dominant concern of change agents is to make sure the program moves from Phase One to Phase Two. They're the "boots on the ground," so they need cover from above, often from someone who has the ear of the CEO, to make sure the change keeps moving forward. The other role played by executive sponsors is as provider of cover for the individual teams. In a large organization, the executive sponsor can be anyone in a position to clear obstacles for the individual pilot teams. It need not be the same sponsor for every team—but every team needs at least one.

In *The Lean Startup*, I emphasized that what people commonly think of as "protecting the startup from the big bad parent corporation" is actually backward. The issue is how to convince the parent company—and its nervous middle managers—that whatever the startup is doing is safe. That's why innovation methods that rely on secrecy rarely work more than once. The only path toward company-wide transformation is to innovate out in the open. But then, how do we clear these obstacles?

In a startup, even one that has grown to thousands of people, the person who plays the role of executive sponsor is often the founder or co-founder, who has both the moral authority and the connections to wave problems away. Todd Jackson of Dropbox, who has seen this in action both there and at Google, says: "You have to have the founders or the CEO say, 'Nope. We're investing in this.' And that has to come from him or her, because if it doesn't, the project will likely get swallowed up by the internal amount of energy and internal inertia that goes into the core product."

In a larger organization, the executive sponsor must be senior enough to clear obstacles, but not too senior to be unable to meet with individual teams.

WHO IS LEGAL?

At one tech company, I worked with a team that wanted to bring a new software product to market in a number of different countries. Their original plan was to launch globally and with great fanfare after eighteen months. During their Lean Startup training, they realized they could gauge interest in those countries much faster with Facebook ads. Their goal was to see if they could get people to enter their credit card numbers and commit to pre-ordering the software before too much time and money had been spent building the new versions.

Everyone agreed on the plan. Then, all at once, they froze. What about legal?

In a rush, the team presented a series of arguments for why "legal" wouldn't allow this experiment. They argued that there was no way they'd be permitted to take a credit card number without actually shipping something. And, once they had the credit card numbers, they'd have to make sure those numbers were kept safe from hackers, since they wouldn't be using the company's usual systems for processing. They needed a way for customers to explicitly agree that if the software was never shipped, they would get a refund. There was a laundry list of rules and compliance issues the team saw as insurmountable. They were ready to go back to the original plan.

So then I asked a dumb question: "Who is legal?" Who had told them about all of these ironclad rules? They were stumped. As in many organizations, their fear was a part of the culture that had been handed down and passed around for years.

Then I asked who we could call to find out whether their fears were actually well founded. Remember, this was software, not a medical device or a jet engine. No one's life or livelihood was at risk, so it seemed worth exploring whether there was a way to run this experiment.

The team decided that the only person who could really answer their question was the division's general counsel. At my insistence, we placed the call and cowered around the speakerphone in a conference room, waiting for "legal" to answer. When the GC answered, the team presented their question in the worst possible way: "Do you mind if we incur unlimited liability to the company by taking people's credit card numbers and charging them for a product we may never ship?" You can guess what the answer to that was.

Before the GC could launch into a full lecture, I interrupted. "Sir, apologies for the confusion, but what this team actually wants to do is take credit card numbers from no more than one hundred customers, each of whom would be charged a maximum of $29.95 if and when the product finally ships." To which the general counsel replied, "You're telling me that the total liability to the company is three thousand dollars, even in the worst-case scenario?" When we replied yes, he said, "Do you realize you've already spent more money than that wasting my time with this phone call? Of course you can run that experiment. Goodbye."

The team exploded with delighted disbelief. Their experiment had been approved. It was a one-time exception, but the experience offered a glimpse of a new way of working. Only much later, in Phase Three, did this company adopt a more systemic policy. For Phase One, simple exceptions would suffice.

ALL HANDS ON DECK—OR NOT

What happened to that software team frequently occurs in Phase One. It's not always going to be smooth sailing; conflicts will arise in the organization with both existing systems and people. I call this the "all-hands-on-deck problem." A company has an issue—perhaps the quarter isn't going well, or the company is about to raise financing and the numbers aren't where they want them to be. The person in charge tells the CEO, and the CEO reports the problem to the board with alarm: "We need all hands on deck! Every person in this company is now dedicated, one hundred percent, to solving this problem!" But what about the small teams dedicated to innovations not tied to the current quarter? There's something supremely unsatisfying about "almost all hands on deck," or giving only "99 percent effort" to an urgent problem. This causes many innovation projects to be canceled.

This is precisely the kind of situation in which executive sponsors are critical to making sure the transformation isn't stalled by conflict and the clash of systems. They can both protect the innovation teams and reassure everyone else that rising to the call in the company's hour of need is also the right thing to do. It's one of the ways in which organizations begin to build the capability to do both kinds of work simultaneously. Without this, long-term, sustained growth is impossible.

7. Translate This Way of Working into Terms the Organization Can Understand

One of the most important things an organization needs to do in the early stages of a transformation is to make the process its own. That includes talking about it in language that makes sense for each individual company. As Beth Comstock says of FastWorks (a name that drew on GE's tagline "Imagination at Work"): "I think with any company, you have to make it your own. We took the best of what was brought to us and adapted it, and I think that's part of the story, too. We added other tools, like a more disciplined growth-board process inspired by venture capital funding and cultural sayings. I think if you judge a culture by their communication, by the words they use, that's how you know you've had a change." Remember, it's not even called "lean manufacturing" at Toyota—it's the Toyota Production System.

Learning to work in this new way is not about the rigid adoption of a series of practices; it's about finding the ways the tools can be adapted and applied to each specific company. When people go to Intuit looking for a model of how to bring innovation into their companies—the company's Design for Delight innovation process has been hugely successful—Bennett Blank, innovation leader at Intuit, explains, "They say 'What can we replicate?'" His answer? "The first thing I always say is, 'You can't replicate. Run your own experiments, apply everything to your own process, and then you'll discover what works in your organization.'" This is really good advice, and it's what has made it possible for the organizations we've been talking about in this chapter to move forward so successfully. In this book, I've attempted to draw attention to the similarities between programs like FastWorks, Design for Delight, and the U.S. government's USDS. But each of these programs is still distinctively different. They reflect the culture and character at their parent organization.

As word has leaked out about my work with GE, I've fielded calls regularly from companies that want to replicate GE's early FastWorks success. But I don't run a consulting company, so I'm frequently asked whom a company should hire to make this change happen.

I tell companies to put someone already on their staff directly in charge of this initiative and to give that person the necessary resources. I believe this is the only way to make a change like this permanent. It has to come from within the organization and be seen as an indigenous development. It has to be designed by people who truly understand the company culture and the levers that make it work. It's fine to have coaches help along the way, but an outsider pushing the organization to change is doomed to failure. As CEO of Hootsuite Ryan Holmes says, "Bad processes won't fix themselves. They often lurk in a power vacuum; frontline employees don't have the authority to make changes, while senior leaders overlook these issues or assume they're someone else's problem. That's why it's so helpful to put someone in charge, even if it's not an official or full-time role—it gives employees somebody to go to."[10]

It was precisely this realization that led Janice Semper to approach her boss and insist that she be put onto GE's transformation project full time. Not only did the individual teams lack someone to lead them, but GE as a whole was trying to effect massive change without an authoritative guide.

About three months after the first group of eight teams I worked with at GE went back to their businesses, Semper and Viv Goldstein asked them to return to company headquarters for an update on how they were doing implementing lean practices. Semper and Goldstein, who both had other roles at the company, had been charged by the executive team with figuring out the next steps in this process everyone was so excited about. "What Viv and I expected to hear was, 'Hey, everything's going great!'

and some good ideas on how we could scale it," Semper recalls. "What we heard was, 'Wow, this was really hard.' Consistently, when they went back into the businesses, it was like organ reject. They were thinking and beginning to work in a different way, but nobody around them understood what they were doing, why they were doing it, or how."

That was the moment when Semper knew that this was about more than just training a few people and waiting for the message to spread. "We realized we needed to redefine and re-articulate how we wanted our employees to think and act and lead." Semper's and Goldstein's jobs from then on were solely focused on helping to create the culture that would support a new way of working. They became co-founders of what would soon be named FastWorks. "We started to look at the process and think about how to take the essence and the root of that process and apply that to GE and make it work for us here," Semper says. This realization led to much larger changes in the coming months.

PUTTING IT ALL TOGETHER: THE GE BELIEFS

After Janice Semper realized that GE needed to redefine and re-articulate how they wanted employees to think and act ("You can't just train people and expect that everything's going to be fine"), she asked herself a critical question: "What are the levers for change?" One of them was the company's long-held GE Values, a list of principles that, as Semper describes them, are "growth values. Historically, they were very deeply entrenched in our HR processes, our talent processes, how we recruited people, how we developed them, how we assessed them." These tenets served as the company's "north star," and GE knew that if they really wanted to change the way people worked, they needed to find "a new North Star."

Rather than tinker with the old list, they decided to start fresh. "This is not incremental," Semper remembers thinking. "This is a leap, a distinct repositioning of the way we need to work."

After looking at other companies that had embraced the principles Semper and Goldstein wanted to articulate—faster, simpler, more customer driven—the team began drafting. They weren't looking to replicate anyone else's ideas but to educate themselves on what was possible.

They narrowed their "MVP" list to twelve major characteristics of companies that were achieving the kinds of results GE was seeking. Next, Semper's team decided to get validation from their "customers"—in this case, GE's own employees. They took their new ideas and engaged directly with "the officers, top two hundred leaders, and four thousand employees in GE's entry-level leadership program." They posed two questions:

- Which of these twelve traits is GE good at?
- Where, among these twelve, are our biggest gaps?

The data was unequivocal: There were seven things almost everyone agreed the company was already good at, and five they all believed GE needed to improve upon in order to thrive. Semper's team zeroed in on the company's weaknesses, which became the focus of its new priorities. "They were very much centered around being much more customer and user driven rather than product driven," Semper says. "They were about being simple and lean and operating with speed and experimenting after creating the best teams possible with voices from all parts of the organization."

When Semper's team started drafting the actual principles, they again took them out to employees for feedback. To distinguish them from GE's old values, they decided to call them something different. "We decided on 'GE Beliefs,' because it's meant to capture emotion and spirit, not just intellect. People have to feel this in every fiber of their being, because it's not just about applying a new process. It's about changing your mindset—your paradigm. How you think about things. Then from there, the behaviors follow."

After a few rounds of changes and feedback, they launched the GE Beliefs at the annual officers' meeting in August of 2014:

1. Customers determine our success.
2. Stay lean to go fast.
3. Learn and adapt to win.
4. Empower and inspire each other.
5. Deliver results in an uncertain world.

The reason GE was able to tackle changes at this level, at this stage, was because the transformation was driven very early on by people completely dedicated to making it happen. I've told you this story because, as I mentioned in the Introduction, it's one I saw firsthand. But it's not only a story about GE. It's about how dedicated founders—selected sometimes by deliberate choice, sometimes by accident—are the engine that powers entrepreneurship within an organization. Every company has levers that make it run. All it takes to pull them is courage.

## CHAPTER 7

PHASE TWO: SCALING UP

SO WHAT DOES the tipping point of the Startup Way look like? When and how do companies catalyze their early successes into scaled-up deployment?

As I mentioned previously, sometimes the process is part of a planned transformation. Sometimes it's prompted by crisis, be it positive, like massive growth in an early-stage startup, or negative, as with the federal government following the HealthCare .gov debacle.

Regardless of how, when the moment for decisive action arrives, the hard work and preparation of Phase One pays off. The steep upward slope of the S curve of Phase Two is no time to be taking baby steps and learning new theories. With luck, when the time comes, the new playbook has been battle-tested, or at least probed and prodded a little bit. Because as much as we like to complain that our organizations move like molasses, when change happens, it can happen surprisingly fast.

It may sound strange to compare the exciting sky's-the-limit potential of a Facebook or Dropbox to the quieter rollout of a new corporate initiative in an established company, but having seen both up close, I can attest to some surprising parallels.

Transformation unleashes a huge amount of latent creativity and energy. It makes impossible-seeming things suddenly possible. The key is to be ready.

PHASE TWO: COMMON PATTERNS

This phase is all about rapid scaling and deployment of the methods, identified through the efforts of Phase One, that are right for an organization. At GE, we went from showing that these ideas worked in one functional domain to proving they could be applied in any domain, through individual projects. We proved that this could become the way the whole company would work going forward, even if the new style hadn't yet been uniformly adopted. In the government, the successes of the Presidential Innovation Fellows program led to a larger deployment of technologists and the creation of not one but two new internal organizations that offer digital support across every agency.

As with Phase One, there's no "right" way to go about Phase Two. But there are key patterns and tasks common to organizations that are working their way through this next stage of change.

- Review and identify challenges faced by Phase One teams and projects.
- Develop and roll out a widespread system for working in the new way.
- Identify and make proper use of executive-level champions to reinforce the new methods.
- Bring internal functions into the transformation process.
- Create an internal coaching program.

- Establish growth boards and begin to use metered funding for resource allocation.

FASTWORKS, PHASE TWO

About a year after I started working with GE, I was asked to attend the annual officers' meeting again, in order to update the group on how things were going and what we'd learned. This time, however, I was also speaking on behalf of the corporate team that had been supporting my efforts and the many enthusiastic early adopters within the company who had become allies in this massive undertaking. I wanted to highlight the accomplishments of the last twelve months but also be honest about the larger systemic problems we'd encountered.

I shared how we'd gathered proof points from every part of the company and how we'd experimented in every business and every region. I did my best to be candid about the problems we were confronting (I was the only outsider present, after all, and could afford to give offense). But, most important, I had as my co-presenters other officer-level champions who had witnessed the transformation firsthand. They brought a credibility to the room that no outsider could match.

Together, we presented a balanced view of the successes and failures of the Phase One pilot projects. Jeff Immelt had requested that the FastWorks corporate team develop a plan to roll out this way of working more widely. He looked at the team's comprehensive proposal to kick off Phase Two, which included training all CEOs and senior leaders, building an internal coaching program, and having each division initiate its own FastWorks process. The team estimated the rollout would take two years. His response: "It sounds great, but I want it done by the end of this year."

It was June.

Immelt wanted a scorecard that showed who had (and hadn't) completed the required training. As Beth Comstock remembers, "Suddenly, it was personal." Just as suddenly, schedules that had been too crammed for a three-day training session miraculously opened up.

The Roadshow

Thus began an incredible whirlwind of activity. I spent nearly half a year on the road for GE along with the roadshow team: Janice Semper, Viv Goldstein, and David Kidder.[1] As we traveled around the country facing rooms of executives, some of whom—let's be honest—did not want to be there, we marshaled our evidence from Phase One to win them over. Even in our most senior executive trainings, more than just managers were present. Each participant was required to work with a real-life project team from her or his division and do the work on site. Entrepreneurship fundamentally requires learning by doing. There were no "hypothetical" projects or simulations allowed.

They built new plans, came up with MVPs, and asked difficult questions. "How do you account for *this*?" "How do you integrate this with Six Sigma?" "How does this relate to commercial operations?" "What if it's federally regulated?" At the heart of each question was the same concern: "How do I know this is going to work when I've had success in my career doing something else?"

The storehouse of examples we'd built from every division and function came into play. Someone would say: "I understand that that's a problem in that other division, but we don't have that problem in my division. My guys would never do that." And, thanks to all of our internal evidence, more often than not I was able to reply: "It's funny you should say that. I've worked as a coach with teams in your division. Let me tell you about the reality they are facing every day." Unsurprisingly, I found that putting it in those terms was an effective way to get people to listen. Just saying, "I'm from corporate, and I'm here to help," wasn't going to fly.

Crossing the Chasm

Most people in product development are familiar with what management consultant Geoffrey Moore called the "technology adoption life cycle," outlined in his book *Crossing the Chasm*. The "chasm" is the recurring problem that between visionary early adoption and pragmatic mainstream acceptance there's an abyss that can be spanned only by a shift in the way a product is marketed and sold. The issue isn't just that the product isn't polished enough but that mainstream customers seek a like-minded reference in order to make the leap to purchase it.

We all have that friend we trust for recommendations of new cutting-edge products. But we also all have friends who are a little too "out there" for us to trust their recommendations. Enterprise sales works the same way: Regular, mainstream customers are risk averse and want to know that something is really going to work before they try it. Only so-called early adopters have a burning need for a new solution that is strong enough to overcome this friction. The same thing is true for new ideas and especially for new management practices. New products can gain early traction with a pared-down MVP and an early-adopter market. But eventually those products have to convince skeptical mainstream customers to give the offering a try—without the benefit of other mainstream customers recommending it.

This same dynamic plays out in Phase Two. And it can lead to tense conversations. People inside companies adopt new methods in the same way customers and markets do. Some are early adopters and many are not. Mainstream managers aren't

easily convinced that what the so-called innovators are tout-
ing as the next big thing is actually all that great. This is to be
expected. The executive sponsors mentioned in Chapter 6 were
invaluable at this stage for this very reason. Just having someone
from each division who participated in the training and could
say, "I believe in this," made a big difference. These testimonials
were much more important than anything an outside consultant could say.

It wasn't only the sponsors who were able to push the transformation, either. By this time, there were enough senior leaders
who took seriously their roles in helping FastWorks spread.

The Whiteboard Method

I recall very clearly the end of a workshop with a division president. He asked each of his P&L leaders to name a single, specific
project to which they would apply Lean Startup thinking in the
coming quarter, and who would be in charge of the project. The
P&L leaders weren't especially eager to make this commitment,
but the president was unrelenting. So eventually each complied,
committing a name, in black-and-white, to a whiteboard at the
president's insistence.

The division president then dropped this bombshell: At the
end of the quarter, he planned to meet individually with each
and every person named on the whiteboard and ask them, "How
are you being held accountable for success by your leaders? What
kind of questions are they asking you in your reviews?" The
key to these questions is that they don't have any apparent right
answers. In any meeting that didn't highlight dramatic change
from today's way of working, he'd want to understand from the
relevant P&L leader why.

Those questions demanded a change in the personal behavior of the P&L leaders and their top staff. As that realization dawned, the temperature in the room seemed to drop several degrees. Everyone realized that this change was nonnegotiable and that failure to take it seriously would result in real consequences. Most important, the group began to brainstorm how they could drive this change down several levels within the organization, because most of the people named on the whiteboard were two or three levels below the executives in the room. The P&L leaders considered what they would have to do, personally, to effect change within the team, from the top down, to the questions they were asking in reviews.

Perhaps unsurprisingly, this division became one of the earliest adopters of the transformation. What may be surprising to you is that the division president came up with the whiteboard idea himself. Because his incentives were properly aligned, he took the process seriously, which allowed him to be not just effective but creative about how to motivate his own people.

The senior-level FastWorks training period lasted about six months, during which we trained nearly three thousand executives and spun up nearly one hundred FastWorks projects. And, as it turned out, this was just the tip of the iceberg.

It was an exciting, if exhausting, time. It was also an experiment—an MVP for training, if you will. Because the team had to put together a plan so quickly and implement it in just a few months, there was no time to spend perfecting the program. The typical way to approach this at a large corporation, of course, would be to build out a huge briefing book, hire lots of facilitators, and roll it out slowly. Instead, the first training session happened mere months after Immelt's request. We ran the workshops during the day, then spent the nights integrating what we'd learned into the next iteration of the training. "After each session, we would huddle and ask, 'What worked? What didn't work? What's not resonating? What do we need to dial up or dial down?'" Janice Semper remembers. "It was tough."

And although I am enormously proud of the fact that I was part of this journey, the really hard work—the behind-the-scenes arm-twisting and the mind-numbing logistics and political machinations—was done by employees of the company. They don't get the glory in the magazines and business cases, but I witnessed their dedication firsthand. It continues to inspire me.

. . .

1. Identify the Challenges Faced by Pilot Teams

By the time a company is into Phase Two of transformation, it will have two major sources of information to draw upon. This is the payoff for letting teams fail and succeed.

The first source consists of all the exceptions that had to be made for a team to kick off its project: compliance, hiring, approvals, etc., many of which we touched upon in Chapter 6. What were the biggest issues the teams faced? The variety of problems tends to be far-reaching, but the message among them is clear: *What was done ad hoc and by decree in the early stages must now be systematized.*

The other source is the results of the early projects themselves. Some will have succeeded and become templates for others to emulate. Many will have failed and produced detailed information as to why.

Any kind of change is hard, so the best way to keep moving forward is to enlist an in-house change agent like Viv Goldstein or Janice Semper to track all this company-specific learning. Their job was to follow their startups' successes and failures, chronicling their observations, then analyzing how and why failures happened—and how they could be prevented next time.

RESISTANCE IS A SPECIFIC KIND OF CHALLENGE

A major challenge that innovation teams face in Phase Two is resistance from within. Most resistance comes from a totally valid place: managers who have been trained throughout their careers to act in a specific way. I'm often tasked with giving executives the bad news that they're paying people to inhibit innovation in their organizations. It's not so easy to change these incentives. And, once they've been changed, the effects of years of that incentive structure don't evaporate overnight.

Middle managers especially have a tough time with corporate change. They're the ones who are required to safeguard the company's "standard work" and also deliver results, often without having the authority to change the standard on a whim. They are under constant pressure from above and below. As we saw in Chapter 1, the major management theory they were likely trained in is one that emphasizes standardization and the elimination of variance. Because innovation is a form of positive variation, there is a built-in conflict that almost every manager in the organization will confront. Rather than view these managers as villains, we have to take their objections and skepticism seriously—and find ways to help them support the transformation rather than hinder it.

2. Implement a Widespread Rollout

The months we spent on the road training executives were, as I mentioned, a way of spreading change in an organization that was very specific to GE. It was directly tied to the company's hard-driving culture and to Jeff Immelt's desire to effect change as quickly as possible. But, of course, it's far from the only way to take things to the next level.

Remember Mikey Dickerson and the HealthCare.gov team? As I mentioned, some of the people in that group had been pulled from the Presidential Innovation Fellows program, which by then was in its second year and had increased from eighteen fellows to forty-three. Having enjoyed a number of successes, Todd Park convinced Jennifer Pahlka, the founder and executive director of Code for America, to act as U.S. deputy chief technology officer for a year. Pahlka was tasked with helping to run the PIF program as well as hammering out the scope and details of a more permanent organization. Through Code for America, she had delivered digital services to local government and brought a wealth of knowledge about how to deal with breakdowns among law, policy, and technology in implementing government plans.

As Haley Van Dyck recalls, the plan was to "build a central team with consolidated engineering resources and design talent and see if we could help agencies transform their most important citizen-facing services." The new group, called the United States Digital Service (USDS), would include two separate divisions: one made up of teams that could be deployed to specific agency projects identified as critical; the other operating on a for-hire basis for faster pairing with agency teams that were interested in working this new way.

Ultimately, those two functions split into two different organizations. The USDS remained in the White House as the on-call team for critical problems, and the services-for-hire division, named 18F (for the intersection at which its building is located in Washington), moved to the General Services Administration.

The moment when digital government went from Phase One, in which all the groundwork, including the plans for the USDS, had been laid, to Phase Two was when Todd Park pulled a few PIFs, threw together a team, and held that meeting about how to rescue HealthCare.gov that Dickerson dialed into at 5:30 a.m. "We said great—let's run the play we were talking about," Van Dyck remembers. "We had figured out a little bit of the model, the hiring authorities, the way to bring people on—all of these things. We were reaching for a tool that we already knew was in the tool belt rather than having to invent one on the spot. We had the air cover and the ability to, at all costs, change the way things were happening."

Six weeks later, the site was up and running. After that, Van Dyck recalls, "We had a very different meeting around the budget request and the idea of building this thing called the United States Digital Service. The [people looking at our funding request] said, 'Yes, we absolutely understand the value and importance of this.'" The crisis made wider-scale reform possible.

The team figured they would start small, hire ten or so people, and pick a few high-impact projects in agencies where there was already strong buy-in. Then the response to their formal budget request came in: They'd been given $20 million of the $35 million requested, which was a huge surprise, because it had been approved by a Republican Congress for a program in a Democratic White House. "We like to call it our Series A from Congress," Van Dyck jokes. "It opened up the doors to an entirely new possibility in terms of what we could actually touch and projects we could take on inside of government." In the summer of 2016, the USDS was awarded another $30 million, a sign that their efforts were not only appreciated but in high demand.

It's important to understand that while the creation of the USDS and 18F were certainly helped by the HealthCare.gov meltdown, they were not merely a product of it. All of the work that had already been done meant that the CTO's office was ready to go when the moment arrived. And while no one was glad the disaster had happened, the silver lining was that it had eliminated a huge obstacle that often impedes change: risk. As Mikey Dickerson says, "There wasn't any more downside . . . and the clear signal and direction from the very top of the agency [was] that nothing is more important to us today than getting

HealthCare.gov to work. You put all those things together, and you can move quickly."

"Just as important, if not more important," Van Dyck explains, "it was an aha moment, I think, for people across the country with skill sets running large-scale digital services that there was a need for their talents inside government and that the projects inside government were not just bureaucratic, paper-pushing exercises. They were actually real, large services that impacted millions of people, people trying to get health care." All the frustration of those early years of chaos and the seeming impossibility of implementing the changes she hoped to effect at a greater scale were rewarded at last.

Because sharing information about new methods throughout the organization is a key part of the second phase (as we did at GE through the trainings, materials developed, and, ultimately, the GE Beliefs), the USDS created the Digital Services Playbook, which the team released publicly on the USDS website the day the organization was officially launched. A list of thirteen key "plays" taken from the private sector and government alike, the playbook offers yet another way for the organization to fan its methods out into government.[2]

3. Identify and Make Proper Use of Executive-Level Champions

In larger corporations, an important role emerges in Phase Two: the executive-level champion. Different from a coach and also distinct from the role of the executive sponsor in Phase One (who is required to be intimately involved with the program on a day-to-day level), the executive-level champion's primary function is to clear obstacles that crop up for teams as the lean way of working spreads. But rather than one-off exceptions, these interactions are more systemic and proactive.

A glimpse of a panel discussion I had with some members of one of GE's businesses illustrates the key differences. The focus was on one project in particular that could not secure the funding it needed. At the end of the presentation, the team leader opened the floor for questions.

The CEO of the business was in the audience and asked, "Can you say what's going on at a more detailed level with this situation?" The manager explained, and the CEO responded, "OK, I'll authorize the budget you need."

What happened next was a perfect example of a phenomenon I call "can't take yes for an answer." The team leader couldn't comprehend what was going on, because it was so far out of the realm of his experience for a decision like this to be made quickly and efficiently. Part of the problem in today's management practices is that many people aren't given the responsibility and the opportunity to think bigger. When this manager was, his response was to argue with the CEO:

"Well, we've got to convince finance to . . ."

The CEO turned to the CFO of the business, also in the room. "Is it okay with you?"

"Yes," came the answer.

"Okay, finance is signed up. What else do you need?"

"Well, we have to get approval to transfer this person. That's HR."

"Okay, then, you need the head of HR for my division? He's here, too. Hi, any objections?" The HR leader had none.

In fact, the CEO had to spend more time convincing the person whose project he was green-lighting that he was serious than he did making the decision in the first place. Remember, this was not a one-time trivial decision. This was an entire program's budget. This was the start of this division changing its entire budget allocation process.

It's key to focus on the role of this executive champion advocating, effectively and publicly, not just for this project's progress but for this way of working in general. Executive championship is instrumental in broadcasting the message that this is the way an organization intends to work.

THE MAGIC REAPPEARING PROJECT

During the intensive training process, we drew heavily on another important resource: teams that had already been through earlier phases. At each of our stops, we held panels that included people who had been working lean in each division and had seen results firsthand.

A curious thing about startups in the context of an existing company is how they have a tendency to disappear. I don't mean get canceled at a "go/kill" stage-gate meeting. I mean disappear off the books entirely.

Remember Michael Mahan of GE Appliances? His team was working on a new line of refrigerators, one of the early GE training projects I coached in a cohort of eight. One day, I was notified that one of the teams could no longer participate in the Lean Startup training because its project had been canceled. I viewed this as our first failure, which didn't surprise me too much. We're talking about startups here (in unfriendly soil, to boot), so a high mortality rate is expected.

However, the canceled project turned out to be Mahan's.

I didn't give this much thought, until the next time I saw a corporate review of the transformation. It listed seven projects. Seven team logos. A seven out of seven success rate. Which meant that everyone pretended the "missing" project had never been part of the transformation at all. I chalked it up to typical corporate double-think.

A few months later, I was presiding over one of the training workshops for a large group of senior and mid-level managers in the company. Part of the agenda included testimonials from successful project leaders. And guess who was among them? Michael Mahan, the leader of our "missing" project, who was back with a big success story—but no mention of when he and the project had disappeared from the lineup.

Mahan later shared what had happened. His project had run into political difficulties and was viewed as a failure by some of the executives in his division. Rather than risk it being canceled, Mahan took it underground, with a team of volunteers who continued to do their day jobs but kept the project alive on the side. Although they were cut off from official coaching in Lean Startup methods, they maintained their startup ethos and executed the plan from our original workshops. As Beth Comstock says, "His project didn't get picked as one of the ones that was being tracked and funded and incubated, but he said, 'Screw that, I'm still going to do it. It's a good idea. I like this tool.' He did a sort of skunkworks with Lean Startup, and it ended up getting him promoted."

In a perfect example of executive championship, Mahan had gone to his CEO to get support for the project, even though it was no longer officially a part of the FastWorks program. His team's idea, as Steve Liguori puts it, was "to come up with the next generation of refrigerators, with radically different functions, LED lighting, crazy shelves that folded up in a snap and moved in all directions. They wanted to try these features out and knew that the quickest way to do it was to get the refrigerators into the hands of actual customers and see what they thought." They wanted to make just sixty, test them with customers for sixty days, then collect feedback. For a company that could make six thousand refrigerators in a week, this should have been no big deal, right?

Even making such a small batch required certain compliance,

however. Electrical components had to be UL-approved, a challenge Mahan's team met by agreeing to use standard electronics in their prototype. Another element they were experimenting with was 3-D-printed hinges. Under normal circumstances, a refrigerator door is tested by a machine that opens and closes it a million times, the approximate number of times the door will be used over its estimated fifteen-year life expectancy. These sixty test fridges were going to go into people's homes for only sixty days. Do the math: if 15 years = 1 million openings and closings, 60 days equals—well, a lot fewer.

Upon hearing this plan, the engineering department, bound to its regulations, announced that no fridges would be shipped until they passed the hinge test, which would take half a million dollars and three months to set up—one month longer than the entire consumer test. When Mahan asked if anyone knew they were only making sixty units, the answer was: "It doesn't matter. It's policy." Mahan kept pushing. "Has anyone explained this to the head of engineering?" Again, it didn't matter, because of "policy."

That was when Mahan made a simple decision that dramatically changed his team's future, as well as his own. Knowing that the head of engineering was literally right down the hall, and bolstered by the support of his executive champion, he decided to ask the question himself. "Do you mind if we don't follow that procedure, because I'm only giving out these prototypes for sixty days?" he inquired. The head engineer replied, "Of course I don't mind. You're just doing a test, right?" It was literally that simple. From there, the team was able to continue, under the radar but still completely within the safeguards designed to mitigate risk (the UL-approved electronics) and liability (the almost-certain truth that any prototype could withstand sixty days of door openings and closings).

Eventually, Mahan's team made enough progress (and the

business was under enough pressure to show they were on board with the corporate transformation) that the relevant executives changed their tune and the project was reintegrated.

When I give workshops, middle managers often find these stories upsetting, because they fear they represent a breakdown in the company's processes, employees violating company procedure, and a loss of control. But senior leaders rarely act recklessly or impulsively, even when they are attempting to solve a problem by exception. As long as an experiment is conducted prudently, without excessive risk of liability, and transparently, under clear executive authority, most middle managers can be convinced that these internal entrepreneurs are an essential resource to the company.

THE HIGHEST EXECUTIVE CHAMPIONSHIP IN THE LAND

In the spring of 2015, Lisa Gelobter was sitting at her desk at BET in New York when she received a phone call from the CTO's office at the White House, inviting her to a roundtable discussion exploring the use of digital technologies to improve the way government serves the American people. A few weeks later, Gelobter found herself in the Roosevelt Room of the West Wing with others from Facebook, Google, and Rackspace; as well as Todd Park, who was then the CTO; the CIO of the United States; and the deputy secretary of the Office of Management and Budget.

Park and his colleagues revealed to the group that this was not a roundtable discussion but a recruiting trip. He and his team wanted those who'd been invited to come work for the government, helping to bring technology to the next level. "President Obama wants this to be part of his legacy. You will never do something so meaningful in your entire life," the team said. Then someone asked, "Who is going to be the champion here? What kind of support are we going to get?"

In walked the president, straight from the Oval Office.

Awed as she was, Gelobter assumed that Obama was there for a photo op. ("I am a totally jaded and cynical New Yorker," she quips.) He'd arrived trailing a videographer and a photographer, after all. He went around the table and shook everyone's hand. "I was like, okay, that's cute," she remembers.

Then he sat down. For forty-five minutes.

"The government is bureaucratic, but the White House isn't," he told the group, selling them hard on the move to D.C. "If I have to call your spouse or your children, I will." Everyone laughed. "I'm not joking," he replied. "As the president is talking to us," Gelobter recalled, "all I can think is: 'You have nothing more important to do with your time than talk to us? This is that important to you?' My mother always said, when you're interviewing for jobs, pick the company where the highest-ranking person talked to you. That's how you know they're actually invested in what you'll be doing. You can't get any higher than the President of the United States."

As you know from her involvement with College Scorecard (see Chapter 4), Gelobter took the job. Obama brought new meaning to the title "executive champion," and, as Gelobter learned, when innovators are protected from above, they can accomplish great things. By removing the obstacle of doubt, Obama made it possible for Park to hire a world-class team. This is the role of the champion: to ensure that those who are leaning into the change have the resources available to clear obstacles that they, their coaches, and their managers may not have.

4. Train Representatives of All Internal Functions

Considering the ways in which his company has changed, Jeff Immelt recently said to me: "One of the things that makes Fast-Works a little bit different than other things we've done is that certain functions in the company could stop it. You could say, if you're one of the enabling functions, 'We don't have the budget,' or, 'I worry about compliance.'" The solution? "You need messaging, not so much for the people who are the practitioners, but for the people who can stop things. You put them on notice and say, 'You're going to fail. You do that at your own peril.' I think that's where culture change is hard, because you've got a movement, and the movement can go quickly, but you're not just trying to get people to come with you. You've got to stop the people who want to block it."

People can be trained in this way of working across the organization; they can enlist the support of executive-level champions to help them make their way. But there comes a point at which it's critical to bring in every function of the company; otherwise, innovation teams won't have the support they need to move forward.

This is why it's also critical to have executives participate in training across functions. Often at a "headquarters" training session, which includes people from IT, legal, and other functions who have never been a part of headquarters discussion before, I catch disgruntled comments from executives who don't understand why they are there. "This is silly. I'm the head of HR. Why am I learning about X-ray technology from a team who's using it to look at broken pipes in the oil fields of Saudi Arabia? What does this have to do with me?"

The reality is, there *will* be backlash. To some, this sounds like just another corporate initiative: In the past, trainings and mandates usually meant more work with fewer people. This is why I always start with a question-and-answer period. I've found that even the skeptics are more willing to get on board once their concerns have been addressed. As I like to say, what we're doing is setting up a framework where skepticism will be either proven or disproven. All we really want is the truth.

5. Establish an In-House Coaching Program

Although Lean Startup can be prescriptive at times, what makes a good practitioner of the method is not following all the rote steps but, rather, living its philosophy. The practices and tactics are guidelines to help teams find common vocabulary and shared tools, but they are, necessarily, high-level.

Every organization is different. Every industry is different. Every person is different. Success at using these methods should be judged by outcomes: the culture of the team, the way the team treats customers, and the impact it has in the world.

Still, there is a role for expertise, for veterans who want to pay it forward. The original lean manufacturing experts who came from Japan were called *senseis*. The startup community is full of people who act as mentors and advisors. And the Lean Startup movement has spawned a cottage industry of consultants and other experts.

In my work with organizations, I have generally recommended the term *coach* to refer to this role. I find it helps cut down on the misunderstandings common among other terms. Once the initiative cascades into Phase Two, developing a cadre of internal coaches who can help teams make the mental shift to the new way of working is essential.

COACHING IN THE STARTUP WAY

I was once working with a startup in the energy sector. They had a breakthrough technology that could, if it worked, lead to dramatic efficiency gains in power generation and transmission. But the technology was not yet proven in the real world. The team was gearing up for a big launch at a trade show, where they planned to debut this new product and start generating the hockey-stick-shaped revenue growth curve outlined in their business plan.

You can probably guess where this story is headed. Although their plan was extremely sensitive to a number of assumptions about customers and what they wanted, this team hadn't actually spent much time with them. From my point of view, the team was flying blind and likely to experience a high-profile flop. These kinds of events are sometimes fatal to startups, because they make it harder to pivot, even if the idea-as-launched is only a few degrees off from one that customers would love.

What makes this story different is that this team was supremely confident. Unlike the Series X team or others that I've written about, this group was not at all interested in examining its assumptions. They felt they knew everything they needed to about customers from their past product successes. And they found my questions irritating. The founders, I sensed, were worried that I was weakening team morale by diluting the faith in their vision.

If there is one piece of advice that the Lean Startup movement is known for above all, it's the importance of getting customers involved early and often. Our most famous slogan is probably Steve Blank's *Get out of the building.*[3] If someone presented a plan like this one at a Lean Startup Meetup, they'd probably be booed off the stage. And yet, when I coach teams, "Talk to customers" is a piece of advice I almost never give. Founders are stubborn. Most either think they've already spent enough time speaking with customers or they've already decided it's not worthwhile.

Instead, I saw my job as helping the team run a good experiment that, from their point of view, would confirm their preexisting beliefs. They were already convinced that they'd sell a lot of units at the trade show, so I couldn't get them to start with an MVP. I also couldn't get them to set up an innovation accounting dashboard (see Chapter 9). I couldn't even convince them to agree on their leap-of-faith assumptions.

I said: "Let's find a way to prove that you're right. You're planning on getting a lot of sales at the trade show. Let's have every-one write down on a three-by-five index card how many sales they think the company will get." I then asked the team to put their predictions into a sealed envelope, which we would revisit the week after the show.

The only aspect of Lean Startup theory I could get them to buy into was to treat their upcoming launch as an experiment, with at least one hypothesis attached. As a coach, I felt that was a start.

The day of the trade show came, and—wait for it—the team didn't make any sales. At our debrief meeting, there was a lot of after-the-fact rationalization. They said that they hadn't really expected to make any sales but that they had gauged a lot of customer interest and collected a lot of business cards. They were convinced that industry trends were on their side. So, as far as they were concerned, their plan was still on track.

Then I asked them to open the envelope with the predictions from the week before.

The energy in the room totally changed. They all looked around the room to see if it was okay to say what everyone was thinking: We failed, big-time.

Once the elephant in the room had a name, the team started to make new plans. They generated ideas for how to change the product. They asked for help in finding ways to get customer feedback without suffering the same kind of embarrassment they'd experienced at the show. They even asked how to get that feedback a little sooner—maybe they could reduce the scope on the next version of the product? Make it a little more minimal, so long as it's still viable . . . They were off to the races. I barely said a word.

Remember: I never told them to talk to customers, because they wouldn't have listened to me, anyway. All I did was help them devise an experiment that would reveal what they needed to learn for themselves. Naturally, most teams are able to devise much better experiments than this one and take much better advantage of their coach's expertise. But as long as a team is making its way down the path of experimentation, it will learn its own lessons.

There's another reason, though, why this style of coaching is especially important for startups. I always tell the teams I work with: I'm going to assume you're right and I'm wrong about your plan. Let's design our experiments to prove that.[4] In addition to the learning benefits I mentioned above, this approach offers another major bonus: Sometimes the team really is right!

COACHING STRUCTURE

In the startup world, coaching has been a long-standing part of our practice. Investors have always maintained networks of mentors and advisors to help teams develop and grow. More recent accelerator programs, such as Y Combinator and Techstars, and more modern VCs, such as Andreessen Horowitz, have formalized this approach into a more structured program of services and support. Advice and mentorship are available to startups in the portfolio, but they are never—ever—substitutes for leadership. Nobody is forced to talk to any specific mentor or do what that mentor says. Advisors take on the role of coaches—not spies, not leaders, not executives, not substitute board members.

When a company decides to build an ecosystem of internal startups, it, too, must develop a coaching program. For a startup growing past product/market fit, this is another one of those "through the looking glass" moments. Even in Silicon Valley, for all the thousands of ways we have of mentoring founders, CEOs, and CTOs, there are comparably few programs for lower-level employees. And we rarely treat those employees as internal founders.

For more established companies, there are armies of outside consultants ready at a moment's notice to enact every conceivable kind of training program. But there is no way for a large enough number of outside consultants to become familiar enough with the company to make the kind of impact we need in Phase Two.

In a company of any size, there are *already* lots of people who are naturally gifted at coaching teams. Ignoring this preexisting resource is tremendously wasteful, since key early adopters combine a knack for the new way of thinking with a deep understanding of the company as it exists today.

A second benefit of internal coaching is to create heft behind transformation. Traditionally, the power of managers in most organizations is measured by the number of their direct reports (or the number of people they influence via matrix management). This creates a tremendous drive for savvy managers to increase their power by arguing for ever-larger budgets and ever-more personnel. But this is a dangerous thing for an initiative that is attempting to be cross-functional. In the early days of transformation, there tends to be resistance from many functional leaders. But once the initiative has experienced its aha moment and shifts into Phase Two, many former resisters change their tune. Now they insist that the transformation can logically proceed only if it is located within their specific department!

No matter where the transformation is based on the org chart, it needs to grow. The greater the number of people throughout the organization whose careers are tied to its success, the more likely it is that the transformation will survive. Internal coaches are a great way to achieve this without having to hire a ton of new people or too many expensive consultants.

Whatever a coaching program looks like, it's critical to make sure that the coaches are more than just occasional participants and that they receive rigorous training. Nothing weakens a coaching program faster than filling it with people who feel that what they do isn't being taken seriously by their peers or the company as a whole. Ed Essey, principle program manager for the Microsoft Garage, notes three problems that tend to come up in this situation: (1) Coaches require a lot of encouragement and support to keep them volunteering. (2) The most motivated coaches tend to leave the company and find a place where they'll be able to pursue the job more fully. (3) Each coach has a different skill set—marketing, or design, or technology—meaning none of them can represent the lean method fully.

By elevating coaching into a real, vital position within the organization, tied to the future growth and success of everyone who works there, companies gain the resources to train people properly in a cross-functional manner and give them motivation to stay in the organization by providing a clear career path.

COACHING AN INTUIT FINANCE
OPERATIONS TEAM: A REFRAMING

A few members of Intuit's Finance Operations team joined coach Bennett Blank at an internal Lean Startup workshop with ideas for solving several customer problems. Over the course of two days, Blank coached the team in Lean Startup techniques and Design for Delight principles, like how to focus on customer problems and the story of each potential solution, using real evidence from real customers. The team was ready to explore their ideas, but one of the challenges they faced was that they were addressing two different customers, one of which was internal: Intuit's phone support staff, who help the company's external customers with billing issues. The team decided to run, with the internal phone support staff, small experiments related to everything from tone of voice, to billing communication, to more traditional features. The end result was that the team made rapid progress and reframed their understanding of this staff as "potential startup customers," in Blank's words. This small change in framing had a big effect on the team's approach as they began to apply Lean Startup principles to this new "customer."

The benefits of this reframing have been ongoing. Blank continued to check in on the team's progress and noticed they became more engaged once they'd been empowered to work in this new way of gaining customer empathy and running fast experiments. The team participated in two more weeklong coaching sessions, along with additional Finance Operations members, and began to tackle additional problems they'd identified after their initial coaching sessions. Soon they came up with several solutions that delivered real business results, and their engagement level continued to rise along with their confidence.

The final stage of the team's transformation came when they began to change the operating mechanisms they used to manage their work. "They began presenting their 'plan' as a series of experiments to be tested, rather than a traditional 'execution' plan," Blank explains. "They were essentially acknowledging the inherent uncertainty of their proposed ideas, while simultaneously providing a plan for reducing their uncertainty through experiments." They also continued to conduct their own two-day sprints every month or so, which continuously led them to the next set of experiments and gave them opportunities to hone their new skills. Now that they've experienced the power of coaching, several team members have made the leap to coaching others, volunteering their time to teach Lean Startup principles to nonprofits and middle schoolers.

COACHING IN ACTION

Here are just a few examples of the kinds of coaching programs that exist at different companies, to give you a taste of what such a program can look like. As I've said, every program will be different depending on company size, culture, and other factors.

Techstars's Mentor Manifesto

Techstars, a tech accelerator program, takes its coaching role so seriously that it published its own manifesto[5] to lay out "what entrepreneurs can and should demand from their mentors" and "what mentors should consider if they want to build effective relationships with the entrepreneurs they're working with."

- Be Socratic.
- Expect nothing in return (you'll be delighted with what you do get back).
- Be authentic/practice what you preach.
- Be direct. Tell the truth, however hard.
- Listen, too.
- The best mentor relationships eventually become two-way.
- Be responsive.
- Adopt at least one company every single year. Experience counts.
- Clearly separate opinion from fact.
- Hold information in confidence.
- Clearly commit to mentor or do not. Either is fine.
- Know what you don't know. Say "I don't know" when you don't know. "I don't know" is preferable to bravado.
- Guide, don't control. Teams must make their own decisions. Guide but never tell them what to do. Understand that it's their company, not yours.
- Accept and communicate with other mentors who get involved.
- Be optimistic.
- Provide specific actionable advice; don't be vague.
- Be challenging/robust but never destructive.
- Have empathy. Remember that startups are hard.

IBM

At IBM, coaches assist teams not only in areas where they struggle, but also in organizing and reorganizing groups of people to be even more successful. The coaches focus on three areas: leadership practices, collaboration practices, and technical practices. Coaching isn't mandatory, but each cross-functional team of eight to ten people is assessed every quarter, and the results are made public via a scoreboard, which provides incentive to take advantage of the program.

IBM also offers a program called "The Agile Doctor Is In," which enables individuals or teams to schedule an hour or two with one of the thirty coaches employed worldwide by IBM to focus on a particular problem that needs solving.

Before the company instituted lean and agile methods, there were thirteen layers between CIO Jeff Smith and the first-line leader in the squads (what IBM calls teams). Now there are five. Smith says the coaches are the accelerators.

Cisco's My Innovation

At Cisco, coaching is part of a program called My Innovation, which works alongside Cisco's other innovation initiatives with the broad purpose of engaging, empowering, and enabling its 70,000 employees to experiment with new ideas. The program includes online resources and a go-to portal for people looking for training or mentors throughout the company. To date, two thousand people have signed up to go through coach training.

While the company is still figuring out how to organize the program, Mathilde Durvy, an innovation program lead, says the goal is to train coaches for three areas: innovation (design thinking and agile prototyping), business (sales and marketing), and technical. Durvy explains that each team is required to enlist coaches who cover all three areas, whether it's one person who possesses all three skill sets or multiple coaches, each with his or her own specialty. The company's coaching resource is typically used by teams that are in the process of developing a new idea, but even those teams that don't make it to the final stages of a project or transformation have found the resource valuable.

6. Set Up the Mechanisms of Metered Funding and Growth Boards

ENTITLEMENT FUNDING VERSUS METERED FUNDING

Almost every company I meet with more than a few hundred employees uses the same budgeting process. There is an annual appropriations process, in which all proposed projects, departments, and initiatives are evaluated. The winners receive funding targets for the coming year, subject to quarterly (or, in some places, more frequent) adjustments. When the company has a bad quarter, it's not uncommon for budgets to be slashed, and there's plenty of adjusting the actual allocations throughout the year.

As a result, managers spend a large amount of time preparing for the annual meeting and considerably more time defending their budget politically. I call this system *entitlement funding* because of an underlying dynamic that always seems to play out. It is extremely hard to get your preferred project onto the "deck" for funding at the annual meeting. But once it's on deck, it's what most managers refer to as a "spigot"—always on, with the flow of funding varying from period to period.

Barring a catastrophic and highly public failure (or perceived failure), the expectation is that the project will continue quarter after quarter, even year after year. Most projects funded in a given year will also be funded in the next year—maybe not at the same level, but they're rarely canceled.

If teams feel entitled to funding, it's almost impossible to generate the energy and focus that startups require. Innovation without constraints is no blessing—startup mortality rates are unusually high for overfunded projects, with many infamous examples.

Let's think about the incentives that entitlement funding creates for project teams. Imagine a team that is debating whether to launch a product now or to delay a little longer. In terms of the team's budget, it's almost always a good idea to delay. If you launch now, you risk catastrophic failure and project cancellation. If you delay, you may face some criticism from management, but as long as your reasons are sound (and there are always an infinite number of sound reasons to call upon), you'll most likely live to fight another day. And with a delay, you may be able to make the product more perfect, increasing odds of success in the future.

The pathological case is the manager who realizes that, by pushing ship dates and accountability deadlines far enough into the future, he or she might be promoted out of his or her current position before ever being held accountable. In that case, his or her successor will be forced to deal with the consequences. If things go well, credit is easy to share. If things go poorly, the successor tends to get the blame.

The other problem with entitlement funding is the sheer cost of managing the politics. The number of meetings the average project team leader endures related to his or her own budget can be staggering.

In companies that are used to working that way, changing the culture is a long-term project. It requires a series of interlocking reforms, many of which we will cover in the remainder of this book. But because the budgetary process is foundational, the key antidote to entitlement funding is what I call *metered funding*.

This is the deal with metered funding: absolute freedom to spend the money, with extremely strict criteria for how to unlock more, denominated only in validated learning.

If you raise $1 million in seed funding from a VC, you will never *ever* get a phone call the next month saying, "Hey, sorry about this, but we had a bad quarter and we need $200,000 back." Such an investor would immediately be run out of town. Aside from that, the reality is the VC would have no ability to retrieve its money; startups are independent companies and once the check clears, that's that.

This freedom is an essential part of what makes startups possible. It's hard to know in advance when a company is going to need to pivot, but it often comes up suddenly. It's important to know how much money is left and to have confidence they'll be able to spend it quickly, without interminable reviews. And startups have a tendency to run pretty "hot"—many of the most famous startups you've heard of came within weeks or even days of running out of money at one point in their lives. Having their budgets cut even by 10 percent at a key moment would likely have been fatal.

The benefits of metered funding when transposed into a corporate context are many:

- Scarcity mindset
- Changes the calculus of who's to blame if a project fails
- Allows managing a set of projects as an explicit portfolio, along with portfolio metrics
- Greatly reduced political burden on teams
- Greatly enhanced focus on "what do I have to provably learn in order to unlock more funding?"
- More conducive to cross-functional collaboration (because everyone is paid out of a common budget)
- Reduces middle manager interference (because no resources are borrowed from the parent company)

Metered funding is much closer to venture investment than to a congressional appropriations committee. But, as most companies who have tried it before have discovered, it's not sufficient by itself to change culture. That's because existing systems are extremely resilient to change. It helps to pair metered funding with other changes, such as growth boards, to make real culture change.

METERED FUNDING

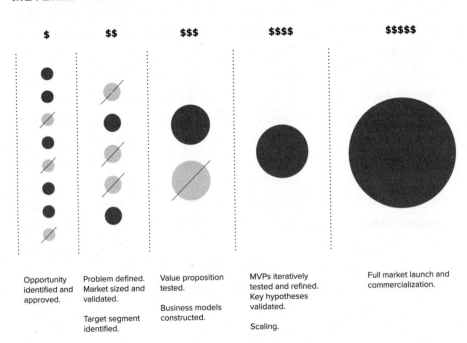

$	$$	$$$	$$$$	$$$$$
Opportunity identified and approved.	Problem defined. Market sized and validated. Target segment identified.	Value proposition tested. Business models constructed.	MVPs iteratively tested and refined. Key hypotheses validated. Scaling.	Full market launch and commercialization.

The Impact of Nonprofit Metered Funding

The Global Innovation Fund (GIF), started in 2014 and headquartered in London, is a nonprofit that invests in the piloting, rigorous testing, and scaling of innovations targeted at improving the lives of the poorest people in developing countries.[6] The projects it funds collectively open up opportunities for millions of people. "We are a hybrid of a charity and an investment fund, targeting social return first," says Alix Peterson Zwane, the fund's chief executive officer.

GIF makes its grant, debt, and equity investments using a

staged approach to funding. "The idea is to combine some of the best of the venture capital–style funding, which follows the ideas and journeys of entrepreneurs, with the rigor of academic peer review," explains Zwane. As project teams produce results, "additional amounts of resources are triggered by additional evidence of social impact." This approach differs from traditional philanthropy, which often funds nonprofits to do specific projects, but monitors activities to measure success, rather than outcomes or impact.

GIF has three levels of funding. In the earliest stage, grants to entrepreneurs looking to pilot their innovation go up to $230,000 (though many are much smaller). "The money is for learning, not outcomes," Zwane explains. The expectation is that key questions about the project will be answered, and that understanding of the probability of success will be increased. For example, GIF funded the pilot program for a Ugandan startup called SafeBoda—"an Uber for motorcycle taxis"—that hopes to reduce motorbike accidents and head injuries by educating people about wearing helmets. "Their vision of success is that their drivers would wear helmets and their passengers would get offered helmets, so you'd see these health benefits of people using their business. And part of the reason people would want to use them is because of the helmet availability," Zwane says. "That's a cool hypothesis. But a key question for the early stage is, will people really wear helmets?"

The next funding level provides grants of up to $2.3 million to innovators who are transitioning from piloting their models to scaling their intervention. That's when startups need to test their business models and cost effectiveness, while also providing rigorous evidence of impact. To follow the SafeBoda example (though the company is still in the pilot-program stage as of this writing), the company might collect data on measurable changes in head injuries as they begin to get a larger market share and others begin to copy them. "If in Stage One your money is 80 percent for learning and 20 percent for outcome, in Stage Two it's more like 50/50," says Zwane.

At the third stage of funding, GIF offers up to $15 million to investees who are ready to take their innovation to scale. This is when entrepreneurs get help growing their businesses and striving for widespread adoption in one, or multiple, developing countries. "You're paying closer to 80 percent for outcomes, and 20 percent for learning," says Zwane. Possibilities for this stage include things like addressing operational challenges as a company grows, working with partners who can help carry the project beyond GIF's third stage, and adapting innovations to meet the needs of a more diverse customer base.

Changing the way aid is allocated and used is difficult but, as GIF shows, by no means impossible. And think of the benefits. "If we figure out how to create incentives to generate impact and to be honest about what we do, we can preserve and protect and nurture political and popular support for development systems," Zwane says. "The real value of using staged funding as a nonprofit is that it keeps your focus on the right things: risk, evidence, and impact."

GROWTH BOARDS

As noted in Chapter 3, every startup has a board it reports to—a group of people to whom it's accountable, on whatever schedule the various stakeholders agree upon. This creates a direct relationship between the financing of the project and its progress. In big organizations, reviews, managers, and matrix performances prompt an environment in which people become adept at changing their PowerPoint presentations to meet the expectations of whichever manager they happen to be meeting with that day. This needs to change in Phase Two.

An internal startup functions the same way as an independent startup: with team accountability. In a larger corporate setting, each person's salary is paid by a particular division. What's missing is a way to hold the whole team accountable. That's where a growth board comes in. Often I've seen growth boards start with a single team and a manager who says, "How do I decide to give my team more money?" From there, it's easy to set up a simple structure. (For more on how to create a growth board, see Chapter 9.)

As more teams start to function in this way and their success stories spread, the structure gets replicated. At GE, for example, we made sure teams were set up with a growth board by the time we were in Phase Two of implementing FastWorks.

One internal team at a large corporation I worked with a few years ago came up with a plan to reduce its time to market by nearly two years by entering into a co-creation partnership with a customer. Instead of going through the normal process of development, demonstration, and sales, they'd decided to learn more, faster, by getting a product based on customer feedback into the customer's hands as soon as possible.

Before long, however, their colleagues in finance began asking them: "What's the ROI?"

The team did the math, and (of course) the ROI for their MVP was negative. Because they were working in a different way, the number reflected only the first stage of their plan. Measuring the ROI of an MVP is like measuring an acorn and then cutting off its water supply because it hasn't yet grown into a tree.

The team members wondered if they could somehow leave the ROI off the chart, but that wasn't allowed. Crossing their fingers, they went in to make their presentation to finance, and immediately their project was canceled.

Leaving off your ROI in a standard corporate setting is never an option. But if you have no ROI in the first place, because you're operating with metered funding and reporting to a growth board, you never have to face the temptation to do so. That's why setting up these mechanisms is so critical at this stage.

WHAT COMES NEXT

At GE and in the federal government, Phase Two created teams devoted to spreading the new way of working far and wide. Both entities trained a lot of talented people in the new way and built an impressive portfolio of both successes and failures. Between the teams themselves, their managers, coaches, and executive sponsors and champions, we're talking about thousands of people.

Yet within these immense organizations, these are still comparatively small numbers. Everyone knows that small teams are always vulnerable to changes in leadership, reorgs, or the emergence of new fads. For teams like these that have "crossed the chasm" and are affecting the lives of managers throughout the organization, backlash and resistance from the rest of the organization can be devastating.

The only way to give this change staying power is to use the early successes and their attendant institutional clout to tackle the deep systems of the company—namely, its incentives structure, how people are held accountable, how resources are allocated. Think about government procurement and how deeply entrenched it is. In most organizations, these systems are considered untouchable by most employees. To make changing them a prerequisite for embarking on the transformation is a nonstarter. But change them we must. How these organizations pulled that off is the subject of the next chapter: Phase Three.

## CHAPTER 8

PHASE THREE: DEEP SYSTEMS

WE ALL UNDERSTAND what it means to found a company. It starts with a vision and, as we talked about in Chapter 3, a visionary leader. Most tech startups that have gone on to huge success have some kind of iconic origin story, whether it's two guys in a dorm room, three founders in a coffee shop, or a couple driving cross-country armed with only a dream and a laptop on which they were hammering out their first business plan.

I believe that every company that has scaled successfully has a second story, too—one that starts after the thrilling ride of turning an idea into reality and finding a place for it in the market.

I call this moment the *second founding*: It's the period in a company's growth when it goes from being just another organization to an institution that's here to stay. It's the moment when the company grows up and adopts a managerial culture. I've seen it firsthand and unfortunately, the whole world has been witnessing what happens when companies fail that test. For too many companies, the second founding is also the moment when bureaucracy and lethargy set in and the most innovative people—hamstrung by frustration—are sidelined or leave altogether. A few companies have been able to make this transition without losing their "startup DNA." What sets them apart, and how can future startups replicate their success? How can established organizations recapture that startup spirit?

This is the work of Phase Three, in which organizations transform their internal processes. The goal: to create functions that are capable of continuous innovation. This moment is about changing the deep systems of the organization to support innovation for the long-term life and value of the company.

This chapter is, in many ways, the most misleading in the book. I've tried to give a glimpse of what a truly large-scale transformation looks like from a number of different angles. But precisely because these transformations are so large, so profound, and so different for every company, it's difficult to be systematic about it. It's not that Phase Three is any less rigorous than Phases One and Two. In fact, it requires quite a bit more. But because each organization's understanding of what systems it needs to change will be based on the outcomes of its particular earlier work, the patterns are not nearly as common. The work of Phase Three is to take what the transformation has revealed already and use it to create solutions that affect every aspect of the organization. These stories illustrate what that process has looked like in a variety of settings.

AIRBNB'S SECOND FOUNDING

Trips, which I first talked about in Chapter 1, marks Airbnb's second founding. But before Trips was launched, it languished for a while because the company wasn't focused on it even as it continued to grow its core business. The urgency Brian Chesky felt about ushering his company into its next phase had sent him back to the inspirations that had made it a success in the first place. Among them was the book that had motivated him to move to San Francisco and start Airbnb: Neal Gabler's biography *Walt Disney: The Triumph of the American Imagination*. Rereading it, Chesky became captivated by the story of how Disney used storyboarding to create *Snow White,* Disney's first fully animated film, a feat no one had thought possible. Airbnb hired a Pixar artist to storyboard an entire trip from end to end, from the perspectives of both the host and the guest: that was how the company found what might be its next big idea. "We realized immediately that we were really absent from most of the trip," says Joe Zadeh, VP of product. From that, the concept of curating an entire trip was born. "What if, instead of trying to build incrementally on top of our existing platform, we rethought end-to-end trips completely from scratch?" Zadeh recalls thinking. The team called the new initiative Project Snow White.

And then, nothing happened. Months passed, and the company's founders had made very little "progress toward the vision" they believed was going to help Airbnb continue to grow. So they launched a startup within their own walls. A six-person team headed by Joe Gebbia, co-founder and chief product officer, and made up of designers, product people, and engineers, went to New York for three months and ran their own internal incubator program. They tested numerous ideas for what the company might do next, and they were expected to demo them back in San Francisco when their East Coast stint was up. Back home, they reformed as "a team called Home to Home . . . to explore and test more ideas, [the most promising of which was called] the Experience Marketplace." It was, as Leigh Gallagher writes in her book *The Airbnb Story,* "a platform where hosts with a particular skill or knowledge set could offer experiences to guests in their city for a fee."[1] Project Snow White was back on the table.

The company formed another cross-functional team (this time with no expiration date) to restart the project, including a designer, an engineer, a project manager, and two people assigned to scout people and experiences. Brian Chesky joined the team as project leader, providing both moral authority and executive support to the new venture.

One afternoon, the team went out to Fisherman's Wharf in San Francisco to talk to their customers. Their first questions, posed to whoever would stop to talk, were simple: "Why are you here?" and "What do you want to do?" They spent two years quietly growing the Trips technology iterating online and offline.

"We optimized that sort of startup scrappiness," Zadeh recalls. "Everybody who was on the team has that. We had this startup within a startup." Chesky had once again learned from his original mentor, Walt Disney, who created Disneyland at a separate company that was later bought back and reintegrated into the parent company.

Though Project Snow White was always operating within Airbnb, the concept remained the same. "This product was designed around the principles of Disneyland," Chesky told Leigh Gallagher. Then, referring to some words of wisdom given to him by Elon Musk, the founder of Tesla, who had described for Chesky the three "eras" of a startup—creation, building, and administration—Chesky added: "Airbnb will never be in the administration era. It will always be in a building era."[2]

To that end, last year the company launched Samara, an in-house innovation and design studio made up of designers and engineers and headed by Gebbia. "We care so much about creating a brand that has longevity to it, we decided it was time to create a space to do just that," Gebbia explained in an interview, "one that was untethered from the constraints of the day-to-day, one that could have the space to take big risks and fail on some of them." His hopes for Samara, which, among other projects, has gotten involved in helping to alleviate the global refugee crisis, is that it will help ensure the company's continued growth and evolution. "We planted a seed in 2008 that's grown into this incredible tree that has global roots in 191 countries" he told *Metropolis* magazine about the company's start. "No tree survives, nor does it become a forest, if it doesn't plant more seeds around itself. We've created Sámara to be the internal design studio to put more seeds out there. We hope that our ideas take us far from the tree."[3]

BUILDING THE PLANE

Part of any second founding story has to do with the journey of the founder or founders, who, like Brian Chesky and Joe Gebbia, must be as invested in the entrepreneurs who work for the company as in their own careers. That shift in attitude represents a critical moment in the long-term success of any organization.

At the same time, though, it doesn't matter how much the founder's perspective changes if the systems to support what the company is attempting don't exist. That fresh understanding of the need for support is what makes it possible for legacy and enterprise organizations to experience a second founding, too. They may have more work to do in terms of restructuring than a hypergrowth startup, but that re-founding moment is similar. The executives who lead that transformation must have as much of a founder's mindset as anyone in Silicon Valley in order to succeed.

Teams working on experiments and MVPs can get temporary funding using metered funding, but what happens when they're successful? People are inevitably going to start asking questions about how working in this new way is going to affect their career equity—their future performance reviews, promotions, how their peers view them. There are going to be challenges with procurement, supply chain, and compliance, which are still set up to work in the old ways. Finance and IT need to look different company-wide, too. If the company is going to ask every division to start allocating some percentage of money through metered funding and a growth board, that's a very different proposition than just having a few teams experimenting with a small amount of money. To replace a multimillion-dollar IT contract in the federal government, the systems that made that contract possible in the first place must change, too.

It's fine, in the early phases of a transformation, to operate by exception. Successful teams need to get off the ground somehow, whether the company is growing a truly new organization or making changes in an established one. Leaders can jump into the air and defy gravity, but without support, they're coming right back down. If you want to fly, you have to get on an airplane. The final phase of transformation is *building that airplane*. Trying to touch the deep systems of the company too soon is suicidal. Leaders can't do it until they've earned the political capital and gathered the proof through all the earlier work that has been done in Phase One and Phase Two. But once they have, the entrepreneurial function that management has put to work on smaller scales can come into play on an organization-wide level.

THE TEN-PAGE ONE-PAGE DOCUMENT

In Chapter 6, we met the software team that was too scared to seek "legal's" approval of their experiment. When they finally did consult the company lawyer, it took him only a few minutes to green-light the experiment.

But that wasn't the end of the story. The team launched their experiment, gleaning a huge amount of valuable data about which countries to go into and which wouldn't be worth the effort. News of the process they'd gone through to gather this data soon made its way up to the division head, who had also been the project's executive sponsor. He could see that the relationship between people trying to innovate and the legal department was broken and that the result was probably a lot of missed opportunities. That particular team had gotten the exception this time. But what about all the teams that weren't being coached in this new way? Or those that didn't even bother to call legal, out of fear or a sense of futility?

The division head decided it was time to end this cycle. He posed a question to me: "Could we work to enlist the general counsel and the whole legal team to make this kind of problem less expensive for the company?" I thought we could. But I knew that the key to making it work would be participation from the legal department itself. A meeting with everyone in the legal department was the next step. The lawyer who had helped the team with their experiment was not, in fact, a fringe member in an otherwise unimaginative department full of people who enjoyed denying projects and putting up roadblocks. In fact, the lawyers said, "We hate being the gatekeepers. We don't like saying no all the time. How can we be helpful to teams doing experimentation?" As is so often the case, they were being constrained not by a lack of ability or interest in doing things a different way, but by entrenched processes that had been built up over years and were intended to mitigate risk. Instead of protecting the company, though, they were hurting it.

My proposal was simple: create a one-page guidance document that laid out, in plain English, a series of parameters within which innovation teams would be pre-cleared to work.

1. If you're doing a tiny MVP experiment with fewer than X customers possibly affected, total liability of Y, and a cost of Z, you're pre-approved.
2. If the experiment is a success and you want do a "scaling MVP" of a little bit greater complexity and bigger numbers for X, Y,

and Z, it's deemed approved in advance as long as: (a) it's built on an initial MVP and (b) you have managerial sign-off.

3. If you want to exceed these guidelines for something larger or more complex, you need to discuss it with legal. Here's the hotline to call . . .

You probably won't be surprised to learn that the first version of this one-page document that the legal team created was . . . ten pages long.

At this point, we began applying lean methods to the process. The legal team thought we couldn't make the document any shorter, so we treated it as an MVP and ran a series of experiments, showing it to teams (the "customers" in this scenario) and asking them to share their feedback. Then we made a new version and showed them that one. After several iterations, we got the essential information down to a single page, in easy-to-understand language.

From then on, teams had a go-to source for legal advice in the early stages of experimentation without picking up a phone or incurring the expense of putting a full-time lawyer on their team from the start. There are, of course, projects for which a lawyer *should* be consulted from the beginning. Some projects have complicated compliance issues that merit a serious review by legal. But for many projects, the team's vague anxiety about what "legal" might do or say, combined with a lack of knowledge about what the rules actually are, can keep people from trying things out. Creating this document reversed the impact of legal on teams: The department became an enabler of faster speed rather than a creator of slowdowns.

There's another valuable aspect to creating a set of guidelines like this. By serving as an incentive structure, it encourages teams to build better experiments.

The typical team has an idea, and they hope to come up with some great numbers to put into their business plan. In order to produce vanity metrics, they think they need to show the experiment to thousands of customers. But when they look at this sheet of guidelines and discover that doing so would require them to call legal—well, who wants to do that? They realize it's actually easier for them to start small—say, by showing one hundred customers instead of seeking permission from legal to show ten thousand. When teams start to think this way, their behavior changes. Legal is now a part of the solution.

FROM GATEKEEPER FUNCTIONS TO ENABLING FUNCTIONS

The way this legal team was operating is typical of the challenges that "gatekeeper functions" present. Now let's take a tour of some of the other repeat offenders that oversee the company's deep systems. The goal of the Startup Way is to help them embrace a customer-service mindset. Gatekeepers delay the work of other functions through reviews, bureaucracy, and rigid rules. Enabling functions help teams accelerate their work. The specifics of what needs to change varies by function, as you'll see. Incidentally, every single one of these examples involves a function that someone, over the years, has told me is impossible to change. Is that really true? Come see for yourself.

Legal

Let's take a look at another organization that changed its legal department in response to customer needs. Pivotal is a software development company that spun off from EMC and VMware in 2012.[4]

Because Pivotal's business model is based on open-source and free software, many legal questions arise: Who owns the copyright? Is the code valid? What IP might leak or is being licensed unintentionally? "Lawyers have an allergic reaction to open source," says Andrew Cohen, general counsel at Pivotal. "You don't want unintended, unknown things to be hidden in your software," he says. The company's legal team embarked on a project to "harmonize IP protection and open-source compliance." Borrowing from VMware, they created a vetting process for software that was being used or contributed, consisting of a series of online questions and a legal review. "Once you did that, you created a repository of pre-checked, pre-validated open source software," explains Cohen. "That was kind of the starting point." This turned out to be their MVP.

From there, two attorneys on Cohen's now nine-person legal team approached the engineers at Pivotal. "They said, 'Hey, here's our open-source process. It's actually too manual and too slow,' " recalls Cohen. " 'You guys are changing software in this model constantly. We're months behind you checking out what people are using, and guess what? The customers now are asking us for a manifest and for details on what's under the covers inside our product. We can't get them a crystal-clear response fast enough unless we work together with you and come up with a better process."

Cohen says it helped that the two lawyers who worked this out with the engineers had an engineering background of their own. Each team agreed that this was really a customer trust issue. "Rather than legal standing back, creating the policy . . . we fully engaged as scientists and experts," says Cohen.

The ultimate goal was to automate the process, which everyone realized would take the burden of the questionnaire and technical details off the engineers, improving their situation as well as that of customers and the legal department.

They started with a single process. "One of the issues when you grab open-source software is just figuring out what license is applicable," explains Cohen. That process was automated and replaced by something Pivotal calls License Finder. From there, the legal department created a filter using green, yellow, and red to indicate which licenses could be used or not. Green sailed right through the system and was good to go. Red almost always couldn't be used; yellow required further review.

Ultimately, Cohen says, Pivotal was able to find something that has less impact on the engineers and builds customer trust without the "army of lawyers" required by other companies. "We're operating at very high scale in terms of the size of our engineering operation, and it's really being supported by two part-time lawyers who also do lots of other things."

Finance

Ledgers. It's not really a word most people associate with start-ups. It sounds . . . old-fashioned. But ledgers are, in fact, the core of finance in any corporation. Because of this, one of the most engrossing projects I've worked on to date was an ERP (enterprise resource planning) software ledger consolidation at GE. It may seem dull from the outside, but if a company has reached the stage where it can drive real change in a function as tradition-bound as finance, it's a demonstration of just how deeply the culture change has permeated the organization.

When I joined the project, the company had embarked on a five-year plan to simplify the network of ERP systems used by all its businesses worldwide. Over time, driven by acquisitions, new business models, and new capabilities, GE was operating through more than 500 ERP systems globally, spanning all major business segments. Integrations, visibility to operations, and financial closing processes were much more difficult than necessary.

For example, in GE's centralized corporate operations, there were more than 40 ERP systems spanning more than 150 countries. Historically, when GE begins operating in a new country, one of the first things it does is to implement an ERP. Then all GE businesses in that country use the same system until they scale enough to use a system of their own.

For this project, the end goal was to have just one ERP system that would allow all of the company's industrial businesses to consolidate in the same way, using a single chart of accounts, so that the finance work could be done centrally out of the company's Global Operations function. The team hoped to make the simplification process 50 percent cheaper and 50 percent faster. "We knew we couldn't go back to the old ways of taking six to nine months to build out requirements, then try to build custom solutions for each business," says James Richards, who was the CIO for finance at GE at the time (he's now CIO for GE Healthcare).

The team started small with a new approach, with just two countries in Latin America: Chile and Argentina. Teams made up of finance, operations, and IT were embedded on location, and each one dove into the project with a goal of getting the software live with standard functionality in a month. Then they went even smaller. Rather than build all the necessary modules of their new software at once (the ledger is just one of the functionalities, which also include accounts payable, accounts receivable, cash management, and supply chain) and then roll the whole thing out on an eighteen-month cycle, they started with just one module for each country. "We looked for the biggest pain point in each place," says Richards. "Or what we thought was going to be the one that, if we didn't get it right, we wouldn't be able to go live in total. Then we targeted the MVP toward that specific area." They remained focused on co-located, cross-functional teams and "short sprints of exposing functionality to the users," he says. "We would take off-the-shelf functionality and go directly into testing mode."

This was a complete reversal from the old method. Now the onus was on the customers—GE's internal customers—to show the team why something didn't work well for them. "That was sort of the key to it," says Richards. "We'd assume that the enterprise software we're deploying works . . . then we will only fix or configure those things that caused us a compliance problem or caused massive inefficiencies in the user base." Once they were nearly finished with one module, the team would move on to the next one. Working in this way, they reduced their deployment time from eighteen months to between four and six months.

With every country they cycled through, the team added another proof point to their case for widespread adoption, using proof points to scale up to more countries. When GE moved to Oracle ERP Cloud, they scaled up again and started working on sets of countries. The project as a whole was "a framework that helped the company move to a different clock speed and ensure people were constantly challenging themselves to go faster with less cost. It was visible across the entire enterprise and celebrated when we had big successes," says Richards.

Many of GE's business segments began leveraging similar approaches, and the global teams have driven those original 500-plus ERPs down to less than 100, an 80 percent reduction in just four years. It didn't happen without some stumbles, but the project benefited from "a strong push from the top of GE for simplification and speed. You would always have some people stuck in their old ways, but then you'd have a whole set of people who were up for anything," says Richards. "That was the group we relied on to sell it to the rest of the organization."

When I tell this story to entrepreneurs or product people,

they're often extremely skeptical (there are usually extensive groans in the audience audible from the stage). We all assume that this team is a typical multiheaded hydra of finance and IT, made up of lifetime bureaucrats who don't have an innovative bone in their body. Yet what I witnessed firsthand was this: the transformation of this team into a startup that is deeply passionate about solving problems with speed and creativity. The change in their demeanor and behavior after a three-day workshop was so striking, even some insiders found it hard to believe. I was even accused of putting something in the water! But this was no magical or pharmacological miracle. It was simply the result of changing the systems, incentives, and mindsets that were holding this team back. It's a "miracle" I've witnessed time and again, even in the most boring, intransigent, or impossible contexts.

Information Technology

On one of my trips to Washington, D.C., I swung by the newly expanded offices of the United States Digital Service. They had many projects under way, and I was catching up with a number of teams. We were talking about moving USDS beyond just concept projects and tackling some of the deeper problems plaguing the federal bureaucracy.

At this point, one of the leaders said, "Tell him about the cave."

They launched into a story: Imagine a stack of paper nearly twice as high as the Statue of Liberty. That's how much paper the United States Citizenship and Immigration Services (USCIS) used to receive every day from the 7 million applications it processes annually. That's right: They were processing millions of applications on paper, by hand.

The technologist within me was horrified. Think of the incredible inefficiency!

But the USDS team assured me I didn't understand the half of it. With this much paper, where do you store the applications when they are being processed? Paper is actually quite dense and heavy. The volume of paper we're talking about is so immense that standard offices can't contain it. Buildings have to be specially reinforced to handle the load.

Including one processing center, which—for structural support—is built into a cave.

At first, I thought this was a joke or maybe a metaphor about the working conditions of civil servants. It actually took me several minutes to understand that the work was being done in an actual cave. And working in this cave are people whose job it is to help move all of this paper between the cave and field offices all over the country, for the purpose of approving immigration applications.

It doesn't seem like the kind of setup twenty-first-century government should have, does it? But this was the situation in 2008, when the USCIS, which is part of the Department of Homeland Security, launched what it called the Transformation Program to build the Electronic Immigration System (ELIS). The goal was to move the agency's processes from paper-based to electronic to deliver faster, more efficient service to people waiting for everything from citizenship to green-card replacement.

At the time, for example, the process for starting a background check went like this: Someone sat at a computer (in the cave, also known as the National Benefits Center) with a stack of applicant folders to the left. He or she opened the top folder, then opened up the background-check software and keyed in the name and date. The contractor printed the screen—in many cases, on a dot matrix printer!—ripped the perforations off the edges of that printout, stapled it onto the folder, and moved the folder to a new stack on the right-hand side of the computer. This same process was repeated numerous times for each application, depending on how many systems the applicant needed to be checked against.

This, and the many other processes like it, prompted the Transformation Program. But by 2014, the program itself was in need of transformation. It had been run according to standard government IT practices since its launch in 2008, with all the typical features: two years of requirements, legacy contractors, and a track record of failure. The new IT system was actually slower than the paper-based process.

That was when Mark Schwartz, the CIO of USCIS, and Kath Stanley, the chief of transformation and a public servant who's been in government for thirty years, decided to try something new, using various techniques that, by now, will sound familiar.

For about two years, the USCIS team worked on restructuring their contractors and doing small releases of features every few months, which brought them to the post-HealthCare.gov moment when Mikey Dickerson was making the rounds in Silicon Valley to gauge interest in government work.

One of the people who answered Dickerson's call was a software engineer at Google named Brian Lefler. "I think for me, personally, working at Google Maps at the time and being very happy, I needed to see HealthCare.gov burn down before I could see there was a problem. Then watching people fix it—I needed to know that my skills would actually be applicable." He signed on for six months, and the first project he took on, along with two other members of USDS, Eric Hysen and Mollie Ruskin, was a two-week sprint at USCIS.

Lefler stayed on to help with this process beyond his official two weeks, and six months later, the department had adopted all of the team's recommendations. By that time the USDS had come into existence. Brian Lefler was now part of a five-person team officially tasked to help the USCIS staff, led by Mark Schwartz and Kath Stanley, implement their transition from paper to electronic systems. They addressed issues from engineering to product and design. "People assume they know what the user wants because it's written down in a document somewhere that someone drafted two years ago," Lefler says. Among other things, the USDS team convinced the agency that it was worth the money to fly people out to "the cave" to watch how the applications were being processed. They also took prototypes out to the cave as they evolved so that workers could try them and provide feedback, creating a continuous feedback loop.

By November of 2014, they were ready for a three-day soft launch of the product, which allowed the team to perform an end-to-end test of the system and target any remaining issues through automated tests the team had developed (which had been continuously evolving) before the full launch of the new I-90 process in February of 2015. When the product launched, 92 percent of the people who used it to renew or replace their green cards said they were "satisfied with the experience."[5] Processing times dropped dramatically, almost instantly. Right after the launch, someone was approved and got a green card in two weeks, when previously there had been a six-month backlog. "We thought it was a bug," Brian Lefler recalls. "We figured it would probably take people a month to get a fingerprint appointment and whatever else, but someone got his receipt from the system and then took it and bullied his way into an appointment center and was like, 'Take my fingerprints now!'"

From there, collaborating with the USDS team, the USCIS continued to add new functions to ELIS. They looked at how to manage security in a world of rapid releases and brought that process from eleven reviews to two. In a period of eighteen months after the soft release of the I-90 application, they digitized almost 40 percent of the system.

The department now has its own in-house team: the Department of Homeland Security Digital Service. Now, instead of having a group of people from USDS parachuted in to assist, they've integrated IT innovation into their department. These days, work being done at USCIS is part of a pool other parts of the department can draw on. As Hysen, who heads the team, says, the old way makes "a lot of contractors rich. It isn't actually helping us meet the needs of people who depend on our departments as quickly and effectively as we can." It's not uncommon to see tours of people from other parts of the DHS, like TSA, FEMA, or the Secret Service, "who have been really stuck for years," according to Hysen, moving through USCIS in order to see how they're working. The agency has 14,000 federal employees supported by 6,000 contractors on a day-to-day basis, and the work they do impacts 4 million people a year. Now, the staff in their eighty-five field offices around the country, many of whom had been using the same systems for thirty years, is using ELIS, and the process of transformation is ongoing.

Human Resources

GE's Employee Management System

GE has a world-class human resources function. Other companies model their own HR departments after it. So you can imagine that when I suggested changes might be needed as part of the transformation, people thought I was a little bit crazy. I found out why in an early meeting with a team building a gas turbine.

The team was making considerable progress at one of the first FastWorks workshops, debating how quickly they could get a new product to market. No one was satisfied with the traditional five-year development cycle. Eventually, the team settled upon a traditional lean technique called set-based concurrent engineering (SBCE)[6] that could bring the initial MVP to market in less than eighteen months.

The team worked hard to identify their early-adopter customers and plan ways to bring them into the development process early. Everyone agreed that the new plan had a higher likelihood of success than the old one, because the team would uncover potential problems with their plans in a matter of months, not years. Excited, I asked. "Are we ready to propose this new plan to the senior leadership?" The answer was a unanimous, "No, of course not."

Why on earth were we not going to proceed? One of the engineers offered a one-word explanation: "EMS."

The engineers patiently explained that working in parallel on multiple components at the same time, as SBCE requires, would cost the company more money because there's necessarily more rework involved when you design components independently of one another. I asked them to quantify the rework cost, which they estimated at $1 million. I was confused: Wasn't that cost miniscule compared to the overall project budget (which was substantially higher)? Wouldn't a modest increase in short-term costs be worth the overwhelming reduction in cycle time and the dramatic reduction in overall costs via validated learning? Everyone agreed that it would.

So this seemed like a win all around, right?

Everyone agreed that it was.

So we're agreed to go forward with the new plan?

Oh, no, definitely not.

Why not?

EMS.

No one could believe that I hadn't heard of EMS (GE's Employee Management System) before now. But what did that have to do with making suboptimal engineering decisions?

One of the engineers finally took pity on me and explained that every engineer in the room had an annual goal he or she worked toward, which was evaluated in EMS, based on a functional matrix of what excellence looks like for his or her job category. In this division, the amount of rework caused by an engineer was one of the key metrics to which the engineer would be held accountable. So any plan that increased rework would negatively affect that engineer's annual review and career. Getting this project to market sooner, while certainly admirable and perhaps even desirable to the company at large, would hamper team members' individual career prospects.

As it turned out, Janice Semper and Viv Goldstein were hearing the same thing from other teams being coached in Fast-Works: The company's performance system, in place since 1976, was "a big part of the culture," according to Semper, but didn't support the new way of working. Don't get me wrong: EMS is an impressive system; it simply wasn't designed to function with the kinds of projects the company was now taking on, where extreme uncertainty demands a new approach.

EMS operated on an annual basis, with employees setting goals at the start of each year and being evaluated on them at the end. As Jennifer Beihl, a member of the HR team described it, "It was completely misaligned with everything else we were trying to do."

People were coming to Semper and saying things like, "I'm applying FastWorks and learning, and in many cases I'm invalidating assumptions. I should pivot but can't because of the way I'm being held accountable." That was when she understood at the deepest level that EMS was literally preventing the change the company was trying so hard to make.

Semper turned to the culture team that had helped create the GE Beliefs (see Chapter 6) to design a new performance approach aligned with FastWorks. She insisted that this new approach be tested with actual employees to prove that it would work—with real data that showed increased productivity, speed, and engagement. The process followed by the culture team is a perfect example of the dual role that individual functions play in Phase Three: *They both support the entrepreneurial efforts of product and project teams* and *create their own entrepreneurial processes to streamline their own functional responsibilities.* (See the org chart in Chapter 5, page 127).

PD@GE (Performance Development at GE)

The team's first step was to establish a senior leader board of about a dozen top executives in order to facilitate an ongoing dialogue about the process and progress of this critically important change. Next, they conducted some external research on how other organizations were changing their approaches to be less hierarchical; they even talked to an orchestra without a conductor to better understand how they could design a process that was more in line with the outcomes the company wanted to achieve.

With some ideas in mind, the team identified three groups of internal customers they wanted to serve with the new approaches, and they went out to roughly a thousand of those people across functions, businesses, and locations for feedback.

CUSTOMER #1: GE employees
PROBLEM #1: EMS doesn't offer a personal connection to goals, individual development, and career aspirations. ("We need a more continuous, fluid process versus an event-driven one.")

CUSTOMER #2: GE managers
PROBLEM #2: EMS doesn't effectively give them the ability to inspire, engage, and lead their teams to the best possible performance. ("Too much time spent looking backward.")

CUSTOMER #3: GE senior leaders
PROBLEM #3: EMS lacks the ability to improve individuals' and teams' performance and develop employees in support of GE's business needs and evolving culture.

The customer responses were very valuable to the team. But they weren't the main learning, which turned out to be the invalidation of a leap-of-faith assumption so fixed that the team hadn't even singled it out as something to specifically ask customers about.

For years, GE had famously used a five-point rating system to sort employees into different categories ranging from "unsatisfactory" to "role model."[7] At the start of the redesign process, the team had assumed that, no matter what else changed, they would keep that model. "Then we learned from our employee and manager dialogues that it was actually a huge pain point for many employees," recalls Beihl. "For the majority of them, the label either meant absolutely nothing or it actually demotivated them." Given that these categories affected compensation and other rewards, the team realized that the old system might warrant a complete overhaul.

It was a startling realization. They'd gone from being gatekeepers to being entrepreneurs, and had also discovered that they had to treat employees as entrepreneurs. This understanding is similar to the way a startup founder needs to go from being the leader of a small team to the leader of an ecosystem of small teams (as we discussed in Chapter 1) in order to guide a company to the next level. Janice Semper remembers that her team "looked at the human resources function, which would traditionally own this process, not as a customer group but as a key enabler to the approach."

MVP Component Testing

Three months into their project, the team launched their first product MVP, a new app that could be used for feedback, conversation, and evaluation. Among the three customer groups they'd surveyed, a clear mandate for maintaining a culture of meritocracy came through. Employees were accustomed to getting feedback from their managers—senior to junior feedback—but they wanted to add upward feedback and colleague feedback to the mix, as well. The team identified two more leap-of-faith assumptions before building their MVP:

1. If we create a way for employees to share feedback as they requested, they will use it.
2. If they use it, they will find it valuable.

Then they built and ran their experiment:

- They created a quick-and-dirty app that allowed for all three methods of feedback (leaving out the other functions they knew they'd want later).
- They trained a hundred employees and managers in how to use the app.
- They gave the trained cohort two weeks to test the app.

What happened when the two weeks were up? "We went back and collected our learnings, and what we learned was that nobody did anything," remembers Janice Semper.

So what went wrong? First, the team tried to pin the problem on the app. Too complicated? Nope. Their test had failed not because the technological tool was bad, but because the behaviors and environment needed to deploy it effectively weren't there. Employees *said* they wanted to give upward and collegial feedback, but when it came to actually doing so, they were too uncomfortable. There was no history of this kind of exchange at GE, and they had no idea how their colleagues would react to it, so they took the safest option, which was to do nothing at all.

The pivot, once the team embraced it (with the mantra "Let's not fight the pivot"), was to focus on the behaviors and culture needed to make the tool useful, rather than expect the tool to create those behaviors. "That particular learning helped us to transition from technology as the center of our performance approach to using technology as simply an enabler of the approach," Beihl says. "It helped us really focus on a performance development approach as a product that is all about behaviors and new conversations and new ways of working." In the old days, she says, the team would, no doubt, have launched the app company-wide, checked the "done" box on their list, and moved on. But in Phase Three, despite the success and momentum organizations feel, testing and validation are more important than ever.

That's why the HR team—now a true startup—embarked on a series of experiments to gauge different approaches to changing behavior, testing on cohorts of employees and managers as small as twenty people, no more than one hundred. What they learned led them to the realization that none of the performance management tools available on the market could support the kind of outcomes they wanted. They made the decision to go back to the app design with their new knowledge, and in three months they had an MVP version based on real feedback to test on a larger cohort. They'd saved not only time but a lot of money that would have been spent buying elaborate software that didn't align with what they wanted to facilitate and measure.

Wing-to-Wing Pilot Test

By the fourth quarter of that first year, the team was ready for a larger test (though still a very small one in relation to the size of GE as a whole). They rolled out their new approach and app, which was designed to facilitate and support ongoing conversation between employees and managers, culminating in a simple year-end summary, to 5,500 employees across five global organizations. A thousand of these employees also used a new "no-ratings" approach the team was testing in lieu of the five-point system. Participants in this pilot were asked to pretend that the final quarter was the full year, in order to go through the process from start to finish.

The learnings gathered from this pilot involved everything from subtle language changes—using the word *insights* rather than *feedback* and giving people the option to suggest that colleagues *continue* or *consider* their actions—to observations that led to a change in the way the tool captured notes made by all parties in the next iteration. "In our old way of working," Beihl explains, "we would have told them they were doing it 'wrong' and helped them 'fix' it. Now we understood how they were actually acting and pivoted the approach to meet that."

There was also good news from an important leading indicator: 80 percent of the employees using the new system had completed their year-end summary by the end of January, while less than 2 percent of the employees still using EMS had.

Based on these successes, in early 2015, the team started scaling up the testing using two basic methods:

- The entire HR function transitioned to using the new system, regardless of whether or not their businesses or organizations were part of the growing cohorts of testers.
- Businesses that had teams in the pilot program were asked how they wanted to scale (through sub-business units, entire business units, etc.). Businesses that had not participated in the pilot were encouraged to put a small team into the cohort. No one was forced to participate; any business that agreed to test the system did so on a volunteer basis. The fact that so many signed on voluntarily was another great leading indicator of success.

Over the course of 2015, the testing groups grew from 5,500 people to roughly 90,000. Within those groups, the employees testing the "no-ratings" evaluation went from 1,000 to 30,000 (we'll talk more about the adoption and effects of that in a bit). In 2016, the app was rolled out company-wide, along with supporting tools to help employees use it effectively.

In two years, the PD@GE team changed not only the method of performance measurement from "a highly prescriptive, formal, annual process to an approach where we provided a framework and we allowed freedom within that framework," according to Semper. They changed the way people in the company think of success. And—just as important—they demonstrated that even HR can act like a startup.

The kind of restructuring at the heart of PD@GE not only makes the company run better but also serves as an efficient means of sending a clear signal across all levels and divisions of an organization that this way of working is the new standard.

COMPENSATION AND PROMOTION

When you go from a system of ratings like the one GE previously had, in which employees were rated annually using one of five ranked labels,[8] to a system that treats learning, honesty, and outcomes as the signs of success, it's hard to envision how that translates into career progress. That turned out not to be a problem, as the "no-ratings" subset pilot testing showed.

The team chose three metrics in particular to measure:

- Managers' self-reported ability to effectively plan, prepare, and differentiate for salary and bonuses
  - 77 percent said their salary planning was either the same or simpler than it had been before PD@GE, and the findings were the same for those using ratings versus no ratings.
- The average merit and bonus increase both for employees participating in the no-ratings test and those who were still given a rating

- These remained unchanged, indicating that the new system allowed for differentiation in rewards regardless of ratings or no ratings.
- Managers' belief that they could effectively connect performance with salary increases using the new no-ratings system
  - 70 percent of managers said they had no problem with this.

These learnings showed that the no-ratings system was a good plan as far as reward was concerned (other metrics showed that employees were having more meaningful conversations with their peers and managers and that managers felt they had a better view of employee impact—also good signs). In 2016, GE decided to scrap its old ratings system entirely.[9]

Compensation as Hiring Tool

Think back to the discussion of equity ownership in Chapter 3. What's critical about incentives for startups is not just the financial piece, but that the people who are working on a startup have a *stake in the outcome,* a sense of ownership over their shared fate. For early founders and employees, equity ownership provides this belief. But for later employees, especially as the company grows, direct equity ownership can become little more than a complex bonus system, because their fractional ownership is so low.

WordPress—the open-source blog platform that powers more than 27 percent of websites—is structured overall in an open, non-hierarchical way. More than 500 people work for the company all around the world, and none of them do so in quite the same way. "I want to create an environment where people have autonomy and purpose," explains co-founder Matt Mullenweg. "Part of that is saying you're not going to tell someone how to do their job. It's all about the output." The same ethos applies to the way WordPress manages accountability and incentives. "We try not to do anything by decree," says Mullenweg. "People can change drastically when they join a team, or a team can change when someone joins." Many of the company's leads rotate in and out over time, but that doesn't involve any kind of change in compensation. Mullenweg wants people to feel totally comfortable transitioning out of the lead role if it isn't a position they're enjoying or particularly suited to. "In many corporate structures, you end up moving up in a company by managing more people. I don't want someone to feel like in order to grow in their career they need to become a manager. And conversely, I don't want them to feel bad for letting it go."[10]

WordPress has structured incentives this way since its founding in 2003. But at more established organizations, it's necessary to change the way people are rewarded. This can be incredibly difficult, especially in a place that has had the same systems in place for a long time. When I talk to corporate executives, they often claim they wish they could provide their employees with "equity" tied directly to the long-term success of their current project. For an internal startup, this is clearly logical. And yet, they claim, the mysterious forces of "finance" would never allow it. But when I speak to the leaders of finance functions around the world, they universally agree the mechanics of how to build this kind of "internal equity" are not especially complicated. What's missing is the willingness of general managers to commit to specific milestones for valuing the project's success.

Working together in a cross-functional way shows a possible path forward: a stake in the outcome for internal startups designed by finance, backed by the conviction of senior leadership.

As Ryan Smith, head of Global Human Resources at GE Business Innovations, says, "Compensation in a big company tends to be a place that is fairly rooted in consistency and process. It can be a hard place to innovate." That, of course, is what makes it a perfect Phase Three project. When you've seen so much success with teams and processes, experimenting with something as sacred as compensation feels less risky. People understand the way experimentation works and often are willing to give it a try.

That was the case at GE Ventures, the company's investment arm, which launched in 2013. The business's leaders knew that if they wanted to get the best people on board, they had to do more than just offer them a standard contract and cross their fingers. "We have a pretty good track record with engineers," Smith notes. "But venture capitalists are not engineers. They're looking for something different from a compensation rewards point of view."

What once would have been a major break with protocol was now more or less another day at the office. "We came to our leadership team with an idea and said, 'We want to compensate this set of leaders in a different way. We want to test this—can we?'" The leadership liked parts of the experiment and signed off on the test, which was quite small (the power of mitigating risk in an MVP applies no matter what is being tested).

Their hypotheses were: (1) This new compensation system will allow us to retain and reward some key and unusual talents inside the company. (2) The new compensation approach will allow us to better recruit new hires.

They ran the test, made a few tweaks based on what they learned, and have now implemented it. "If the outcome we're going for is rewarding, retaining, and hiring the best talent in the world," says Smith, "this has allowed us to do that in a market we've never been in before. When you're not able to innovate in new spaces, you're not able to meet the business objectives. It just so happens that the objective we're trying to drive in this case is to get the best people and hold on to them."

Procurement

As I mentioned at the start of the chapter, that kind of transformation can and does occur in every function. I've seen incredible results across organizations of all kinds, even procurement and supply chain. In government alone, projects like RFP-EZ[11] (Request for Proposal-EZ), one of the first Presidential Innovation Fellows projects, which created an online marketplace where small businesses could bid for government work; and the Agile Blanket Purchase Agreement (Agile BPA),[12] which gives the entire government access to contractors and vendors who provide agile delivery services like DevOps, user-centered design, and agile software development have both cut the requirements and time needed for purchasing, leading to faster resolution of critical problems. But that's not all.

Even the Nuclear Codes Need Procurement Reform

It may seem highly improbable that procurement reform, which many consider inherently uninteresting, could be connected to something as critical and sensitive as generating nuclear codes. But not only is it possible, it's true! In 2016, Matt Fante, chief innovation officer of the Information Assurance Directorate at the National Security Agency (NSA), launched a startup incubator, which is now called I-Corps (for Innovation Corps). For one of their first projects, one of Fante's NSA colleagues in the Nuclear Command Control mission proposed changing the way the "no-lone zone" worked. The no-lone zone is the physical area where the nuclear codes are generated on an ongoing basis.

This is a solemn responsibility. The old system in place when the project was proposed required two people to be present in the room at all times (thus, "no-lone") to keep the systems equipment of the nuclear command and control process running securely. Sometimes three people were needed to accommodate breaks and lunch. They were effectively trapped in a tiny, secure room for many hours. "What those people wanted most was their freedom. Could we offer them freedom? The team quickly figured out that this was the biggest pain point for the customer," Fante recalls.

The I-Corps team started working with the idea of building a KVM (keyboard video mouse): One person shows up and uses the equivalent of a smart card to log in. The second person does the same, and the system is live, energizing the video, keyboard, and mouse. Unless two people are present, the KVM will not authenticate, the systems are inoperable, and ultimately you achieve the same end goal as when two people sit in a room all day long. The team named the device they were designing Orthus, after a monstrous two-headed dog in Greek mythology.

Though the team was working to develop the product, they were not receiving some of their supplies in a timely manner because of the NSA's uniquely unwieldy and secure government supply-chain process. At one point, in need of something called a break out board, Fante went to the team, asked for a USB cable, then proceeded to cut the cable in half. "Here's your breakout board," he said.

With the new sliced-up cables, that team was able to finish an MVP in seven weeks and start iterating, resulting in a working tool that met the customer's needs in a short time frame. Fante and his team built one of these systems, then worked on twenty-five the second year, and will look to continue to scale after that. "This offered a whole new way to be productive, all with a $200 device," he says. "Getting it to utility in a year, in that environment, is unbelievably cool." This kind of speed is very unusual in this context.

As a result of this experience, the team now has processes in place that allow them to buy components more quickly while they're searching for value and solutions. "Then we go through the full-blown acquisition process when it's time to execute," explains Fante.

The Closet at Seattle Children's Hospital

Procurement reform has also taken hold in health care. What started with the reorganization of a single closet at Seattle Children's Hospital (based on the methods of the Toyota Production System) has spread through the system and become a full-blown philosophy that meshes lean manufacturing and Lean Startup ideas to form a cycle of continuous improvement called Seattle Children's Improvement and Innovation.[13]

In 2006, when Greg Beach moved from the clinical engineering department to the supply chain at Seattle Children's, he brought with him a deep background in lean methodologies. The hospital became one of the first in the country to adopt lean principles, overhauling its system one department at a time.

Early in this adoption process, Beach arrived at the supply-chain side, expecting things to be running smoothly. Instead, he found a unit without metrics or a work standard. "People came in at seven or eight and went home at three thirty, and what they did between those hours was not quite defined," says Beach. "I would get calls in the evening from our chief nursing officer saying, 'You're out of diapers, and this is a pediatric institution.'"

Beach quickly learned that some of the nurses took ordering into their own hands. They'd call suppliers, put orders through the system, often ordering far more than was needed so they could stockpile supplies around their unit to ensure they wouldn't run out. Sometimes those piles of supplies just sat, unused. "The people who should be taking care of patients or doing laboratory analysis were actually in the ordering business," he said.

That's when the supply-chain department turned to Toyota. Beach and his colleagues took a trip to Japan. There they learned how Toyota's staff was empowered to come up with ideas for improvement, and they were given suggestions for how to reduce waste and effectively manage inventory.

As a result, in 2008, the supply chain at the hospital made the switch to what they call the "two-bin system." Two bins are set up full of each necessary item. When the first bin is empty, a second full bin behind it is pulled forward. At that point an order, relying on a bar code attached to each bin, is automatically placed with the vendor for replacement supplies.

While this small adjustment sounds simple, it involved many layers of change within the organization (just imagine the level of cross-functional coordination required). But it was worth it: This modification alone resulted in a reduction of 80,000 workforce hours a year. "That's almost forty people who were given back to the hospital, to get back to the bedside, to do their work, to do their nursing and do what they do best," says Beach. Because they aren't distracted with opening boxes and ordering supplies, the nurses can be more focused on their jobs.

Seattle Children's has regional clinics and a satellite ambulatory surgery center, each of which is set up with the two-bin system, which has been replicated by other hospitals around the country. The ordering, receiving, and distribution of all supplies are now streamlined, as well. "The goal was to reduce search and travel time for nurses," says Beach. Thanks to a new building, where all supplies are warehoused and sorted, search and travel time was reduced by 50 percent.

Beach says they've recently worked on creating supply carts stocked with commonly used items so nurses don't have to leave patients to retrieve supplies as often. In the intensive care unit and the emergency department, these carts enable nurses to stay within a given room longer, and reduce the number of times they have to remove and replace their gowns and repeatedly wash their hands, thereby helping to prevent infection.

COMPANY-WIDE INNOVATION

Ultimately, the goal of the Startup Way is to enable the entire organization to function as a portfolio of startups. This is the key to making the kind of long-term bets that provide growth and sustainability. Just as with a cohort of startups in a place like Y Combinator, expect that innovation projects in a larger organization will also have a high mortality rate. But the projects that survive from year to year can have dramatic impact.

The Creation of GE Sustainable Healthcare Solutions

In 2011, Terri Bresenham, president and CEO of GE Sustainable Healthcare Solutions, went to India as CEO of GE Healthcare India to help implement new solutions in a market where GE Healthcare was struggling. She had an engineering background, which meshed well with the large engineering team on the ground at the time.

When Bresenham arrived, her team was enthusiastic about the new way of working because they had already begun to experiment with ways to make health care more accessible in a market where it remained limited for an estimated 5.8 billion people worldwide and out of reach for roughly 600 million in India. The R&D team had developed a very-low-cost portable EKG machine that could perform a test for less than 10 rupees (20 cents).

In 2012, John Flannery, then the CEO of GE India and now the CEO of GE Healthcare, decided to fund an "in country for country" (ICFC) innovation program as part of a global initiative led by the GE Global Growth Organization, which had created a fund for emerging markets. Along with all the other regional businesses, Bresenham and her team presented their work, including the EKG machine and other projects they were developing, and Flannery awarded them $6.5 million from the innovation fund for India. That may sound like a significant investment, but consider that the total R&D budget was $1 billion, and you'll understand what the team was working against. "Skeptics challenged that low-end products might dilute our brand, have anemic returns, or not be big enough as a market even to pursue," Bresenham recalls.

Seed money in hand, the R&D team decided to focus on a single area of care in order to keep things simple: a suite of infant and maternal care products—"very low-cost, critical devices that are needed at birth for resuscitation, ventilation, and thermal regulation that, when used together, could reduce infant mortality rates." When I first encountered this team in an early round of FastWorks projects, their goal was to reduce the cost of these products by a minimum of 40 percent. The successes they had—including the design for a heating element for the baby warmer, which has since been patented—led to more projects, all of which have not only improved patient care but also increased revenue. As Bresenham puts it, "It's a win-win. There's a positive financial outcome for GE and a positive clinical outcome for patients." In 2012, global revenue for these lower-priced products was $30 million; by the end of 2015, that number had reached $260 million.

Those successes led to the creation of a new business for the company, GE Sustainable Healthcare Solutions (SHS), which launched in early 2016 with an investment of $300 million and which combines health care in India, South Asia, Africa, and Southeast Asia. "We created an entire business around the portfolio," Bresenham explains, "exclusively focused on creating affordable technologies and solutions for developing economies that leverage new approaches, some innovative technologies, and more relevant care delivery systems." This new business is run in the FastWorks style at the highest level and is itself an experiment. "We're internally experimenting with organizational structures to further enable our teams to work in ways more conducive to emerging markets," Bresenham says. "For example, a network of teams versus a traditional hierarchy of manager and subordinates." Each major region has its own chief marketing officer, and these CMOs work together and take ownership of specific strategy areas on behalf of their peers: (1) improving collective accountability for the overall business, and (2) allowing translation of learnings across various markets much more quickly. All of the funding for SHS is done through a growth board, too, which ties back to that initial decision to fund the team. If John Flannery hadn't made that choice, GE would have lost out not only on new market share and growth (more than 35 percent of customers who recently bought a new low-cost CT scanner had never before purchased a GE product) but also on the chance to affect millions of lives for the better.

HOW THE STARTUP WAY ENCOURAGES CULTURAL ACCLIMATION

True success at adopting the methods of the Startup Way means more than just applying them to already-existing products and processes in an organization. The most impact happens when the ideas and way of working become deeply baked into a company's

DNA. Innovation is no longer being applied only to specific projects or even divisions—it's just, as Viv Goldstein at GE puts it, "the way we work now." The new way of working becomes, in other words, part of the culture. Ben Horowitz, co-founder of the VC firm Andreessen Horowitz, defines it clearly: "Dogs at work, yoga, organic food—that's not culture. [Culture] is the collective behavior of everyone in the organization. It's what people do when left to their own devices. It's the organization's way of doing things."[14]

I want to share a few more stories that illustrate the Startup Way of thinking at low levels in the organization. These stories are not, in themselves, big breakthrough projects. Rather, they show a glimpse of the gains that are possible when small acts of innovation, testing, and iteration are applied throughout an entire organization. Imagine each of these little vignettes happening again and again among thousands or hundreds of thousands of employees. Each act is small, but the sum total of impact is enormous. And then consider: how many world-changing breakthroughs started ever so small.

FastWorks Everyday

About two and a half years after we started rolling out FastWorks at GE, the company launched FastWorks Everyday, designed to help employees ask a different set of questions not just around product development but around everything they do—from creating a presentation to posting a job listing. It's as much about mindset as it is about accomplishing specific tasks. When employees do that, Goldstein says, "It becomes the foundation for this whole culture change across the company." Like the rollout of FastWorks itself (remember the road show?), FastWorks Everyday has grown through iteration, not by mandate. Employees choose to go through the training, and more than thirty thousand of them have. They can take either an online class, which is supported by discussion boards and follow-up conversations, or an in-person class of six to eight hours. GE is scaling the program up and has created a cohort of FastWorks Everyday facilitators who run the classes. As the momentum spreads, they're collecting another whole archive of proof points and stories that illustrate how powerful this way of working is for those who might be skeptical.

At the corporate level, Ryan Smith (see earlier in this chapter for his story of testing compensation strategy) found himself applying FastWorks to job listings for Current, the company's new digital energy startup.[15] "We said, 'Let's try something different.' If the outcome we're trying to drive to is a different, new, more contemporary, startup-like business, we need to keep up with what's going on in the marketplace." With a small group, they piloted embedding videos into job descriptions, with plans to gather feedback and scale if it went well. To make the decision, he notes, "We didn't sit back for six months, put together a gigantic business case, review it with twenty people, get a hundred million dollars in funds. We said, 'This is a great idea; let's go try it with twenty jobs, and let's do it fast. Let's learn from it, and then we'll see if we want to scale it.' Those are FastWorks behaviors."

"We Decided to Treat Culture as a Product."[16]

Another sign of true cultural embrace of these principles is evident when they extend to employees who aren't necessarily involved in Startup Way processes. The hypergrowth tech startup Asana is built on the notions of mindfulness and intentionality. "Most companies end up with a culture as an emergent phenomenon," says co-founder Justin Rosenstein. "We decided to treat culture as a product."[17] Co-founder Dustin Moskovitz (who was also a co-founder of Facebook) adds, "From the beginning we were intentional about wanting to be intentional. A lot of companies have that conversation several years into their existence. We'd already had it in the first couple of weeks. Then we went about trying to manifest it and keep it extensive."

Asana works to regularly reassess and redesign its core values, and when the company makes a change, it launches the new value throughout the organization in the same way it would launch any other kind of product. Then it goes through the process of feedback and iteration on the road to resolution. Asana calls these problems "cultural bugs" and works to eradicate them the same way it would a problematic piece of software. When some junior employees came to management saying they felt "falsely empowered"—they had decision-making power, but their decisions were too frequently overridden by higher-ups—the company launched a process to restructure the way that power was allocated. Asana was started by some of the best founders in the world. This is what can happen when they turn their entrepreneurial talents beyond products: to the structure of the corporation itself.

Social Innovation at Intuit

In 2013, Brad Smith, the CEO of Intuit, was the host of the annual American Heart Association benefit. It might not be immediately clear that this event would present an opportunity for innovation, but Intuit was so steeped in innovation by that time that it was possible for the company to leap outside the boundaries of its traditional work. Six weeks prior to the benefit, Smith pulled together a team of five people—two designers, an engineer, a product manager, and an innovation leader—and asked them to help him host the most successful fund-raising event the AHA had ever had.

In about a month, the team came up with a mobile app for

the volunteers to use to keep track of all the ways money was coming in, connected to a screen projected in the main room that showed the total amount raised. "Every time someone gave money for anything during the event, the numbers on the screen ticked up in real time." The team had two hypotheses: (1) If the progress toward the goal was highly visible to everyone in the room, people wouldn't allow themselves not to reach the goal. (2) By heightening emotion in the room, the screen display would motivate attendees to work together as they realized they were all giving toward the same goal. To test it, two weeks before the actual event, they ran a mock benefit ball, including a fake auctioneer. Each invitee had a persona that told who they were and how much money they wanted to spend. After the mock benefit, they made adjustments based on what they learned, then launched the tool at the benefit, where it worked flawlessly.

The fund-raising goal was $1 million, and team engineer Justin Ruthenbeck recalls, "They were at $947,000 and the auctioneer said, 'Is there anyone who can help us?' A few tables worked together and said, 'Hey if you give twenty-five we'll give twenty-five. We'll give thirty-five and you give thirty-five.' They were playing with each other, and at the end of the night the benefit broke the one million mark and made $170,000 more than the previous year." From there, the tool was used at all the AHA's West Coast benefits, and after that Ruthenbeck and his team made it self-service so that any organization can use it free of charge.[18]

ONE MORE THING . . .

I hope you find the stories in this chapter inspiring enough to want to dive into the difficult work in your own organization, no matter what phase of transformation you find yourself in now.

However, there is one more topic I have reserved for the end of Part Two, because it is not nearly as inspiring. It is tedious and detailed labor, and it is the glue that makes all of the techniques I've shared so far work.

It is the collection of mechanisms and methods that come together in a framework called *innovation accounting,* and it is the subject of the next chapter.

WARNING: Do not try this at home until you have mastered the math that makes it possible.

## CHAPTER 9

INNOVATION ACCOUNTING

IN THE EARLY days of IMVU, the company I co-founded in 2004, we were attempting to raise money from some of the top venture capitalists in Silicon Valley. As we traveled up and down Sand Hill Road, we brought a pitch deck that summarized our progress to date. It included a few of the graphs I mentioned back in Chapter 3, when I told the story about how we were embarrassed by our very small numbers in spite of the fact that they showed clear progress, but we still earned the trust and investments of the VCs who not only understood our thinking as a team (it's all about the team) but also knew how to read into those tiny numbers in a more sophisticated way.

These investors understood that the real lesson of our pitch was not that our company had already achieved a large "asset value." Looking beyond the vanity metrics, they could see that (1) our per-customer metrics were actually very promising,[1] and (2) the change in metrics over time indicated that something important had happened that was causing the hockey stick to take off. It wasn't definitive proof that we had found product/market fit, but it was a promising leading indicator. It meant that, if the early results held true as we scaled, we would have a large business. In other words, we had addressed two important parts of the startup valuation formula: our probability of future success and the presumed magnitude of future success.

Recognizing these early signs of success as worthy of further investment is the key skill that powers successful venture capital. Still, in most corporate contexts, finance teams would happily pull the plug on a project like this. A very common line of criticism for corporate projects in their early days, when the gross numbers are small, is that even if the early results are promising, the sample size is too insignificant to matter.

What is needed in a startup project is a new way of interpreting early results, one that solves this basic repeated dilemma that all innovation teams face. In fact, once we get the right framework in place, teams can use my favorite reply to these frequent critics: "You say we have too small a sample size. Excellent. We're glad you agree our budget should be increased. Let's scale up the experiment and get a larger sample." This works because the criticism implicitly grants the premise that the early results are promising.

THE FATAL PITCH

I've witnessed this same negotiation, almost word-for-word, in three very different contexts. It happens when a Silicon Valley startup is pitching a VC for funding, but also when a corporate team is pitching their CFO, and even when a garage inventor is pitching his or her spouse. Every entrepreneur is accountable to somebody, because entrepreneurs have the terrible but consistent habit of spending *other people's money.*

The pitch starts out with great fanfare, like this:

Dear [VC/CFO/Spouse], have I got a deal for you! If you give me [this team of five/one million dollars/our whole life's savings] and a year's time, I promise you the most amazing results. We will make billions in revenue, we'll have millions of customers, and we'll be on the cover of magazines! It will be just like that famous movie or business-school case you remember about how great startups are!

In startup circles we call this making the "plausible promise"— how much impact can be promised that is large enough to activate the investor's greed but not so large that the founder doing the promising sounds like a crazy person. The key to the promise is to know just how big the numbers need to be. I've worked with companies where a new $25 million per year line of business would be considered a game-changer and others where it would be so small as to be a rounding error. Good entrepreneurs are skilled at honing their pitch so they get it *juuuuust* right.

So let's say the answer is a green light. The startup gets the money and time. And now let's fast-forward. Let's say a year has passed. What do we know for sure about our promising new venture? I can almost guarantee:

1. All the money is spent, right on schedule. You rarely hear about startups in any context giving money back because they couldn't think of a way to spend it.
2. Everyone was very busy (another entrepreneurial superpower). Milestones came and went and lots of things got done.
3. And, if you've followed the stories in this book, you can probably guess that most of the time, the business results that were promised up front were not quite up to scratch.

Think back to my conversation with the VCs at IMVU. It's always the same story: "So, [VC/CFO/Spouse], there's good news and bad news. The bad news is, we missed our account-ability targets by a wee bit. Instead of millions of customers, we have hundreds. Instead of billions in revenue, we have thousands. But, but, but, the good news! We have learned so much! We are on the brink of success, and if you just give us another year and another $10 million, I promise . . ."

This is one story that, no matter who the audience is—from the hippest neighborhoods in San Francisco to the most boring corporate boardrooms—always gets laughs and not a few groans. We all know what's going to happen next. This entrepreneur is going to be fired. The experience we had at IMVU is very much the outlier: Most startups simply do not survive a perceived fail-ure of this magnitude.

Now, when entrepreneurs—corporate or venture-backed—get together in private, we love to breathe scorn and complain about the "vulture capitalists" and gray-suited CFOs who are constantly—constantly!—pulling the plug on promising new ventures right before they have a chance to succeed. And, in fact, the history of technology is littered with lore about these kinds of mistakes, like the time the founders of Twitter were so embarrassed by their early modest results that they gave several of their investors the chance to take their money back.[2] Some even said yes!

But let's look at the problem from finance's point of view. In normal corporate situations, a manager who misses his or her quarterly targets—even by a little bit—is in big trouble. In most organizations, a 10 percent miss in one quarter is prob-ably not enough to get you fired on the spot, but woe befall any manager who makes a habit of it. And this policy has a certain logic to it. As we saw in Chapter 1, twentieth-century manage-ment figured out a system of accountability to make sure that no manager could just skate by on external events or luck. Only those who can make and beat a reasonable forecast (vetted by finance, of course) on a consistent basis are worthy of praise and promotion.

So how do entrepreneurs look from this point of view? We are talking about managers who miss their accountability targets not by 10 percent but by 2, 3, 4 *orders of magnitude*. Who then have the chutzpah to ask for more funding when they missed by only 10,000 percent!

A team may come to finance with almost no customers and almost no revenue and ask to be treated as a success. Yes, it's possible that this team has learned amazing things, but it's also possible that the team just set the company's money on fire and spent the time on a beach doing nothing. From the point of view of traditional accounting, these two possibilities are indistinguishable. Their vanity metrics are the same: close to zero. How is finance supposed to adjudicate which is worth further investment and which is not? The true answer to how finance decides, in almost every organization I meet, is the same: politics.

So this is not really the fault of our colleagues in finance. If your accounting system literally cannot tell the difference between the next Facebook and Bozo the Clown, you are suffering from total paradigm breakdown. It's time for something new.

INNOVATION ACCOUNTING: WHAT IS IT?

The Lean Startup has spawned a lot of cool slogans, some of which fit nicely on a bumper sticker. *Pivot! Minimum Viable Product!* And even Steve Blank's famous *Get out of the building!* (I kid you not, you can buy T-shirts with these slogans on them.) I can tell which parts of the book most people read by how often I get questions and fan mail about these concepts.

One of the most important concepts in *The Lean Startup*, though, doesn't fit on a bumper sticker. And, perhaps unsurprisingly, I don't get a lot of fan mail about it, either (although the special few communiqués I do receive are amazing). You see, it involves a lot of math. It's about accounting.

Few things in this world are perceived as more boring than accounting, and people who pick up a book about innovation and startups are usually looking for something a little more exciting. Believe me, if it was possible to accomplish the goal of creating an engine of continuous innovation without accounting reform, I'd be all for it. But, based on my experience, that is impossible.

In transforming our organizations and our way of working, we need to transform accounting, too. We need something that aligns finance with this enterprising model. I call it *innovation accounting* (my colleagues who work in finance always ask me to add this disclaimer: not to be confused with "innovative" accounting, which you could go to prison for, so do be careful).

Innovation Accounting (IA) is a way of evaluating progress when all the metrics typically used in an established company (revenue, customers, ROI, market share) are effectively zero.

- It provides a framework of chained leading indicators, each of which predicts success. Each link in the chain is essential and, when broken, demands immediate attention.
- It's a focusing device for teams, keeping their attention on the most important leap-of-faith assumptions.
- It's a common, mathematical vocabulary for negotiating the use of resources among competing functions, divisions, or regions.
- It provides a way to tie long-term growth and R&D into a system that follows a clear process for funding innovation that can be audited for its ability to drive value creation.

Innovation accounting enables apples-to-apples comparisons between two or more startups, in order to evaluate which is most worthy of continuing investment. This is a way of seeing a startup or innovation project as a formal financial instrument, an "innovation option"[3] if you will, one that has a precise value and reflects a range of future costs and financial outcomes.

Innovation accounting is a system for translating from the vague language of "learning" to the hard language of dollars. It puts a price not just on success but also on information.

Innovation accounting allows organizations to quantify learning in terms of future cash flows—and to make the explicit tie back to the equity structure we discussed in Chapter 3. In other words, IA gives finance a way to model the variables that go into making up a startup valuation: asset value, probability of success, magnitude of success. Early numbers, like revenue, are likely to be really small, with a possibly negative ROI. This is really politically dangerous for innovation projects, so we have to be able to explain—in a rigorous way—how those small numbers can turn into big ones without doing naïve extrapolation.

However, it's important to note that innovation accounting is not the same as an equity calculation. When we calculate the net present value (NPV) of potential future earnings, we are assessing the magnitude of possible success—but not the probability. In this way, innovation accounting acts as a scorecard that can track a team's progress as it marches down the "innovation field" marked by two end zones:

zero -> current IA value -> equity value -> fantasy plan

A word of warning: This chapter is necessarily incomplete. It provides the high-level tools to build an IA framework unique to your organization, in order to encourage the hard work of learning the math involved. It's not rocket science, but it does have to be done properly to be effective. Just as you can't learn traditional cost accounting in a few minutes by reading a business book like this one, innovation accounting, too, requires careful study and, because it is a new emerging discipline, careful experimentation.

THE THREE LEVELS OF INNOVATION ACCOUNTING

Whenever I attempt to teach this material to teams, I introduce it gradually. There's too much complexity in the full framework for even sophisticated teams to start using it at once. So I typically break the concept down into three "levels." At any scale—from the team level on up to the enterprise level—coaches and managers alike have to be adept at using the right level of complexity when holding teams accountable. And, as teams grow in sophistication, they are able to mature their practices to match.

Level 1: Dashboard

Every flavor of innovation accounting is designed to demonstrate validated learning in a rigorous way. As you'll recall from Chapter 4, this requires showing a change in customer behavior from experiment to experiment. Those behaviors are the *inputs* to the business model, the leading indicators that drive future outputs like ROI and market share.

The innovation accounting process begins with a simple dashboard full of metrics that teams can agree are important. Many teams aren't yet aware of the drivers behind their revenue projections. They're focused instead on the financial goals or "outputs"—things like ROI, market share, and margin—and not on the power required behind the scenes to grow them.

This ends up causing many teams to pad their predictions in

an effort to get funding. If the fantasy plan looks promising at the beginning, you'll get more money up front. Instead, teams would do better—and companies, too—if more were looking at the actual drivers of growth and trying to understand how, over time, these drivers could help make a business successful. Innovation accounting allows us to track this sort of progress and eventually translate what we learn into a language that finance departments can understand.

The key piece of data in this process is the per-customer input, something that can be measured in a sample of any size; it's the same currency whether you're looking at one customer, ten customers, or ten times that many. And, critically, you can show changes to it over time much earlier than you could show other significant gross numbers.

Per-customer learning metrics include:

- Conversion rates (such as the percentage of customers who try a free trial of a product who subsequently become paying customers).
- Revenue per customer (the amount of money customers pay for a product on average).
- Lifetime value per customer (the amount of money the company accrues from an average customer over the entire "life" of his or her relationship with the company).
- Retention rate (what percentage of customers are still using the product after a certain amount of time).
- Cost per customer (how much it costs to serve a customer on average).
- Referral rate (what percentage of existing customers refer new customers to the product, and on average how many referrals they make per unit of time).
- Channel adoption (what percentage of the relevant distribution channels carry the product).

Many startups begin with a complicated business plan. They often look at projections in a fancy spreadsheet and try to work backward from there. Instead, a more effective means of starting out with innovation accounting is to begin with a simple dashboard. At this early stage, teams can choose whichever metrics they prefer, as long as they are simple and actionable.

Need help coming up with initial metrics? At a minimum, every IA dashboard should attempt to answer the four "key questions" described in the "Innovation Accounting at Scale" section, which starts on page 280.

Metrics don't even need to relate to one another at this point. The idea is simply to start with something manageable, begin looking at the numbers over time, and have a plan. For example, this week, aim to reach three customers with several questions that will clarify your objectives and their needs. Next week, five customers, and by week three, seven, after which those numbers on a percentage basis to see if they are improving or not. This is similar to Y Combinator's obsession with having their startups measure growth on a week over week basis.[4]

This dashboard, while simple, is powerful. For one thing, it starts the process of seeing customers as a "flow" through the experiment factory. Instead of saying, "Let's get the product done and then show it to x customers," get used to saying, "We test our latest product with five customers every week. When we're ready, we can increase to ten customers per week or even decrease back to five." The point is to set up a cadence of regular releases and regular customer contact. It's never okay for the rate to drop to zero customers, but it's fine to take a step back if needed. Some things will break when we go up a scale, and that's to be expected. Simply lower the rate.

The second power of this dashboard is its focusing effect. If customers won't even try our product, it really doesn't matter what their repeat purchase rate is. It doesn't matter what their ninety-day retention looks like, or anything that happens later. The dashboard gives a basic sense of what's working and what's not.

To use a Level 1 dashboard to hold a team accountable, simply ask this question: Which metrics are improving over time? For example, a team that is trying to prove that they can charge a price premium for a new product might do an initial MVP where nobody is willing to buy. So revenue per customer is $0 for the first test. A few product revisions later, perhaps revenue has grown to $1. This is progress—even if the goal is ultimately to get it to $10 or $100 or higher.

LEVEL 1 DASHBOARD

HLS MVP 1: Street corner lemonade stand/ tables and chairs

Milestones:			Launch of Instagram Campaign	Drop in Prices	Introduction of Super-food Line	Hiring of Marketing Intern	New Location	
	Week 1	Week 2	Week 3	Week 4	Week 5	Week 6	Week 7	Week 8
# Passersby	100	100	125	150	175	200	400	450
# Customers	0	0	5	20	35	45	60	75
Conversion rate	0%	0%	4%	13%	20%	23%	15%	17%
Price per lemonade	9	9	9	5	6.5	6.5	7	7
# Orders per customer	0	0	1	1	1	2	2	2

Level 2: Business Case

Level 1 is not meant to be comprehensive. Rather, it is a necessary first step to help teams understand the process of innovation accounting. With Level 2, we go a bit deeper. Level 2 depends on having a thought-through business plan and having identified the leap-of-faith assumptions that power it (see Chapter 4). Now it's time to start seeing those LOFAs as inputs that drive the business case.

Think about the stage from when a customer first hears about a product to the time he or she actually purchases it. In Level 2 innovation accounting, a dashboard is built to represent the complete interaction with the customer. The dashboard should include a complete set of the input metrics that make up the business plan.

For example, a common Level 1 dashboard will have only metrics relating to revenue, not to costs or long-term retention. As every salesperson knows, you can always boost revenue by making unrealistic or unaffordable promises up front. A Level 2 dashboard is meant to try to prevent these kinds of mistakes.

This dashboard should provide a comprehensive understanding of what's happening in a business. And it should be detailed and clear enough that anyone in finance could understand it. The most important thing is that this set of inputs matches the drivers of the spreadsheet in the back of the business plan.

In particular, every metric in the dashboard should correspond to a specific LOFA from the business plan, and there should be no extraneous metrics included. A common Level 1 mistake is to cherry-pick only the metrics that make a team look good. For example, it's easy to drive sales if you wildly overpromise in the initial marketing and slash pricing. But this will inevitably show up as bad retention, repeat purchase, or margin. A Level 1 dashboard might not include these later-stage variables, but a Level 2 dashboard must.

In particular, it's essential that the dashboard encompass the value hypothesis and the growth hypothesis (from Chapter 4). Making these two concepts quantitative is a big improvement over the common way investors and entrepreneurs alike talk about product/market fit. For the value hypothesis: What is the specific customer behavior that indicates *delight* with the product?[5] In Level 1, we might use a proxy variable for this, like net promoter score (NPS)[6] or GrowthHackers founder and CEO Sean Ellis's "very disappointed" survey.[7] These are good indicators of customer satisfaction, but they are hard to translate into dollars and cents. How do we know what NPS score is "good enough" to convince people to invest more time and money into a project? By contrast, a Level 2 value hypothesis indicator should measure a behavior like repeat purchase, retention, willingness to pay a premium price, or referral. What threshold is "good enough"? That's easy to answer now: whatever number is required to make our business plan's spreadsheet add up.

ENGINES OF GROWTH

The growth hypothesis, likewise, can be put on a secure quantitative footing. We can ask: Given that a customer delights in our product, what specific customer behavior will cause us to acquire more customers? We are searching for behaviors that follow the *law of sustainable growth*: New customers come from the actions of past customers. This can happen in one of three ways:

1. The "sticky engine of growth"—Word of mouth referral is higher than the natural attrition rate (and so growth compounds).
2. The "paid engine of growth"—We can take the revenue we get from one customer and reinvest it into new-customer acquisition.
3. The "viral engine of growth"—New customers can be recruited into the product as a side effect of normal usage, as in products like Facebook or PayPal, as well as fashion or other trendy products.

For each of these "engines of growth," there is a specific number that indicates that it can grow sustainably, and this number defines the threshold for product/market fit. Unlike the traditional product/market-fit advice that "you'll know it when you see it," this allows us to answer a more difficult question: How do I know how close I am to product/market fit?

LEVEL 2 DASHBOARD

HLS MVP 2: Simple landing page with order button

Milestones:			Launch of Instagram Campaign	Drop in Prices	Introduction of Super-food Line	Hiring of Marketing Intern	30 Min Delivery Guarantee	
	Week 1	Week 2	Week 3	Week 4	Week 5	Week 6	Week 7	Week 8
# Site visitors	500	250	1,750	1,800	2,750	3,000	5,000	7,500
# Customers	0	0	100	500	1,200	1,250	2,500	5,000
Conversion rate	0%	0%	6%	28%	44%	42%	50%	67%
Price per lemonade	9	9	9	7	7	7	8.5	8.5
# Orders per customer	1	1	1	1	2	3	3	3
Referrals per customer	0	0	0	1	2	2	3	3
Cost per lemonade	2	2	2	2	4.5	4.5	4.5	4.5
Web development	1,000	250	500	0	250	0	750	0
Delivery transport	100	100	100	100	100	100	2,500	2,500
Marketing budget	0	0	500	150	500	1,000	1,000	1,000

Level 3: Net Present Value

In Level 3 innovation accounting, the goal is to translate learning into dollars by rerunning the full business case after each new data point.

Everyone has a starting business model somewhere (often a spreadsheet in Appendix B of the business plan—a time-honored tradition—in two-point type). There is value in this spreadsheet: If done properly, it shows how certain customer behaviors aggregate over time and result in a positive future impact. Rarely do we revise it as the project progresses to show what's actually happening. But that's what this level of innovation accounting requires. The goal here is to re-run that initial spreadsheet with new numbers learned from experiments and see how things change. In all likelihood, when we do this with our very first MVP, the hockey stick will become a flat line (a depressing but necessary first step). From that point on, every new experiment means a new set of inputs to this model.

Each new run of the model yields a new graph, and a new set of projections. And these projections can then be rendered into net-present-value terms using standard finance tools. Changes in this NPV calculation represent the direct translation of learning into financial impact.

For example, small improvements in a key conversion rate will take the business from x to $2x$ or $10x$ in dollar terms. Suddenly, the plan becomes much clearer—and more exciting. With every new learning, the information translates into financial terms by rerunning the model. The ultimate result is an accountability system that finance cares about. Everything can be translated into future impact—and its attendant cash flow.

Let me repeat this key idea: A Level 3 dashboard literally makes everything we learn translatable into net-present-value terms. If we learned how to change our product's conversion rate from 1 percent to 2 percent, we can say with precision how much that is worth if the product scales the way we hope. And we can also give revised estimates as to the time line of achieving that scale. Over time, we are effectively refining the spreadsheet in the business plan to get more and more accurate (as we plug in fresh data).

Most important, this establishes a "playing field" that allows us to see progress over time. Imagine our first MVP comes back with bad news, and the new NPV calculation is effectively zero. I've been there! Instead of seeing that as bad news, we can see that as the establishing of one end zone of the field. The other end zone is the fantasy plan of what we promised when we got started. Every new MVP, every new test, reveals a new NPV, which is, with luck, closer to the fantasy plan.

And now, when we negotiate with finance, VCs, or other stakeholders, we have a way of showing progress. Only they can judge if our progress is fast enough to give them confidence that we are truly changing the ultimate probability of success (since they still have to use judgment to decide if they think our recent progress will continue). But at least now we have a common framework and language for having that assessment be done in a rigorous way. Most teams I work with—from Silicon Valley to the factory floor—are, most of the time, completely stuck in the mud. They are getting a lot of work done. They are shipping new products and new features. But if you look rigorously, they aren't really moving the key metrics that matter for their business. This may sound depressing, but it's actually wonderful news to find out, because teams that have this realization are able to pivot more easily than those that aren't sure if their current strategy is working. In other words, finance has a constructive role to play here in helping teams be more effective, instead of just being a gatekeeper that slows everyone down.

LEVEL 3 DASHBOARD

NET INCOME, MILLIONS

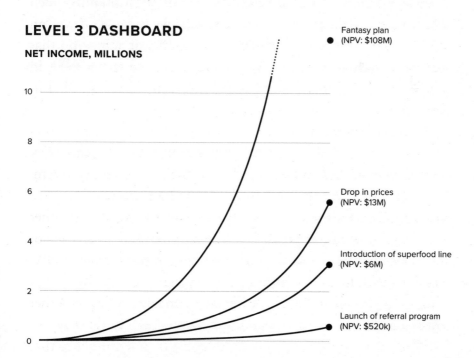

.   .   .

So far, I've been talking about innovation accounting as simply a way for individual teams to report their progress and communicate in financial terms. But IA is also extremely useful for seeing how projects, portfolios of projects, or even whole enterprises are changing over time. And, most important, it gives us the ability to summarize these disparate initiatives using a common vocabulary and accountability framework.

INNOVATION ACCOUNTING AT SCALE: "THE BINGO CARDS"

Another advantage of using innovation accounting (IA) is that it creates a common vocabulary and set of accountability standards that can be used for innovation projects across the whole organization. Recall the "three scales" that form one axis of the progress chart in the introduction to Part Two (page 145). IA allows us to develop dashboards and standards across all three scales. We can even use it to judge the success of the overall transformation effort.

The "bingo card" diagrams on the next two pages show how experiments played out over not just the three scales from team to enterprise level but also the four time horizons that represent the progress of adoption: execution, behavior change, customer impact, and financial impact. The leading indicators (see Chapter 6 for more on these) in each time period predict the leading indicators in the following time slot, acting as a focusing mechanism that will allow teams, businesses, and companies to see immediately if something has gone off track.[8]

"BINGO CARD" OF KEY QUESTIONS

	EXECUTION ＞	BEHAVIOR CHANGE ＞	CUSTOMER IMPACT ＞	FINANCIAL IMPACT
	"Did we do what we said we were going to do?"	"Are our people working differently?"	"Do customers (internal or external) recognize an improvement?"	"Are we unlocking new sources of growth as a company?"
PROJECT TEAMS	Have we set teams up for success? (dedicated resources, clear leader, cross-functional, metered funding, etc.)	Has the training trickled down to the people doing the actual work?	Are customers feeling a difference?	What are the leading indicators of financial or productivity performance?
BUSINESS UNIT / GROWTH BOARD	Have the division and functions implemented the Growth Board process?	Viewed as a portfolio, are the projects in this business using the process successfully?	How do we prove that the division/function as a whole is improving customer satisfaction and outcomes?	Are we unlocking new sources of growth, share, or dramatically reducing costs?
CORPORATE/ TRANSFORM-ATIONAL	Who has been trained and have their leaders bought into the system?	Has it become "the way we work" for our employees?	Is the company delivering for customers in a simpler, faster way?	Is the company achieving growth and productivity?

"BINGO CARD" OF SAMPLE KEY METRICS

	EXECUTION ⟩	BEHAVIOR CHANGE ⟩	CUSTOMER IMPACT ⟩	FINANCIAL IMPACT
	"Did we do what we said we were going to do?"	"Are our people working differently?"	"Do customers (internal or external) recognize an improvement?"	"Are we unlocking new sources of growth as a company?"
PROJECT TEAMS	Project team trained Clear leader and Exec Sponsor Project structured to win	Faster cycle time Earlier/greater customer engagement Faster pivot/ persevere decision Clear LOFA	Faster time to market/first revenue Increased customer satisfaction Customer referrals	ROI / Margin / Share NPV of Business model (audited valuation) Productivity savings
BUSINESS UNIT / GROWTH BOARD	% Funding allocated through Growth Boards % Projects adopting Growth Boards	Project success rate Employee morale Identifying and eliminating wasteful projects Per-project cost pre/post launch	Win rate Customer satisfaction vs competitors Share of wallet Improved time to market Decreased cost to market	Growth Productivity / SG&A Portfolio performance (overall ROI) Market leadership Audited portfolio valuation
CORPORATE/ TRANSFORM-ATIONAL	% Company (functions, employees, businesses) adopting the new method % People trained by level % High-quality coaches	New product success rate Change in gatekeeper functions behavior Simplification in all processes Employee morale	Brand impact Customer satisfaction vs competitors Division and functions moving at market speed	ROI SG&A Growth Share price

Each column and row in the first diagram serves as a leading indicator for the next. Teams provide leading indicators for change at the divisional level, and divisions for the corporate level. In order to use the charts to identify and focus in on a problem area, answer the question in each square successively until an unsatisfactory answer comes up. Then go back to the previous square to determine what change is needed to move forward.

Each of these key questions gives rise to a set of metrics designed to answer it. These metrics, which make up the second "bingo card" diagram, are obviously team-, division-, and scale-dependent. But this framework allows an organization to create an org-wide dashboard that shows how it is performing across many portfolios of teams.

As we saw above, these charts act as a focusing tool. I've seen far too many internal process (such as IT) teams that roll out a new "product," mandate its use across the whole company, and then try to start measuring its productivity impact. But because they skipped a few key questions, they didn't realize that nobody was using the new system. If nobody is using it, then anything we measure in the later stages—such as customer satisfaction or productivity improvement—is just measuring noise.

I also see the opposite problem: teams that never get around to measuring their business impact at all. Think of all the corporate training programs that are content to show vanity metrics of how many people have completed the training—never mind if those people have changed their behavior as a result.

By creating a common framework that works across all the kinds of entrepreneurship, innovation accounting gives the "missing function" a playbook to use in many different places (and a few surprises, too, which are discussed in the next chapter).

The Role of Finance

Some of the metrics that this approach requires are already being tracked in the normal course of business operations. Some will require additional work that serves just to measure whether the new methods are working. Whose responsibility is it to develop these metrics and establish consistency across the whole portfolio or even the whole company? If this were any other kind of project, the answer would be obvious: finance. A finance function that wants to support innovation (instead of hindering it) will have to do this work, hopefully in partnership with the new entrepreneurship function. For the largest organizations, this will have to include establishing an "innovation audit" process to ensure this new kind of standard work is being adopted everywhere.

It is for this reason that, at GE, the initial rollout of Fast-Works involved the Corporate Audit Staff (CAS). It was not just an engineering, HR, or marketing initiative. Finance was on board from the start. Every single one of the early FastWorks projects had a high-potential leader from CAS assigned. At first blush, this might sound strange—who wants an accountant on a startup team?[9] But being able to build the kinds of models that innovation accounting requires was a huge help to those initial cross-functional teams.

An IA audit works differently from a traditional financial audit. It ensures that teams are doing innovation accounting at the right level for their project stage. Early-stage teams with small budgets can get by with a dashboard that simply tracks three to five key metrics against their learning milestones. But for projects with larger investment levels, teams should have a fully developed business case and a Level 3 IA dashboard that shows the financial value of the validated learning they have achieved so far.

The key to this is not to compare the interim progress (which will often be quite modest) to the fantasy plan in the business case, but rather to compare it to the previous milestone. In this way teams can show progress over time. Growth boards can value the overall worth of their portfolio, and the company can have confidence that its investments are likely to pay off in the future.

Just as a venture capital portfolio is valued based on the paper valuation of each company (during subsequent financings), a company portfolio can be valued based on the audited net present value of what it has learned. And this brings us to a technique I've alluded to all along in this book, the system that allows leadership to hold the team accountable and to allocate funding for long-term growth (rather than short-term accounting gains), and can work across an entire division: the growth board.

WHAT IS A GROWTH BOARD?

A *growth board* is simply the purely internal version of a startup board: a group of people who meet on a regular basis to hear from teams about their progress and to make funding decisions. "Growth boards are operationalized venture capital funds," explains David Kidder, co-founder and CEO of Bionic, a company that installs an integrated solution of growth boards and lean methodology inside large enterprises. (Kidder and I worked together closely to help establish growth boards at GE.) "The growth board introduces a decision framework for executive leadership that enables them to manage a portfolio of early-stage startups like a venture capitalist would."

In a startup, the board generally hears from company founders. An internal growth board in a bigger organization creates a single point of accountability for teams that are operating as startups. Growth boards are the venue for all of the innovation accounting techniques in this chapter.

The Dropbox Growth Board

In Chapter 1, I told you the story of how Dropbox went through its second-founding moment and had to re-learn some entrepreneurial lessons in order to find success with developing new breakthrough products like Paper. Adopting a board structure was key to this transformation.

"The idea of having a board for authority—and calling it a board—was pretty powerful," says Aditya Agarwal, the company's VP of engineering. At any given time, Dropbox has seven or eight innovation initiatives going on. Each of these projects has a leader for engineering, one for product, and one for design. Then, depending on the specific situation, a board made up of leaders from these functions plus some combination of the company's top executives—Agarwal, Todd Jackson, and co-founders Drew Houston and Arash Ferdowsi—meets with each team every two months. "We hold them accountable and give them strategic guidance on how to evolve or just point out the need to evolve or change their plan," explains Agarwal. For projects that leadership feels need more regular guidance, board meetings are held once a month. This board also decides which projects get more funding to continue pursuing their idea and which teams need to scrap what they're doing and move on to something new.

On occasion, Dropbox has experimented with treating these internal boards more like external startup boards, including external participants (akin to independent directors on a board). I've seen that model work in other companies, too, where the role is fashioned as an "entrepreneur-in-residence." But from the point of view of most internal startups, anyone not in the direct chain of command of the team leaders is an "outside director." So bringing in expertise from other domains, such as the main executive sponsor's peers in other functions, is quite powerful. And most companies have at least some people with venture capital or external startup experience (especially in corporate development or licensing functions), whose voices can also play the "outside" role quite well.

What matters is not the exact composition of the board but that its membership is consistent from meeting to meeting. It's better to meet less frequently than to have members miss meetings. Just as in a venture investor board, the most important attribute of a good growth-board director is conviction. Members of the board should be individuals who have a point of view about their investments, who will stick with teams—as long as they are showing real progress—even when the metrics are small. Board members also have a clear opinion about what kinds of leading indicators are valuable and will drive much better returns (like the executive in Chapter 6 who saw that faster cycle time would necessarily lead to improved products and happier customers).

HOW GROWTH BOARDS OPERATE

Apart from its legal and compliance obligations, a startup board has three primary responsibilities:

1. To be a sounding board for the founders and executives, helping them plot strategy, and hosting the pivot-or-persevere meeting (see Chapter 4).
2. To act as the central clearinghouse for information about the startup, taking on the burden of reporting on behalf of the founders to key financial stakeholders like general partners and limited partners of the investment firm (see Chapter 3).
3. To be the gatekeepers of future funding, either by writing checks themselves or by encouraging (or vetoing) sources of outside funding (see Chapter 3).

Recall from Chapter 4 the executive sponsor who had a regular check-in with one of his internal startup teams that was going through Lean Startup training and ended up applying the methods he used in those meetings to a tricky phone call about a failing project. This was not an institutional exercise; nobody outside his division was even aware of the board. But he wanted to have a venue where he could ask key questions: *What have you learned?* and *How do you know?*

Over time, that ad hoc growth board became a template for the company to replicate. And, as the process became more incorporated into the fabric of the company, it became more sophisticated. This evolution roughly mirrors the Phases One through Three structure discussed in Chapters 6 through 8, but I have seen these elements adopted in a number of different ways.

A growth board, then, has these same three responsibilities:

1. To be the single point of corporate accountability for an internal startup. Some growth boards are bespoke and designed to serve only one team. Others are long-lived and/or service many teams at once. Some even intentionally bring cohorts of teams through the board at the same time, as in a startup accelerator.

    Regardless of its form, every growth board should aim to be the venue for pivot-or-persevere decisions for the internal startups it oversees. The best boards are able to push founders to think deeply about their progress and question whether they really have achieved *validated learning* or just wishful thinking. This is different from a stage-gate ("go/kill") review and is not effective if adversarial or imperious.

2. To act as the single clearinghouse for information about the startup for the rest of the corporation. This responsibility requires some real work by the executives who sit on the board,

and many executives and teams take months or even years to get comfortable with this role.

The key is for every team that has a growth board to feel comfortable deflecting the infinite asks for status updates they get from middle managers. It's not that team members are refusing to answer; it's that they've been told that any requests should be routed to Senior Executive X, who sits on their growth board. Middle managers rarely ask for status updates idly; such requests are almost always a prelude to requests for a change in plan. Making these requests of low-level, low-status managers in the company is relatively cost-free. But making the same requests of a high-level executive is much more expensive, politically speaking. The existence of a growth board forces middle managers to think carefully about whether they really, truly have a problem that needs solving, while giving them a clear and direct path to getting it solved if they do.

3. To provide *metered funding* to startup teams. I discussed the benefits of metered funding versus traditional corporate entitlement funding in Chapter 7. For the most advanced growth boards, metered funding is the ultimate tool to drive culture change in an organization. An internal startup that is funded—as well as coached—by a growth board has a true scarcity mentality. In order for metered funding to work, growth-board funding decisions have to be simple: denominated in a fixed budget of either time or money. For example, one of Todd Parks's strategies was to use a "ninety-days" fixed budget in government. Teams would be disbanded after ninety days unless they showed sufficient promise.

I recommend: The startup is allowed to spend its growth-board money on whatever it wants, without micromanagement. But it must bear the full costs of anything it uses: salaries, equipment, facilities. This is not a matter of allocating partial overhead costs from the parent organization, either. Recall from Chapter 6 that the only people who should be working on a startup are full-time dedicated employees or part-time volunteers (who are not paid to do so). There should be no part-time costs—unless the startup decides to hire part-time or contract labor from the outside. I've seen internal startups go to outside vendors, like IT, when internal gatekeepers are intransigent. As long as they are spending their own money, this is fine.

However, the ironclad rule of the growth board has to be: The money is yours, but you *cannot get a penny more* if you do not show validated learning. That is why this is an advanced technique. Most teams simply won't believe this rule until they see it enforced. But also, *most executives* are not able to prevent themselves from throwing good money after bad. And remember, most subordinates have elevated convincing their boss to fund their projects to a high art. The arguments for one more try are always compelling. But the whole point of innovation accounting is to have these decisions made in a rigorous fashion. Both the teams and the executives in the growth-board process have to learn and grow in order to do so.

In the same way that no two venture capital firms have the exact same process, no two companies approach growth boards in the same way. And just as a rigorous entrepreneurship process (like the Lean Startup) doesn't remove human judgment from startups, so, too, are growth boards still fundamentally about the people who make them up. They are a focusing mechanism that helps teams and boards get better at what they do. Over time, I have seen executives start to make much better funding decisions at the same time as their teams are becoming more efficient in the use of startup-style funding.

David Kidder of Bionic, who has led more than one hundred growth boards for GE, Citi, and other large enterprises, offers these tips for companies that want to set up growth boards:

1. *Small Group, Right People:* Growth boards should consist of six to eight members at the C-suite level. The group must be nimble, have the authority to act, and project to the organization that this work is not only allowed but highly valued.
2. *Frequent Meetings:* Growth boards should meet at least once a quarter; as the number of teams increases, a subgroup may also meet more frequently.
3. *Action Oriented:* Growth boards must make go/no-go decisions at the meeting. Requests for follow-ups, additional opinions, etc., should be the exception, not the rule.
4. *Fact Based:* Growth boards must overcome their biases about what the "right" answer is, and use the evidence uncovered by teams to make decisions.
5. *No Attendance, No Vote:* Only growth-board members in attendance may vote; no delegates or proxies allowed.

GE Oil & Gas

Eric Gebhardt, now vice president of product management at GE Energy Connections, was a FastWorks champion for GE Oil & Gas during the rollout period. As he watched the teams succeed and fail and adopt new strategies, he and his executive team had a realization. "We saw that there should be an operating mechanism for leading FastWorks," he recalls. "So we kind of stepped back and said, 'If we look at FastWorks as a way for individual projects to act like startups, we need a model that is similar to venture capital.'" The question became, "How could we put a venture capital model on top of the startup model for all the individual projects so we could make sure we kept our strategic focus as well as our entrepreneurial spirit?"

The answer very quickly became: growth boards. Gebhardt's division moved from individual team boards to what they called "portfolio leaders," who would lay out a growth thesis for each portfolio, then assess how various projects fit the thesis.

With some initial seed money from Lorenzo Simonelli, president and CEO of GE Oil & Gas, as well as his full support, the team undertook the first round of boards. The initial setup assigned a growth board to each of Oil & Gas's tier 2 P&Ls: surface, subsea, measurement and control, turbomachinery, and downstream. Each group then defined a growth thesis over time, after which the board looked at the project portfolio as it existed on the day of creation and at what the input stream was.

The question they tried to answer, Gebhardt explains, was: "How do you get your input stream coming in to match the growth thesis as well as possible? It was a fundamental shift in how we operate."

In addition to changing the way things were run on the finance level, the new setup also served as a great way to educate not only teams but also leaders in the principles of FastWorks. (We'll talk more about this in Chapter 10, which discusses how the transformation of each internal process should be run as a startup itself.)

"One of the benefits was that we approached growth boards the FastWorks way. We set assumptions around what a good growth board would look like, and we thought about how we could validate or invalidate these in each round and learn along the way. I would say we assumed that we'd get a five-minute pitch, ask two minutes of questions, then talk for five minutes and be able to make an exact up or down decision immediately. What we discovered was that the board didn't have context for how the projects would fit in. That's how the whole idea of having a growth thesis came about—to show 'How does this fit into a portfolio?'"

There were also some practical, everyday learnings about the best ways to present to the board. "At first we said, 'Do it free-form, and we'll pick the best pieces'; then we came up with a couple of templates and ways to structure the discussion better," explains Gebhardt. "We brought in external experts in the area to get diversity of thought. I think our humility in saying up front with teams that it's not going to be perfect, and how they saw us changing and getting better each time, was very beneficial. It wasn't easy, but, as tends to be the case, as each team went through the process and reported back, others got on board."

The Oil & Gas team did one more round of growth boards with great results. What happened next is a perfect example of how transformation spreads. They gave their third round of funding directly to the product companies within the division and said: "You run a growth board. Go and invest the money and then come back to us and tell us how you're spending it."

By empowering the people at the next level, they placed their trust in them (while remaining on standby as coaches, of course). The results were immediate. "We moved it down the chain of command," Gebhardt says, "and that really unlocked a lot of the innovation."

Oil & Gas Metrics—and Results

Let's look at two very simple metrics the Oil & Gas team used to measure their progress.

1. What percentage of projects are canceled, and how long does it take to stop them?
   - *Before growth boards:* Only 10 percent of the division's projects were being killed. That meant 90 percent of the projects delivered something, regardless of whether or not someone wanted it.
   - *First round of growth boards:* 20 percent of the projects were eliminated after a ninety-day cycle and for a lot less money.
   - *Second round of growth boards:* 50 percent of the projects were stopped, many of them after only a sixty-day cycle.

2. How are projects being killed?
   - *Before growth boards:* They weren't, for the most part, being canceled, for all the reasons we've discussed thus far.
   - *First round of growth boards:* Projects were terminated by the growth board.
   - *Second round of growth boards:* The responsibility shifted to the teams. "The teams would come in, and they would almost pitch the case like they wanted us to stop them."
   - *Third round of growth boards* (after the seed money had been handed down to product companies): The teams would come to the board and say, "We've already stopped the project." This was a major step in many ways, according to Gebhardt. "The fact was that they felt better and better about being able to make that decision, they were secure it was the right thing to do, and they realized they were saving money for the company and that we would actually thank them for what they were doing."

All of that took just nine months. Nine months from expensive, never-ending zombie projects to self-sufficient product teams making their own well-informed decisions about whether to proceed.

From there, the program continued to expand, tailored to the needs of the Oil & Gas division. They divided their investments into three phases:

SEED PHASE: Learn as much as possible about the market, business model, and the technology involved.

LAUNCH PHASE: Develop technology. (At this stage, some products would be tracked through a stage-gate process, especially large things like blowout preventers or gas turbines, which have a critical safety process.)

GROW PHASE: Scale up learnings and production.

"Discover 10X" at Citi

Grounded in the discipline of venture capital and the principles of Lean Startup, Citi's Discover 10X program (D10X) seeks to identify solutions that are at least ten times better for its clients and customers. D10X was conceived, launched, and shaped by Citi Ventures as a structured model to create a rich portfolio of validated growth concepts across Citi's businesses. Citi has implemented this way of working at the highest level, and today, it's its own entity, including multiple portfolios, overseen by six growth boards. David Kidder and Bionic partnered with Debby Hopkins, former chief innovation officer at Citi, to install and manage the growth boards within the D10X program. As Vanessa Colella, Citi's current chief innovation officer and head of Citi Ventures, the company's venture capital and innovation arm, explains, most of the ideas are run within each unit, but some come through the enterprise growth board, especially when they would apply company-wide.

Each of these growth boards holds a meeting—called a Deal Day—every six to eight weeks. These are pitch meetings during which teams can present their ideas to a panel. It's a continuous, year-round process, meaning there's a Deal Day almost every week somewhere within the company.

Through Deal Days, the growth board will give the go-ahead and a small amount of funding to a number of teams. Unlike many other companies with this kind of innovation, Citi doesn't have a set number of hours or weeks or even dollars allotted. It varies depending on the project. For a team that is progressing, each Deal Day represents another step along the way. Approximately 30 to 40 percent of the ideas survive the first round, and these ideas then go through subsequent stages of validation.

When it comes to the financing of these new ventures, Colella says the long-term vision is that the cost will become fully embedded in the business units. The growth boards offer seed funding; as ideas move toward launch and as they are generating income or next steps for businesses, they move back over to those units for funding.

The process of client validation and customer validation that Citi has put in place is very inexpensive. "We're talking about many of our teams spending as little as a couple thousand dollars validating," says Colella. "Because until you go to the later stages of building products and launching, it should be inexpensive to test. It's a fairly rapid cycle of very small amounts of funding to move forward. One of the things that we've been able to create by building D10X is a rigorous process that allows for experimentation with low risk."

For example, Colella says there was a team that had an idea about offering an existing product to corporate clients who were already part of institutional investor services. Many of Citi's large corporate clients have a lot of the same needs as institutional investors, such as different bank accounts and global operations. Things can become complex for clients when they begin trying to manage their Citi presence in a variety of countries, markets, and currencies.

The D10X team's idea that perhaps there was a way to offer corporate clients the same services available to institutional clients was met with tremendous enthusiasm from the growth board. "We said, 'Great, we'll fund your idea. Go out and talk to a handful of corporate clients,'" recalls Colella. But what the team learned was that while clients agreed that their businesses were complex, they used multiple bank accounts—something this initiative would eliminate—in order to deal with the complexity and the related regulations. The team quickly validated that this was not a need of Citi's corporate clients. They weren't on the path to building a solution that would solve their clients' problem, so the project was ended.

Colella says the biggest change in the growth boards since they began is seeing people at all levels being comfortable not knowing all the answers and being able to say they think they can probably go out and find them. "That's important, and we've absolutely seen our leaders excel at pushing and prodding and questioning their teams," says Colella. "I think it's even more significant that the questioning has become acceptable at more junior levels in the organization."

The growth boards have also heightened Citi's ability to act on its pledge to serve the customer. "This process has given us language to talk about validation and customers in a way that is completely different than just saying, 'We're going to be customer-centric,'" says Colella. "It's given us a process and a system to validate what our clients need, even in many cases where they don't yet know what they need."

CORPORATE GROWTH BOARDS

I've intentionally let this chapter be complicated because I want to give you a sense of the full theory of innovation accounting—even though length restrictions (and the sanity of the non-mathematicians among us) require that I skip over a lot of the details. I want to be clear that not every company that adopts this new way of working takes on so much accounting complexity. Some organizations (and many famous VC firms, for that matter) are run off Level 1 dashboards. They depend much more on the judgment and character of the people making the investment decisions. There's a reason why even the most successful VC partnerships are quite small by corporate standards. To maintain these practices at larger and larger scales, more of the theory underlying this chapter is needed.

Every organization will have to find its own way. What I want for you, as a reader, is to be armed with the more complex answers, should you ever need them.

And I want to make one last suggestion.

One of the scourges of internal innovation teams is that existing divisions of the company want to impose "taxation without representation." They often want control over the project (because they are afraid of negative consequences to the status quo), but they don't want to provide funding for the project (because they would much rather invest in the short-term things that are working today). This combination gives rise to the problem outlined in Clayton Christensen's *The Innovator's Dilemma*.

Innovation accounting suggests one possible way to solve that problem. Along with division- and function-level growth boards, which allocate funding and hold teams accountable within their existing structures, how about a corporate-level growth board that can fund and accelerate new startups that no existing division wants to fund. Create "M&A" and "IPO" analogs, just like an external startup. If, at some point in the life of an internal startup, a division wants to exert control over its destiny, let them acquire the internal startup out of their M&A budget. IA will give finance a rigorous methodology for assigning it a fair price. And if no division wants to pay this price, create a mechanism to allow the startup to "IPO" and become a new stand-alone division—if its results warrant.

If you've gone that far, why not use these "M&A" and "IPO" events to encourage finance to create real internal startup equity that is tied to the success of the project. Not—as in so many ill-conceived corporate bonus plans—as bonuses paid out for interim short-term milestones, but as real equity tied only to long-term performance.

For most organizations, these ideas are too radical to be considered, so I leave them here as provocations. But especially for the next generation of founders, who are considering the kind of organization they want to leave behind, why wouldn't you want your best employees to experience the rewards, the focus, and the growth that comes with true high-stakes entrepreneurship?

Which naturally raises these questions: Exactly which employees should be considered entrepreneurs? And if we create this new "missing function," what should its scope be? What activities should it be responsible for? The answers may surprise you. They are the subject of Part Three.

PART THREE

THE BIG PICTURE

IT MIGHT SOUND *reasonable to ask: What does Phase Four or Five of the Startup Way look like? Or, alternatively: When is the transformation done? Both questions are reasonable and yet, in my experience, not quite right.*

Once this way of working becomes embedded in the everyday fabric of an organization, it's no longer a transformation. That's not to say that new tools and techniques won't be introduced. But precisely because the Startup Way of working is extremely flexible, with teams self-organizing around new ideas and coaches spreading the practices that work, those later processes won't be nearly as disruptive or challenging as the original transformation that created the platform for them to spread. The cycle of continuous innovation will be completely ingrained and able to absorb change and growth.

So what happens next?

The organization needs to move from continuous innovation *to* continuous transformation*: to an ongoing cycle of change that can transform not just a function or a project or a team, but the very structure of the organization itself.*

CONTINUOUS TRANSFORMATION REQUIRES A RIGOROUS APPROACH

Founders who have been through the process of building a company culture from scratch have a huge advantage when it comes time to transform. Part of the advantage is the moral authority they bring as founders, and part of it is the skills and muscles they build in making it happen.

One benefit of reinvigorating an organization with the methods I've laid out is that you're effectively re-founding the company (see Chapter 8 for more on the second founding). That means the people who drove the change are a tremendously valuable resource. As the story of Janice Semper heading up GE's Performance Development startup shows, leaders who take on this kind of process are themselves permanently affected by it. They learn to think in a new, more experimental way. They're able to empower teams to try bolder projects and to hold teams accountable using the rigorous process of innovation accounting. In the future, when major change looms—as we know it will—these are the people any wise leadership will know to turn to for guidance. The people who work closely with them are likely to be the leaders of future transformations.

Every organization should have an active program of experimentation in new organizational forms and management methods. These programs should themselves be MVPs, embarked upon with caution and strictly defined liability, and helmed by the kinds of people who could one day become founders of the next company-wide transformation.

RIGOROUS TRANSFORMATION IS ENTREPRENEURSHIP

So who, exactly, are these people? They are entrepreneurs. A corporate transformation is—in every way—a true startup, with the same kind of risk, rapid growth, and profound impact that an external startup contains. The ROI on these transformations can be massive, and they require the same kind of governance, funding, and process models as startups. Excellence at founding a transformation requires a skill set similar to what is needed to build a new startup from scratch.

If you follow this line of reasoning, I hope you'll see that we need to treat organizational change as a key part of the "missing function" of entrepreneurship. We need to develop career paths and accountability systems for this kind of role. And we need to provide cross-training for people whose main entrepreneurial experience is in building new products or building new kinds of companies. This cross-training, by the way, is not only needed in established enterprises. It is also a huge part of the power of Silicon Valley (see LinkedIn co-founder Reid Hoffman's blitzscaling *thesis[1]) To date, cross-training has taken the form of esoteric knowledge passed down from investors and founders to the next generation. But we can all benefit from systematizing and bringing this method out into the open (as I think* The Lean Startup *demonstrated).*

THE BIGGER PICTURE

In Part Two, we focused in and looked very closely at the mechanisms for creating transformation and what the results can look like. In Part Three, I want to look at the larger questions. Where should the engine of continuous transformation be located in an organization? And once it's up and running, how can it be used, depending on what kind of organization it's in, to change not just business practices but the laws and systems that support all of us? How does an economy made up of these truly modern organizations function?

I believe this kind of transformation has broader implications beyond just the scenarios we've already considered. Once we're comfortable with ongoing change at the scale shown in this book, we can begin to think outside the boundaries of single organizations. We can consider how innovation and transformation might be able to affect society as a whole. How can we use them to change the way we support people, design policy, and create an operating base not just for companies but for our country? How can we ensure a cycle of continuous transformation in society? What would a world filled with institutions working this way look like?

These are, of course, enormous questions with enormous implications. But that doesn't mean they're too big to tackle. Remember: At the beginning of the book you probably thought cultural transformations like the ones at GE and the United States Citizenship and Immigration Service were impossible. So let's try one more experiment together: to think even more comprehensively about what the Startup Way—and the entrepreneurs it unleashes—might accomplish.

CHAPTER 10

A UNIFIED THEORY OF ENTREPRENEURSHIP

CAN I BE real for a moment?

Come on! What are the odds that, sitting here in California, writing this book, I've invented the One True Management System for All Time? What are the odds that future disruptions in communications, work, manufacturing, and even science itself will be easily met with this single structure? A cursory look at the rate of change being driven by exponential technologies should give us pause before declaring victory. And how many ambitious management "gurus" have come and gone in the last fifty years, each promising a kind of permanent nirvana if you just follow their advice?[1]

I do not want to be your "guru." To me, that's an incredibly foolish way of looking at the matter. So let me propose another way.

One of the companies I worked with came back to me after they had been through several major revisions of their Lean Startup system over the course of several years. The company had followed more or less the trajectory I outlined in Part Two, with a "1.0" version superseded by a "2.0" and then a more advanced "3.0" system. As the company was readying version "4.0," they wanted to discuss what would happen in future years as they refined what they had learned or even—heaven forbid!—added new techniques borrowed from other, non–Lean Startup sources. I think they were preparing to let me down gently, hoping that I wouldn't be upset at their lack of orthodoxy. But, of course, nothing could make me happier than to see new ideas integrated into the fabric of the company—provided they actually work.

This is the hard truth for all founders, of transformations and startups alike. At a certain point, when your transformation has grown powerful enough to affect an entire company, when it has totally won out over whatever culture it was designed to replace, it is also itself *too big* for radical changes. At GE, for example, any modification to the FastWorks program has to trickle down to hundreds of thousands of employees. It's only human nature to start to see any modification as a risky move that could prove costly if it's not correct.

We've already discussed the solution to this problem, albeit in other domains. The right approach once a transformation has achieved scale is to *start a new transformation,* with a new founder and a new startup team. Test, experiment, and learn. See how or if the new approach improves on the previous one. And, depending on what those experiments show, integrate the new approach into the existing system or replace that system entirely. As always, experiments give us the luxury to think boldly without taking excessive risk but also the ability to scale up in a hurry if our bold bets pay off.

In other words, just as *The Lean Startup* argued for a shift in thinking from innovation to *continuous innovation,* I hope this book will leave you with a hunger not only for transformation but for *continuous transformation.* Or, as Viv Goldstein puts it, the appetite to create an endless process loop that's about "constant change. Because it's about constantly challenging yourself and constantly challenging the status quo."

In fact, I think we are better served by seeing transformation as a fact of life for the foreseeable future. I predict that twenty-first-century managers will live through as many organizational transformations as new-product platforms and come to see organizational forms the same way we see our smartphones—as something disposable that's top of the line for a few years, then rapidly surpassed. The final lines of the "Fake Steve Jobs" parody "an open letter to the people of the world," written on the occasion of the release of the first iPad, put it well: "Hold your iPad. Gaze at it. Pray to it. Let it transform you. And do it soon, because before you know it we are going to release version 2, which will make this one look like a total piece of crap. Peace be upon you."[2]

But unlike the endless reorgs of late-twentieth-century management, tomorrow's organizations will not be able to afford the immense waste, politics, and bureaucracy that result from cavalierly rearranging the deck chairs. We have to pursue a new discipline of rigorous change, always ensuring that the new structure outperforms the old.

Here's the good news, which has taken me as much by surprise as it has anyone else in the past few years: The very skills that are required to do the Startup Way transformation are deeply transferrable. They are better seen as a permanent organizational capability than as a one-time event.

CORPORATE ENTREPRENEURSHIP

Think back to the original definition of a startup I settled on more than five years ago: a human institution designed to build a new product or service under conditions of extreme uncertainty.

As I'm sure you've gathered by now, I believe that it's the context in which you work that makes you an entrepreneur, not any surface quality.

So, in any given organization, who meets this definition? I think there are some obvious candidates, like managers who lead project teams whose task is to develop and launch a radically new product or service. In that case, the uncertainty is caused by the team itself: we don't really know if customers will want this new product. But this is easy to extend to related cases. What about a new product introduction, into a new market? I once worked with a team attempting to bring a series of American-made products into postwar Iraq. On the surface, the team had a pretty reasonable plan, based on their previous success working in other countries at a similar level of development, as well as other countries in the Middle East, like Saudi Arabia and Qatar. On the other hand, this was postwar Iraq! The reality on the ground was intensely complex, the politics were opaque, and many of the well-crafted rules in the playbook from, say, Saudi Arabia, didn't translate especially well.

This same situation happens in business model innovation, as recent examples like Dollar Shave Club demonstrate. Any new project that endeavors to experiment with a new strategic approach introduces uncertainty.

I hope so far all of this seems unobjectionable, basically reprising the argument I laid out in the earlier chapters of this book. But now I want to venture into somewhat more exotic terrain.

If you follow my claim that many organizations—including many recently founded startups—have the same structural defect, then I think you'll see why so much of the last five years of my life has been taken up with the task of trying to evolve legacy organizations into the new shape of the modern company.

What if I told you I have a great idea for a new business: a radical new IT system that will dramatically improve corporate productivity in a given industry. All that is required is that customers commit to integrate this new software program into their existing workflow at great cost and over the course of several years. But, in the end, the payoff will be so immense that I am convinced the customer will be glad to have endured the pain, and the company will be glad to absorb the cost of the dozens of full-time employees that will be diverted to this new project. (This hypothetical description perfectly matches a large-ticket IT disrupter like Palantir.)

In that story, I am clearly an entrepreneur. But hopefully, by this point in *The Startup Way*, you see where I am going. The scenario also describes a not-insignificant number of purely *internal* IT projects. Any large-scale software development is inherently uncertain, especially when it operates in the domain beyond "requirements"—like something that radically alters existing workflow. And, in too many organizations, productivity improvement is a code word (or feared code word) for layoffs or workforce reductions, so it has the nice surprise of the extra uncertainty that reluctant employees bring to the table. Isn't the IT manager in charge of such a project an entrepreneur just the same?

Now replace the parable in the previous paragraph with another functional area, such as HR. Recall the story from Chapter 8 about Janice Semper leading the new Performance Development project at GE. That has all the hallmarks of a true startup adventure, despite having none of its surface characteristics.

That's why I've tried so hard to draw connections between the transformation of a legacy organization into a more modern form and the development of a new startup organization from scratch. They really are two sides of the same coin.

So, what do we call this work of "evolving" an organization to become better adapted to the world in which it finds itself?

A lot of best practices for reorganization fall under the general heading of *change management*. But this particular evolution requires something different. I've struggled over the years to explain why this change in particular is so difficult, so all-consuming, that it requires a special sort of person to pull it off. It requires:

- Leadership skills of a most distinctive kind, since transformation pits its leader against the hostile reactions of experienced people whose lives and careers are deeply invested in the status quo.
- Audacious experimentation, since beyond the general framework I've presented so far, every organization has to find its own distinctive shape, its own unique adaptations to the specific context in which it operates.
- The boldness to invest in sweeping, company-wide change—and the patience to wait until just the right moment to make this commitment. The discipline to start with small experiments that might hasten the arrival of the right moment without growing too big, too bloated, too fast.
- The most difficult kind of cross-functional collaboration: enlisting functional leaders in the creation of new and competing functions, thereby breaking down old functional silos and requiring old enemies to make common cause.

But after all that backbreaking effort—*it may not work*. There are so many, many ways to fail: executive sponsors who get cold feet, market shifts or changes, competing internal reorganizations, a coordinated counterattack from powerful enemies within the company, and, most important, shifts in external competition and market conditions that can disrupt even the best-laid plans.

Is this starting to sound familiar?

I believe that corporate transformation—the complete over-haul of an organization's existing structure—is *corporate entre-preneurship*. And it is just as difficult, uncertain, and potentially exponentially rewarding as any other kind of entrepreneurship.

A UNIFIED THEORY OF ENTREPRENEURSHIP

Here's a grandiose way of talking about all of these ideas together. Today, most organizations (no matter their size) do some amount of the following activities:

• Build entirely new products and seek new sources of growth.
• Build new "internal products" such as IT systems and HR policies.
• Do corporate development: buying other companies and start-ups, spinouts, corporate venture, tech licensing/tech transfer.
• Do corporate restructuring or transformation, such as build-ing a corporate team (like FastWorks) to introduce a new way of working.

I believe that those four activities have more in common than many people realize. In fact, they have so much in common that they should be managed centrally and under the auspices of a single overarching function. These are the pillars of the "missing function" of entrepreneurship; by pursuing excellence in all of them, a modern company truly begins to differentiate itself from what came before.

Now, as I said in Chapter 2, when I first introduced the "missing function," this was not merely a question of org charts and business cards. I'm not sure it matters whether a company formally creates the position of chief entrepreneurship officer. In some places, "corporate innovation" sits with marketing;

elsewhere it is owned by the chief technology officer. These details are not essential. What matters is that the organization does the following:

1. Assigns responsibility for the entrepreneurship function to somebody (too many orgs have nobody).
2. Gives these people real operating responsibility instead of designating them merely as futurists or instigators (as too many "chief innovation officers" are).
3. Builds a career path and a specialized performance development process for entrepreneurial talent (producing a common standard that can be used across the pillars, no matter which function or division is affected).
4. Facilitates cross-training of entrepreneurs across the pillars. (This is why VCs who have had real-world operating experience as founders are so highly prized, though I should note the many VCs who have succeeded despite not having it. What matters is the mindset, not the résumé.)
5. Offers training, mentorship, support, coaching, and best practices designed to foster excellence in entrepreneurship across the organization.
6. Somewhat counterintuitively, takes responsibility for educating the *non-entrepreneurs* in the organization, who, though not necessarily acting as drivers of change, will still need to adopt a more entrepreneurial way of working.
7. Gives entrepreneurship a seat at the table when the other functions—especially gatekeeper functions—are setting company policy. This is incredibly important for finance, legal, HR, and IT in particular.

Together, those commitments form the overarching structure of entrepreneurship as a corporate function. On page 316 is an org chart that shows every element of the *unified theory of entre-*

preneurship. Pay special attention to the nine activities now managed by the entrepreneurial function.

CONTINUOUS TRANSFORMATION

The courageous folks you've met in earlier chapters—people like Janice Semper and Viv Goldstein at GE, Jeff Smith at IBM, Ben Blank at Intuit, and former U.S. CTO Todd Park—are all examples of corporate entrepreneurs just as real as the startup founders you see on the covers of magazines. We've discussed the folly of sending new-product teams to do battle against competitors with one or both hands tied behind their backs. It's equally foolish to send your transformation champions to do battle internally without the backing they need.

They need the same things every entrepreneur needs: limited but secure funding to get started, clear access to scalable resources (when the need is proven), appropriate standards for strong accountability, a commitment to the truth about whether their transformation is working or not, a cross-functional dedicated team, and a growth board to which to report progress. And as I've now seen across many organizations, they really benefit from a community of like-minded entrepreneurs working on unrelated startups under the same corporate umbrella.

So, if company leaders don't have someone working right now on a transformation in your organization, that's an oversight that should be remedied immediately. (Maybe you are that future change agent.) If the company has such a change agent in play, but she or he isn't being treated with the respect and authority of a real entrepreneur (perhaps she has only a part-time mandate to drive change, perhaps he's not experimenting but merely rolling out company-wide directives from HQ), that's fixable if leadership gets on it right away.

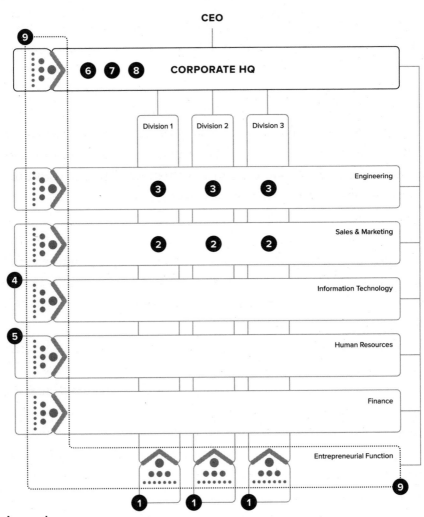

CEO

CORPORATE HQ

⑥ ⑦ ⑧

⑨

Division 1 Division 2 Division 3

Engineering

③ ③ ③

Sales & Marketing

② ② ②

④ Information Technology

⑤ Human Resources

Finance

Entrepreneurial Function

① ① ①

⑨

Legend

① New products
② Existing products in new markets
③ Products that act as insurance against future disruption
④ New IT systems
⑤ New policies and initiatives from gatekeeper functions (HR, finance, legal)
⑥ Investing in and acquiring new companies, IP licensing, joint ventures
⑦ Incubating potential new divisions
⑧ Promoting corporate transformation along the lines of the Startup Way
⑨ Advocating continuous transformation to adapt to an uncertain future

Growth Boards

Internal Startup Teams

But let's say you already work at one of the companies featured in *The Startup Way*. Your company has embraced entrepreneurship as the "missing function" and has a major transformation like FastWorks underway. You have a cross-functional board of senior executives overseeing startup founders who are seeking that exponential impact of a new way of working. Maybe you're already in Phase Three of the Startup Way, and the CEO and other senior leaders have committed themselves publicly and incontrovertibly to the new way of working.

Lucky you! I guess it's time to relax, right? There's nothing more you can do. You might even feel that you came to this book a little too late: You could have been that change agent if the opportunity had presented itself. But now all the glory—and the attendant career rewards—have already been handed out to someone else.

Whoa—stop! What I've outlined here isn't the end—it's the beginning.

This is the secret double benefit of a successful transformation. Not only does it pay for itself many times over in the tangible benefits we discussed in previous chapters, such as improved time to market, win rate, productivity, and profitability. It also plants the seed for the new corporate capability of continuous transformation. The people with the battle scars from having succeeded at it once are ideally suited to become the board members of future transformation, mentors to future change agents, or even repeat founders themselves if—*and only if*—the company is prepared to invest in them, value their skills, and find an appropriate organizational structure to support them.

Let me say it again.

Continuous transformation—an organization's capability to test and learn from experiments having to do with its own structure and processes, promoting the best-proven techniques company-wide while limiting or discarding the rest—is what will give that organization the ability to thrive in the modern era. It's my last suggestion as an addition to the toolbox of the entrepreneurial management function.

Let's formalize and systematize that approach, so that we build up a critical mass of like-minded entrepreneurs who can tackle the full heterogeneous range of challenges we're likely to face in the twenty-first century and beyond.

.   .   .

This is the true promise of the Startup Way: a management system that contains within it the seeds of its own evolution by providing an opportunity for every employee to become an entrepreneur. In doing so, it creates opportunities for leadership and keeps the people best suited for leadership in the company, reduces the waste of both time and energy, and creates a system for solving challenges with speed and flexibility, all of which lead to better financial outcomes.

But the most important use of the Startup Way isn't to create better and more profitable companies. It's to serve as a system for building a more inclusive and innovative society. That is the focus of the final two chapters.

## CHAPTER 11

TOWARD A PRO-ENTREPRENEURSHIP PUBLIC POLICY

IT IS MY fervent hope that this book will be read by present and future policy makers. Some of them might be tempted to skip over the early chapters and come straight to this one (Welcome!), and that's certainly fine with me. Few of the policy makers I've been privileged to meet—both politicians and civil servants alike—think of themselves as entrepreneurs; I hope those who have read the preceding chapters will challenge this self-assessment.

One recurring theme of this book has been the importance of seeing entrepreneurship as a tool for developing business ecosystems. Within a company, this means setting up structures and incentives to grow the next generation of entrepreneurial leaders. On Sand Hill Road, this means building a community of investing professionals who can identify and mentor the next generation of technology startup founders. In the preceding pages, I've argued that these two ecosystems are not as different as they seem. Now I'd like to add one more ecosystem to the mix: that of public policy.

The entrepreneurial principles we've discussed can and should be used in developing policy as well. In fact, we've already seen several examples of this entrepreneurial mindset applied in policy domains: stories about how government agencies used lean methods to create the means for *delivering* policy that had already been made—the Affordable Care Act, the College Scorecard, the immigration paperwork at USCIS. This is an important step, and I urge all policymakers to follow these examples.[1]

This chapter is about how we might be able to run fruitful policy-making experiments that will help leaders face their current challenge: creating conditions that will allow the next generation of entrepreneurs to thrive. The idea of innovation anywhere shouldn't apply just to the products and processes of business. As economist Mariana Mazzucato writes:

> It is a truism that the winners write the history books. The winners from Silicon Valley—the VCs and the entrepreneurs—wrote the story lines that justified the rewards they took. But their stories are not a useful guide for policy making elsewhere. For that, it is necessary to look beneath, at the shoulders they were standing on, and devise symbiotic ecosystems between public and private actors that recognize wealth creation as a collective endeavor. Because an entrepreneurial society first needs an entrepreneurial state.[2]

IT'S ABOUT POLICY, NOT POLITICS

A pro-entrepreneurship public policy scrambles our traditional political categories. In some ways, to foster startup-driven economic growth, we need pro-business policies that are the traditional province of conservatism: less regulation, more competition, more public-private partnership. But we also need some pro-worker policies that are the traditional province of the left: workplace protections (such as abolishing non-compete employment contracts), portable health insurance, sensible immigration. Then you have a series of reforms that, in theory, ought to enjoy widespread bipartisan appreciation because they benefit everyone, but in practice tend to get caught up in grandstanding and partisan warfare: patent reform, more responsive and effective government, open data and open APIs for government data, education, infrastructure, and R&D.

If you want more people to become entrepreneurs, you need to think about what they were doing five minutes before they founded their company. A few legendary titans of industry go on to found a new successful company, but the law of large numbers says the vast majority of people who create successful startups were not themselves CEOs or founders beforehand. What were they? Students, ordinary workers, immigrants, mid-level managers.

Entrepreneurs cannot afford to wait to see those reforms through: Our whole business ecosystem will live and die by the choices we make in this coming generation.

As a citizen of the world, I am very confident that the entrepreneurial ecosystem will flourish. The democratization of startup knowledge and the low-cost tools to experiment at scale that we discussed in Chapter 1 practically guarantee it. For every reform, *some* jurisdiction on the planet is experimenting with it. Witness the idea of the "startup founder's visa," which originated in Silicon Valley but was implemented in many other countries long before we ever had a feeble version of it in the United States.[3]

Still, as an American citizen, I worry about our ability to maintain U.S. leadership in this most critical area. Startups are, in a very crude sense, made up of three ingredients: products, capital, and labor. If the early twenty-first century has shown us anything, it is that products and capital are both extremely porous across borders, but labor is decidedly not. Consider the next generation of technology breakthroughs and their attendant products. As a global consumer, I will enjoy the fruits of those breakthroughs no matter what country they are produced in. The limited partners who finance the venture capital asset class will have no problem finding ways to get their money invested in these products, as recent experience in developing economies like India and China has shown. But the jobs that are created by those startups—and, therefore, the spillover economic effects—will be mostly local, tied to the country that fosters their development. Silicon Valley, California, USA, has long been the envy of the world because we have harnessed these effects to our benefit. But we are now in a race against time. If we do not proactively invest in the public policies that allow us to maintain this position, we will lose it.

It is through that lens that I want to share some ideas about what a truly pro-entrepreneurship public policy that not only encourages citizens to innovate but can also be used to deliver better policy outcomes might look like.

WHAT MOTIVATES ENTREPRENEURS?

What causes someone to take the speculative leap required to start a new company or to work in a new way? I've coached hundreds of people through this thought exercise. Over and over again, I see them weighing the same three sets of factors.

1. Vision and Upside

A longing to improve the world is critical: That's vision. But where do people get the ideas that lead to real, valuable change? And what role models inspire them to think they're qualified to pursue those ideas? Anything we can do to help people find and believe in valid ideas for improvement will increase the rate of entrepreneurship.

Of course, for someone willing to endure the pain of entrepreneurship, the payoff has to be correspondingly large (although not always financial, as we saw in Chapter 3 on the "stake in the outcome"). This has implications for both education and fiscal policy.

2. Skills and Resources

Vision can be a daunting thing. Many people never pursue their dreams because they can't see a way to get started. Providing a way is one of the big impacts that the Lean Startup movement has had to date, encouraging would-be entrepreneurs to "Think big. Start small. Scale fast." Any policy that helps people take those tentative first steps will have big returns on the rate of entrepreneurship, even if most experiments fail.

It's also important to recognize that even though innovation is sometimes cheap (at the beginning), having access to the resources required to get started is an enormously privileged position to be in. There's a reason that famous entrepreneurs in history, like Henry Ford, came from upper-middle-class backgrounds: They were rich in family connections to fall back on in the event of failure and had easy access to the startup funds and equipment they needed to get started.[4] As entrepreneur and investor Jason Ford writes: "It's time for more entrepreneurs like me to stop telling the story of how they climbed their way to the top. To stop taking credit for flying to the moon all by themselves, as if the entire support structure they were born into had nothing to do with it. And it's time for all of us to find ways to empower more of the world's highest-potential entrepreneurs with their own rockets so they can show us the stars."[5] I believe that genius is widely distributed. Opportunity is not.

3. Risks and Liabilities

All entrepreneurs, whether they admit it or not, are obsessed with failure. It's impossible not to think about all the ways your venture might fail and the myriad consequences, personal as well as professional, that might follow. Of course, part of the art of entrepreneurship is to assess the risks rationally, filter out those that are endurable (like embarrassment) from the ones that are more serious (like fraud or a faulty product), and maintain confidence in the face of these realities.[6]

As for liability, being able to quit your job and start a company with no salary is a luxury only some people enjoy. There's a reason we have the famous pop-culture image of the twenty-something tech founder (not coincidentally, almost always white and male) working in his parents' garage. It's much easier to start a company if you have no dependents and no mortgage or rent.[7] And it's definitely easier if you don't have to worry too much about how failure is going to look on your résumé. In some cultures, a failed startup is not only an embarrassing episode in one's early adult life (as it was for me), but a professional death sentence that makes it impossible to find gainful employment in the future.

As a result, anything that cushions people from the consequences of business failure will pay dramatic dividends in terms of the rate of entrepreneurship. Such cushioning is not easy to accomplish without creating moral hazard, however, as many critics of government programs have pointed out over the years. We have to be smart about it.

.   .   .

For a public policy to be considered truly pro-entrepreneurship, it has to affect at least one of the three sets of factors I just described. To convince people to try entrepreneurship, we have to affect their lives before they're at the moment of making the choice, or the choice doesn't truly exist. Those are the levers we need to move to create not just innovative companies but an innovative *culture*. A lot of current pro-business policy has to do with profitability, but that's only one aspect of a healthy economy. And not all profitability leads to increased dynamism in the economy: Think of the many rent-seeking behaviors that make it harder—not easier—for new companies to form.

We hear a lot about "unicorn" companies, startups that grow into billion-dollar successes, or even hundreds of billions of dollars. But the truth is, these near-mythical success stories are not what create a continuously evolving system of opportunity. In fact, the way policy is set up now discourages people from trying their new ideas. According to the U.S. Census Bureau, 700,000 fewer businesses were created between 2005 and 2014 than between 1985 and 1994. The number of startups that contribute disproportionally to job and productivity growth has been falling since 2000.[8]

We can do better. What follows is a set of ideas that are a sketch of what a truly pro-entrepreneurship environment might look like. It is not my intention to create a complete list; I have tried to avoid regurgitating the most obvious suggestions and to limit myself to ideas that are a little bit out of the mainstream discourse about startups. And I have done my best to keep politics out of this chapter. I believe that one of the benefits of developing a pro-entrepreneurship public policy is the opportunity to cut through today's partisanship.

NURTURING HUMAN CAPITAL

Health Insurance

Over the years, I've tried to talk a fair number of people into taking the entrepreneurial plunge. Before the passage of the Affordable Care Act in 2010, health insurance often came up as a dominant inhibiting factor. Many would-be entrepreneurs have dependents who rely on them for health coverage or have a pre-existing medical condition themselves. These are not minor concerns (see "Risks and Liabilities" on page 324).

There is the striking evidence that the inhibiting effect of uncertainty about health insurance is more than just anecdotal. For example, a RAND study examined the rate of entrepreneurship in the United States population by age cohort. The rate holds steady for most ages, but here's what happens among older Americans: The rate of entrepreneurship spikes as soon as people turn sixty-five and become eligible for government-sponsored insurance in the form of Medicare.[9] Think about this statistic for a moment—do you really think sixty-five-year-olds are more creative or entrepreneurial than sixty-four-year-olds?

Health Care Delivery

A new generation of entrepreneurs is experimenting with new health care delivery systems that offer the promise of world-class treatment *and* prevention at a lower cost and a much higher level of delight to patients and doctors alike. Like any startup-led disruption, these innovations face massive resistance from entrenched interests and old business models. Companies like Honor, One Medical, athenahealth, Forward, Heal, and Oscar Health can all be accelerated or hindered by policy choices. I believe it's in our best interest to encourage them. The health care system we have now is expensive, wasteful, and unevenly distributed. Through experimentation and innovation, we can find better ways to bring better care to more people—if policy makers are willing to support these experiments.

Introducing Entrepreneurial Skills into School Curriculum

In the lower grades, exposure to entrepreneurial skills is often as basic as teaching kids that failure is not only okay but often an opportunity to learn something you can use when you try again (something adults have a hard time accepting, as we've seen!). Even that idea can be radical in an environment in which test scores are the focus of the curriculum and excellence is tied to funding and enrollment. But it's crucial to creating a new generation of citizens who are willing to experiment their way to amazing outcomes. Creating what psychologists call a "growth mindset" is the key to encouraging kids to take risks and learn from their mistakes—which sounds a lot like the mindset of an entrepreneur.[10]

At the university level, I've witnessed the changes happening firsthand. I spent time as an entrepreneur-in-residence (EIR) at the Harvard Business School, where Tom Eisenmann introduced Lean Startup principles into the curriculum. It began with a class called "Launching Technology Ventures" back in 2011 and developed into a required Startup Bootcamp for first-year MBAs and courses in entrepreneurial sales and marketing and product management.

At Stanford, long a center for innovation, Steve Blank launched a class in the spring of 2016 called "Hacking for Defense," in which students applied Lean Startup methods to building complex, mission-critical prototypes for things like wearable sensors for Navy divers and next-generation bomb detectors. The teaching staff shared all of their materials and lesson plans online for other universities to use. As Blank explains it, "Our goal was to scale these classes across the country, giving students the opportunity to perform a national service by solving real defense and diplomacy problems using lean methods." To date, twenty-three additional colleges and universities plan to offer the class.

It's also inspired other courses, such as "Hacking for Diplomacy" at Stanford; and "Hacking for Energy" at Columbia, NYU, and City University of New York, which focuses on innovating in the energy industry.[11]

Blank is also the founder of a government education program called I-Corps, at the National Science Foundation, which has brought Lean Startup practices to researchers to teach them how to turn their discoveries into businesses. As Blank says, "I-Corps bridges the gap between public support of basic science and private capital funding of new commercial ventures. It's a model for a government program that's gotten the balance between public-private partnerships just right."[12] More than one thousand teams have been through the program. It has been so successful that on their last day in session in 2016, Congress passed a bill called the American Innovation and Competitiveness Act, which made the program permanent. Under this bill (signed into law by President Obama in January 2017), I-Corps will move into more federal agencies, state and local governments, and academic institutions. And let's not forget all the ways in which entrepreneurs are experimenting with the application of entrepreneurial techniques to improve education itself. Companies like AltSchool, Panorama Education, and Summit Public Schools are using innovation to build new school systems, measure them, then learn and apply that learning for the benefit of students across the country.

Immigration

Forty-four percent of Silicon Valley startups have immigrant founders.[13] Fifty-one percent of startups worth a billion dollars were founded by immigrants.[14] Many more of the most successful American startups have at least one immigrant founder. Openness to immigrants is one of the cultural values that predict future economic growth on a city-by-city basis (one of several data-based indexes that Silicon Valley routinely leads the pack in). As Richard Florida writes in *The Flight of the Creative Class,* the United States "doesn't have some intrinsic advantage in the production of creative people, new ideas, or startup companies. Its real advantage lies in its ability to attract these economic drivers from around the world. Of critical importance to American success in this last century has been a tremendous influx of global talent."[15]

Yet the United States has no category for a startup visa, and startup founders have traditionally found it quite difficult to come and stay in the States. Which is why most successful immigrant founders have had to figure out a way to get access to another visa category. This makes U.S. immigration policy, as it affects entrepreneurs, especially shortsighted.

Many would-be immigrant founders are already living in the United States—as students or as H-1B workers. Take a common case: a graduate student pursuing a high-tech PhD at one of the country's elite universities. Such a person, between her various undergraduate and graduate degrees, may have spent as many as a dozen years in the States. Upon graduation, having invested a massive amount of resources into her education, at the very moment she would like to switch from being a consumer of resources to a job creator, do we send her back to her home country? It's illogical.

Remember, if such people found a company in their home country, they will probably have easy access to the American market to sell products into. They will probably have easy access to American venture capital. We will be their customers. *But the jobs will be created overseas.*[16]

Labor Relations

One of the most striking claims of Frederick Winslow Taylor's *The Principles of Scientific Management* (1915) was that no workplace that had been organized under the principles of scientific management had ever had a strike, because when workers were treated "optimally" there was never any need for labor strife. With the benefit of hindsight, we now know this claim to be overblown: Many companies organized according to those principles have indeed endured strikes over the years. But the utopian idea that a more enlightened style of management would prevent conflicts between labor and management endures. It's especially prevalent in Silicon Valley, where very few companies are unionized and where most workers, at least the well-paid white-collar ones, have little sympathy for unions.

It's hard to talk about unions without being drawn into the hyperpolarizing world of partisan politics, but let me do my best. I believe a new kind of union-management relationship is available for organizations that are willing to break the mold and try some experiments. I think of it as a "pro-productivity" union: a trade of more flexibility for more investments in workers, the tying of wages and benefits to productivity improvements in the company, and a proactive agenda to create entrepreneurial opportunities for all union members. The goal of a "pro-productivity" union is to align its members financially with the health of the company and encourage managerial flexibility to enhance the long-term profitability of the company.

Or what if the union itself ran incubators to encourage their members to take this leap whenever they have a good idea? As a condition of participating, the company founders could agree to become union shops if an idea succeeded. This system could eventually become self-perpetuating.[17]

UNEMPLOYMENT INSURANCE AND STARTUPS

On a call-in talk show on C-SPAN, I was invited to opine on various topics related to entrepreneurship and public policy. Under our current system,[18] anyone who becomes involuntarily unemployed is entitled to a certain number of weeks of unemployment insurance payments (exact terms vary by state). The idea is to provide a cushion for workers to fall back on in between jobs. Once you find a new job, the payments stop.

But this universal income program has some obvious incentive problems. The first is that the sooner you get a new job, the less money you receive. Some argue that the program is effectively paying people *not* to find a new job.

But from an entrepreneurial perspective, the situation is even worse. What if you decide to start a new company while you are unemployed? Even though the company is unlikely to have a lot of resources to pay you, the government considers you employed and thus ineligible for insurance payments. So here we have a situation where we are paying citizens *not* to start a company.

I proposed, on the air, that citizens should have the option to convert their UI payments into a small business loan on generous terms if they would like to start a company. I think this policy would be especially sensible in times of mass unemployment. A community full of unemployed people lacks income and resources, but it doesn't lack needs that could profitably be serviced by new startups. And, during the short time that UI payments were widely active in that community (acting as a macroeconomic stabilizer), new startups specific to that situation would have ready-made customers available.

Even apart from the situation of mass unemployment, giving the "regular" unemployed the opportunity to switch into entrepreneurship would accomplish many important policy goals: helping people transition to a new career, finding novel ways to reuse their past job skills, and (even for the startups that fail) promoting the increased human dignity that comes with productive work rather than simply receiving a handout. There's abundant evidence that working improves self-esteem and satisfaction with life and decreases depression by significant numbers.[19] It also provides a great opportunity to provide entrepreneurial job training, co-working facilities, or other accelerator-type benefits to encourage this community of would-be founders.

On C-SPAN, these ideas did not receive a warm reception. Some of the responses I heard were along the lines of, "What if people don't pay back the loans?" and so on, despite the fact that the money would have been "lost" in the form of UI payments, anyway. Even if a small percentage of individuals pay the loan back, that's a net win for the government balance sheet! Moreover, those very entrepreneurs may become significant creators of new jobs.

SMALL-BUSINESS LOANS

If the government wanted to dramatically increase the number of entrepreneurial experiments going on among its citizens, the easiest way to do so would be to inject startup capital directly into the hands of ordinary citizens. Many countries do have programs like this: The country provides funding to either state-run venture capital programs, or it becomes a major limited partner in private funds. But this model has had only limited success, because it runs into the same problem as all government-directed investing: politics.

How could we solve this problem while at the same time catalyzing a large number of startups? How about a government-run microloan system available to every citizen? It could start quite modestly, maybe even as low as $100. But each time you repay the loan in full, the amount of credit available to you could increase (imagine it doubled every round). Failure to repay would cause you to lose access to the program but would not cause bankruptcy. Even if the total amount of credit available to each individual was strictly capped at a relatively low amount, the number of startups that could be funded could be quite massive. In earlier eras, a program of this size and scale would have been quite difficult to manage logistically. But modern technology would make it quite simple. And, of course, the program could be administered privately on behalf of the Federal Reserve, in the same way that banks today already act as the Fed's private interface to the citizenry.

I honestly don't know how many people don't pursue their entrepreneurial dreams for lack of $1,000 that they could afford to lose. But I think the number could be large. The cost to find out would be pretty small, and this program could easily be piloted in one community or city to find out.

UNIVERSAL BASIC INCOME

A policy idea that is all the rage in Silicon Valley right now is the universal basic income (UBI), the idea that governments could guarantee to every citizen a secure income that is unrelated to their ability to work.[20] Even a modest UBI would probably pay huge dividends in the category of more startups formed, by simply reducing the risk inherent in failure. If you could not become unemployed and thereby destitute, the worst-case scenario that most frightens would-be entrepreneurs would be moot.

Oulu, Finland, is now running an experiment to see how UBI might encourage entrepreneurs. Finland has the very problem I touched upon above: Because it offers generous unemployment benefits that don't allow for earning additional income, laid-off workers often do better financially by cashing their government checks than by trying to get a startup off the ground. At the start of 2017, the government selected roughly two thousand unemployed workers from fields ranging from technology to construction and enrolled them in a pilot UBI program to see what will happen.[21]

Y Combinator is also running an experiment with basic income, having selected one hundred families in Oakland, California, who will receive $1,000 to $2,000 a month as part of a five-year program designed to look at how ready money affects people's "happiness, well-being, financial health, as well as how people spend their time." The data and research methods will be shared at the project's end so others can learn from and build on the experiment, which is testing the idea, as Y Combinator president Sam Altman says, that a basic income could "give people the freedom to pursue further education or training, find or create a better job, and plan for the future."[22]

In France, an experiment that allowed people to keep their unemployment benefits while starting a new business saw an increase of 25 percent per month in the creation of new companies.[23] And the Dutch and Canadians aren't far behind—both countries also launched experiments in 2017.[24]

REGULATORY RELIEF FOR STARTUPS

"Sliding Scale" Regulations

Regulation can destroy startups without even meaning to. In many jurisdictions, the number of steps required to incorporate a new company is staggering: business licenses, employment reporting, tax collection, mandatory training, and more. Quite apart from the cost of these regulations is the psychological burden of (1) having to learn what they all are, and (2) worrying that you've missed one and will be found liable. In most places, ignorance of the law is no defense, but today's laws have become so byzantine and complex that full knowledge of the law is a full-time job. Most venture-backed companies can afford to pay competent legal counsel to avoid these problems (and, increasingly, a part-time CFO is de rigeur, as well). But what about startups that are not yet ready for venture financing? Today, we strictly limit the pipeline of startups that might one day seek venture financing by inadvertently increasing the friction that prevents people from getting started.

In California, a number of laws have been carefully written to exempt companies with few employees from many regulations. Specific thresholds vary by category, but several important ones kick in only when you reach fifty employees. This is a good compromise: Tiny companies are usually pretty limited in the amount of damage they can do, and once the company has success, it can afford counsel to make sure it meets its obligations.

I think this idea can be greatly extended and updated for a twenty-first-century economy. First of all, arbitrary employee counts aren't as useful as they used to be, thanks to the increased leverage we discussed in Chapter 3, where small teams can have a disproportionate impact. And, in many cases, having just one threshold where many regulations kick in all at once is rough. I think we'd be smart to think about regulation that works on a sliding scale, starting with extremely loose standards for extremely small companies (as measured by some combination of employees, revenue, and market cap) and then gradually becoming more strict as the company grows.

A responsive government should want to make it *extremely easy* to get started in business. Since most countries require startups to file tax returns (usually documenting the extent of their losses, in the early years), why not use this information to proactively communicate with the company's founders? Imagine a simple, web-based signup to begin a corporate entity's life with a regulator who took responsibility for providing targeted communications that were stage-appropriate about what regulations the company needs to follow and which ones are coming up as the company grows. By both making starting the company easier and relieving the psychic burden of so much uncertainty, you'd get more startups, period.

To take this idea even further, I think there are a number of policy "deals" to be had, where high-growth startups are granted targeted regulatory relief in exchange for making human-capital investments that policy makers desire. This could follow an idea that has been circulating around Washington, D.C., to create a new kind of statutory entity for a "growth startup corporation" distinct from existing classes like a C corp, LLC, or partnership. These "G corps" would be available only to companies that are human-capital intensive, have equity that is widely shared with all employees, invest in worker training, and so on. In exchange, they would be able to "grow into" various rules and regulations only as they scale.

Non-Compete Agreements and Patent Law

A specific quirk of California law allows for one of the key elements of a thriving entrepreneurial culture: The courts won't enforce contracts that include non-compete clauses.[25] What this means is that anyone is free, at any time, to take his or her ideas elsewhere. What could be better for innovation? Patent reform is also urgently needed. While intellectual property is obviously critical for innovators, patents can also be used in ways that stifle creativity and competition.[26] "Strangulation" lawsuits, in which large companies file patent infringement suits against startups that can't possibly afford to defend themselves, need to be stopped—or at least postponed.

Bankruptcy Reform

Whenever I travel to a country that allows personal liability for corporate failures, this is the top issue that every entrepreneur I meet wants to talk to me about. In some countries, a failed startup on your résumé makes it hard to get a job, hard to get future credit, even hard to get a bank account. This limitation is extremely counterproductive. The more forgiving the bankruptcy code, the more likely are people to take advantage of it by engaging in more risky behavior. This situation can make policy makers nervous—but it is precisely the situation where more risk-taking is, on the whole, worthwhile.

Civic Reforms

PHILANTHROPY, NONPROFITS, AND OTHER WORK FOR SOCIAL GOOD

You heard about the use of lean methods to help raise money for the American Heart Association in Chapter 8 and about the work done by Global Innovation Fund in Chapter 7. Airbnb's Samara is also following this path with its refugee work. There's no reason why the Startup Way methodology can't be used for all kinds of social good. One of the offshoots of the broader Lean Startup movement has been a grassroots community called Lean Impact, dedicated to bringing Lean Startup ideas into the social sector.

Ann Mei Chang was the chief innovation officer and executive director of the U.S. Global Development Lab at USAID. We are collaborating on an upcoming book, tentatively titled *Lean Impact*. Based on her experience in both Silicon Valley and the social sector, she believes real change can come from applying lean methods to areas that will make huge differences in people's lives—including saving them. Her experiences at USAID have proved formative. "The way the traditional grants work reinforces a waterfall development model," she says. "You have to design a whole solution up front and then run with it for three to five years." The questions she's taking on include how to balance experimentation with funders' need for certainty, ways to speed up measurement of what works when it comes to social impact, and paths for growth that can enable social innovations to reach massive scale. And, for funders, how to fund based more on outcomes than on activity. "USAID provides humanitarian aid and development assistance from the U.S. to other largely poor countries," Chang says. "The U.S. Global Development Lab was set up about three years ago to see how modern tools and approaches could accelerate our progress. The principles for the Lab are very much in line with Lean Startup as we believe data-driven experimentation is equally applicable in global development to drive innovation so we can deliver more impactful interventions at scale."

OPEN DATA

We've seen many examples in this book—in this chapter, even—of people publicly sharing their discoveries and systems for others to use, adapt, and learn from. If we truly want to encourage everyone to innovate, we need to set the example at the highest level. That's what the government's open data project—known as "Government 2.0"—is about. As Tim O'Reilly has written, "How does government itself become an open platform that allows people inside and outside government to innovate? How do you design a system in which all of the outcomes aren't specified beforehand, but instead evolve through interactions between the technology provider and its user community?"[27]

In 2009, the Obama administration created Data.gov, which contains constantly evolving data sets on everything from climate to agriculture to education. In the 2013 Executive Order that

President Obama signed making open government data the default mode, he wrote: "Openness in government strengthens our democracy, promotes the delivery of efficient and effective services to the public, and contributes to economic growth. As one vital benefit of open government, making information resources easy to find, accessible, and usable can fuel entrepreneurship, innovation, and scientific discovery that improves Americans' lives and contributes significantly to job creation."[28]

That is a truth we need to defend going forward. Good, true information is the foundation of innovation—it's what the Startup Way, like the Lean Startup method, is based on. The areas that real data can affect are limitless, ranging from public safety to health care to global affairs. As Todd Park has said, "If you are in these spaces and do not know this stuff is available, then it's like being in the navigation business and not knowing that GPS exists. . . . Entrepreneurs can turn open data into awesomeness."[29]

CAPITAL MARKETS, CORPORATE GOVERNANCE, AND SHORT-TERMISM

Recently, I met the investment officer in charge of a large insurance company's investment portfolio. Because the company offers insurance contracts that mature over decades and centuries, they naturally have a long-term perspective on investing. When I inquired about how they invest assets, the investment officer surprised me by revealing that only a small percentage of their portfolio is invested in public securities. Instead, the company prefers hard assets that require a stewardship model and that pay off reliably over tens or hundreds of years. "Like what?" I asked. "Forestry, for example," was his answer.

I assumed he meant agricultural companies or maybe lumber as a commodity. It took him several minutes to help me understand that he meant *literal forests*. Once I did, it became clear to me that having these assets in their portfolio gave the company a unique perspective on the disease afflicting our public markets. In a forest you can easily—at any time—maximize your quarterly returns. You simply cut down all the trees. Of course, this is the ultimate short-term solution since once you've done it, the forest will have almost no remaining value.

Yet this is what too many of our public companies are doing: cannibalizing their long-term value by destroying their own brand, squeezing vendors, shortchanging customers, failing to invest in employees, and using the company's resources to enrich insiders and activist investors via financial engineering. All of these activities share the same problem: *They work only in the short term.* In companies that have grown a sufficiently large and productive "forest" over years or decades, there's an awful lot of firewood to be cut down before the damage becomes evident.

This is the inevitable result of treating companies as if their obligation to *maximize shareholder value* means *maximizing quarterly returns.*

As I discussed in *The Lean Startup,* these kinds of bad incentives trickle down from the public markets and infect everything that public companies touch, including the environment, politics, public safety, and, of particular concern to me, the whole entrepreneurial ecosystem. If the goal of a startup "exit" is either to be acquired by one of these public companies subject to short-term pressure or to IPO and then be subject to them directly, then founders will inevitably face pressure to maximize their company's attractiveness to those systems.

Even worse, the corporate development departments of public companies then wind up anointing the next generation of leaders in startup hubs simply by being the ones who decide which companies to acquire for outsize valuations. It's corrosive.

After LinkedIn made the decision to sell itself to Microsoft, one of the company's executives confided in me that they felt they would have more freedom to innovate and less pressure to deliver in the short-term as a wholly-owned subsidiary than as an independent company. Only certain megaconglomerates have the sheer size necessary to resist these pressures. And if current trends continue, within a few years only the megacorporations will be left on the public exchanges. The total number of public companies in the United States has fallen by almost half since 1997, and the trend continues year after year.[30]

Companies that do IPO are doing so many years later in their life cycle, which is causing a number of bad things to happen:

1. *A lot more private financing, with no audited financials or transparency.* Our grandparents learned the hard way what happens when too much money is chasing exponential growth without oversight, governance, and disclosure. Although the documented instances of fraud are few so far, the temptations are immense.

2. *Lack of liquidity for limited partners.* Without a robust secondary market governed by any kind of governance and disclosure standards, all secondary market transactions happen in the shadows. This is another market ripe with opportunities for fraud: If the founder of a company wants to sell you his or her shares, ask yourself what he or she knows that you don't know.

3. *Lack of liquidity for employees.* With employees having to wait even longer for liquidity, there is now a whole new variety of ways for them to be deprived of any share of the company's eventual success. For example, most stock options are today set up with two bad design features: a ten-year expiration and a ninety-day exercise window. When companies used to routinely go public between roughly four to seven years of existence,[31] these terms were just fine. But as the time to do so stretches longer, these two terms create two new ways for

employees to wind up with options that they cannot exercise. Once a company has an extremely high valuation, exercising stock options gets expensive. And, as we'll see in a moment, even for employees who can afford the exercise price, the tax consequences can be severe. If there is no liquid market for the underlying stock, the employee can be forced into bankruptcy for lack of liquidity to pay these taxes. It's a huge mess.

4. *Lack of access to growth for public investors.* This is perhaps the worst consequence of all, from a policy point of view. Ordinary investors are simply shut out entirely from this ecosystem. In a world of low-growth investment opportunities and fears of "secular stagnation,"[32] it seems especially cruel to prevent ordinary citizens from accessing the fastest-growing investment opportunities—especially younger citizens investing for retirement who have the time horizon to take maximum advantage of the risks involved in companies like these (with appropriate portfolio management). And yet, because these companies are not listed on public exchanges, all the investment opportunities are limited to "qualified investors"— meaning, for all intents and purposes, those who are already wealthy. It's simply unfair.

Part of the solution to this set of problems is the new kind of management system outlined in this book. But no matter how good a management system is, the available incentives it comes up against every day will lead it back to short-term thinking. In order to address those incentives, we have to address the policy problem behind them.

If companies are going to stay private longer, we need to create a new status between late-stage financing and IPO. I call it the "pre-public offering" (PPO). The PPO allows companies to start the process of engaging with large institutional investors earlier in their life cycle. It permits some early liquidity, but only when investors have real financial disclosures. Both early investors and employees should be able to convert some portion of their equity into a well-defined security with consistent rights and sell it at well-defined times; the company can oversee auctions, possibly once a quarter or twice a year, rather than continuous trading. Most important, only those who receive disclosure will be permitted to trade, eliminating the temptations to fraud that the current system allows.

THE LONG-TERM STOCK EXCHANGE

When I was writing *The Lean Startup* in 2010, I did a lot of research on Toyota. Everything I read made it clear that the foundation of the company's success is its philosophy of long-term thinking, which is made possible by its particular (and, by modern standards, unusual) corporate governance structure. Not coincidentally, it's the same kind of thinking that, as I've said elsewhere here, undergirds successful CEOs like Jeff Bezos, and the philosophy of investors like Warren Buffett and Andreessen Horowitz.

As I went about my work in those years, I kept thinking about that philosophy, and about the fact that what I really recommended in *The Lean Startup,* alongside all the catchy lingo and early days of startup excitement, was that people should try to emulate Toyota by building companies that will last decades or even centuries.

But building a company that will last for generations simply isn't compatible with the way our current public markets are structured. The emphasis is on the short term, and the pressure that puts on companies is immense. In my work with managers all over the world, I see that short-term pressure up close, and all the ways it acts as a malignant gravitational force, warping and distorting the management system of an organization.

It isn't enough just to improve management practices. We have to solve these incentives as well. Many managers I've met and worked with know they're being asked to do the wrong thing, but they continue to do it anyway because they feel trapped in a system of incentives that makes it impossible to do anything else. It's not a surprise to me that the current system is in decline, resulting in so many fewer companies going public and the ones who do taking far longer to do so. It's creating that result because it's distracting companies away from fundamental value creation. And *if companies are distracted from fundamental value creation, they're empirically less valuable.* The result is that it's not just the companies that suffer, but their investors, too, because the company is not doing what it needs to thrive. And, in a low-growth world, this is also a bad policy outcome, since the broader public is barred from taking the kinds of prudent risks that delivered growth in previous generations. Remember, the Amazon.com IPO raised only $54 million.[33]

In last chapter of *The Lean Startup,* I offered a number of ideas about how to go forward that I hoped people would pick up and run with in a variety of areas: education, public policy, research, etc. One of them was an idea designed to address the problem I've just laid out: a "long-term" stock exchange that would function as a new venue for going public and create a new social contract to govern the behavior of companies and investors together.

Almost every idea I suggested at the end of *The Lean Startup* has at least been tried in the years since the book was published. But there's one notable exception, one idea so radioactive that no one wanted to go near it. It happens to be the same idea that wouldn't leave me alone and has kept me up at night since I published it: a new stock exchange. And so, a few years ago I decided to take that idea on myself by creating a company that would embody the new principles. It's called the Long-Term Stock Exchange (LTSE).

The Long-Term Stock Exchange is a national securities exchange that uses its listing standards to change incentives for managers and investors to be more long term. We weight corporate governance power toward long-term investors, who have more of a say than short-term investors. We reform executive compensation to make sure that managers are aligned with their investors over the long term, and we make a number of disclosure and good governance reforms that allow companies to focus on the fundamentals instead of managing to the quarter.

This is a startup in a highly regulated area, so there are limits to what I can say about our progress. If you'd like to learn more about our progress (and I hope you will!), please go to LTSE.com.

MINIMUM VIABLE POLITICS

I believe we can join all of the reforms in this chapter to help our country move toward what Samuel Hammond, the poverty and welfare analyst at the Niskanen Center think tank has called a system of "Minimum Viable Politics"—a whole new kind of MVP. We need to find a way to bridge the distance between the pluralism and the many varied interests that are both parts of our society. As Hammond writes, "The small area of overlap that remains . . . represents the shared set of values or potential rules compatible with a liberal society." But what is minimized is not the government itself or the amount of money it spends but "the ability of one individual or group to use the political process to impose their contestable moral or metaphysical views on another."[34] This gets back to what I said at the start of this chapter about how a pro-entrepreneurship public policy scrambles our political positions, because it draws from both sides of the aisle, seeking to address the needs and concerns of everyone in our society rather than just certain constituencies. As far as vision goes, it doesn't get more valuable than that.

EPILOGUE

A NEW CIVIC RELIGION

THE STARTUP WAY has been dedicated to helping business managers and leaders face the challenges of the twenty-first century. But what we have faced so far pales in comparison to the change that's coming.

We have to get ready for this new future, uncertain though it is. I try repeatedly throughout this book to emphasize that the org chart I am advocating here is not the end of management. Nor is it the be-all, end-all management system. Rather, it is the first one that contains within it the seeds of its own evolution.

By encouraging constant experimentation with organizational structures themselves, we are much more likely to be able to use new technological breakthroughs to create new and more powerful organizational forms. In order to do this, we have to see entrepreneurship as a core requirement of all employees, because we never know where new and surprising ideas will come from.

And we are going to need this adaptability in the years to come, for we are in danger of confronting the four horsemen of economic stagnation:

THE STARTUP WAY

AN EPIDEMIC OF SHORT-TERMISM: A lack of sustainable investment, companies that stay private, and poor circulation of illiquid returns result in a reduction of investments in the next generation. Short-termism is exacerbated by the overfinancialization of the economy and the rise of management through financial engineering instead of customer value creation.

LACK OF ENTREPRENEURIAL OPPORTUNITY: The rise of high-growth startups coincides with a massive reduction in opportunities for regular small business. Traditional ladders of advancement are being closed off, and new ones are not replacing them fast enough. Knowledge about startups is widely diffused, but the opportunity to take advantage of that knowledge is not.

A LOSS OF LEADERSHIP: Business and political leaders are focused more on preserving the results of past investments than on investing in the future. I fear a lack of R&D and science, a lack of shared prosperity, a false drive to protect capital rather than to spread opportunity, and a lack of breakthroughs in science and technology that might save us.

LOW GROWTH AND INSTABILITY: What happens to our social contract when only individuals with the highest educational attainment are eligible to work—at any level—in the new breed of company that drives most of the economy's growth? As corporate structures change, it will become unclear how people are going to find new opportunities. A retreat from globalization and low investment returns across all asset categories will contribute to a rising sense of despair for those left behind.

Loss of leadership, of course, is directly connected to bad management, and research now shows that poor management is directly related to low growth and productivity. We need to

develop and share better, future-embracing management practices, among which I include the kind of entrepreneurial system
described in this book. As Noah Smith has written, "Structured
management turned out to account for 17 percent of productivity differences between companies—half again as much as differences in employee skill levels, and twice as important as use of
information technology."[1]

I don't want to pretend that entrepreneurship is a magic cure
that, by itself, will solve all the problems I've listed here. But I do
believe it is one important component of the solution.

Our project in the years to come will be to advance a positive
vision of what liberal democracy can deliver with the new tools
that technology is placing at our disposal. Its pillars must be:

- Broadly shared prosperity.
- Democratic accountability.
- Scientific inquiry and truth-telling.
- Long-term thinking.
- Universal entrepreneurial opportunity.
- Profound investment in the public goods that benefit every-
  one: basic science, R&D, education, health care, infrastruc-
  ture.

We must be guided by real research into which solutions are
likely to work for society's greater good. We must harness all
of the tools of human culture and creativity to this vision: the
arts, rhetoric, leadership, and education. And, of course, we must
embrace change and disruption. We should understand technological development as a constant source of renewal and enlarged
possibilities.

We must plant the seeds of this new vision now. I hope this
book helps to show how entrepreneurship can be part of this
solution by:

- Creating new sources of growth and prosperity.
- Cultivating a new cohort of leaders among all generations who are not bound by convention or obligation to the ideas of the past yet are yoked through long-term incentives and mindset to the possibilities of the future.
- Integrating scientific thinking into every kind of work.
- Providing new opportunities for leadership to people of every background and circumstance.
- Helping public policy become more long-term in its objectives.

The good news is, this new organizational form is more effective, treats talent and energy as a precious resource, and is designed to harness the true source of competitive advantage in the years to come: human creativity. Every organization owes this simple bill of rights to its every member:

1. The right to know that the work I do all day is meaningful to someone other than my boss.
2. The right to have my idea turned into a minimum viable product and evaluated rigorously and fairly.
3. The right to become an entrepreneur at any time, as long as I'm willing to do the hard work to make things happen with limited resources.
4. The right to stay involved with my idea as it scales, as long as I am contributing productively to its growth.
5. The right to equity ownership in the growth I help to create, no matter my role or job title.

Organizations that cannot incorporate these technologies *and* management practices rigorously and scientifically will give way to those that can. (Ask your neighborhood taxi company how it feels to be on the wrong end of this competition.)

Our goal as a movement should be this: to change management practice to become more adaptive, more humane, more rigorous, and more efficient. If we are successful, I believe the benefits will be immense for society at large:

1. A change in incentives from short-term to long-term.
2. A reversal in the decline of new-business formation by making entrepreneurship more accessible to all.
3. A reversal in the trend toward the bureaucracy of large organizations and, therefore,
4. More growth through organic breakthroughs in customer delight, rather than simply mergers, reorgs, and financial engineering.
5. The opportunity to redesign our economy to be more inclusive, more sustainable, and more innovative—all at the same time.

Achieving these goals across every kind of organization is not the job of politicians or managers or founders or investors alone. It is going to require a vast movement of like-minded idealists and visionaries to integrate these values into the very fabric of their organizations, in every industry, geography, and sector. The transformation will take many years to come to fruition. We will face resistance from all quarters. Seek out allies and innovators—they are all around you. Don't forget how far we've come or how far we still have to go.

And, most of all, have faith that the changes we seek are achievable. I've witnessed them with my own eyes, in fits and starts, in the score or more of examples I share in this book. I hope you will take inspiration from them and use them as a launching pad to greatly surpass what we have accomplished so far. So go. Get started.

APPENDIX 1:
ADDITIONAL RESOURCES

BOOKS

The Lean Series

In the years since *The Lean Startup,* a number of books have appeared to help managers translate the general principles into specific functional domains. Through a partnership with O'Reilly Media, we have published a series of books with this purpose: theleanstartup.com/the-lean-series.

Alvarez, Cindy. *Lean Customer Development: Build Products Your Customers Will Buy* (2014).
Busche, Laura. *Lean Branding: Creating Dynamic Brands to Generate Conversion* (2014).
Croll, Alistair, and Benjamin Yoskovitz. *Lean Analytics: Using Data to Build a Better Startup Faster* (2013).
Gothelf, Jeff, and Josh Seiden. *Lean UX: Applying Lean Principles to Improve User Experience* (2013).
Humble, Jez, Barry Reilly, and Joanne Molesky. *Lean*

Enterprise: How High-Performance Organizations Innovate at Scale (2015).

Klein, Laura. *UX for Lean Startups: Faster, Smarter User Experience Research Design* (2013).

Maurya, Ash. *Running Lean: Iterate from Plan A to a Plan That Works* (2012).

Further Reading

Chopra, Aneesh P. *Innovative State: How New Technologies Can Transform Government.* New York: Atlantic Monthly Press, 2014.

Blank, Steve. *The Four Steps to the Epiphany: Successful Strategies for Products That Win.* Palo Alto, CA: K&S Ranch, 2013.

Blank, Steve, and Bob Dorf. *The Startup Owner's Manual: The Step-By-Step Guide for Building a Great Company.* Palo Alto, CA: K&S Ranch, 2012.

Christensen, Clayton M. *The Innovator's Dilemma: When New Technologies Cause Great Firms to Fail.* Boston: Harvard Business Review Press, 2013.

Cooper, Robert G. *Winning at New Products: Creating Value Through Innovation.* 4th ed. New York: Basic Books, 2011.

Ellis, Sean, and Morgan Brown. *Hacking Growth: How Today's Fastest-Growing Companies Drive Breakout Success.* New York: Crown Business, 2017.

Florida, Richard. *The Flight of the Creative Class: The New Global Competition for Talent.* New York: HarperBusiness, 2005.

Gabler, Neal. *Walt Disney: The Triumph of the American Imagination.* New York: Knopf, 2006.

Gallagher, Leigh. *The Airbnb Story: How Three Ordinary Guys Disrupted an Industry . . . and Created Plenty of Controversy.* Boston: Houghton Mifflin Harcourt, 2017.

Gothelf, Jeff, and Josh Seiden. *Sense and Respond: How Successful Organizations Listen to Customers and Create New Products Continuously.* Boston: Harvard Business Review Press, 2017.

Jeff Gothelf also works as a lean consultant, mainly focusing on building and training evidence-based, customer-centered executive and product teams. These teams often utilize lean principles and agile software development. jeffgothelf.com

Horowitz, Ben. *The Hard Thing About Hard Things: Building a Business When There Are No Easy Answers.* New York: HarperCollins, 2014.

Klein, Laura. *Build Better Products: A Modern Approach to Building Successful User-Centered Products.* Brooklyn, NY: Rosenfeld Media, 2016.

Laura also works as a consultant with product managers, designers, or entrepreneurs struggling to make decisions about what to build next in order to deliver value to your customers. Users Know: usersknow.com. Or listen to her podcast, if you enjoy listening to people argue over the details of user experience design.

Liker, Jeffrey K. *The Toyota Way: 14 Management Principles from the World's Greatest Manufacturer.* New York: McGraw-Hill, 2004.

Maurya, Ash. *Scaling Lean: Mastering the Key Metrics for Startup Growth.* New York: Portfolio, 2016.

Ash Maurya has been an entrepreneur for more than a decade, and throughout that time he has been in search of a better, faster way for building successful products. Ash started sharing his learning on this blog, which then turned into a book, and subsequently into a series of products aimed at helping entrepreneurs raise their odds of success. ashmaurya.com

McChrystal, Stanley. *Team of Teams: New Rules of Engagement for a Complex World*. New York: Penguin.

McGrath, Rita Gunther. *The End of Competitive Advantage: How to Keep Your Strategy Moving as Fast as Your Business*. Boston: Harvard Business Review Press, 2013.

Moore, Geoffrey A. *Crossing the Chasm: Marketing and Selling Disruptive Products to Mainstream Consumers*. New York: HarperBusiness, 2014.

Ohanian, Alexis. *Without Their Permission: The Story of Reddit and a Blueprint for How to Change the World*. New York: Grand Central, 2016.

Olsen, Dan. *The Lean Product Playbook: How to Innovate with Minimum Viable Products and Rapid Customer Feedback*. Hoboken, NJ: Wiley, 2015.

Osterwalder, Alex, and Yves Pigneur. *Business Model Generation: A Handbook for Visionaries, Game Changers, and Challengers*. Hoboken, NJ: Wiley, 2010.

Pound, Edward S., Jeffrey H. Bell, and Mark L. Spearman. *Factory Physics for Managers: How Leaders Improve Performance in a Post–Lean Six Sigma World*. New York: McGraw-Hill Education, 2014.

Reinertsen, Donald G. *The Principles of Product Development Flow: Second Generation Lean Product Development*. Redondo Beach, CA: Celeritas, 2009.

Saxenian, AnnaLee. *Regional Advantage: Culture and Competition in Silicon Valley and Route 128*. Cambridge, MA: Harvard University Press, 1994.

Shane, Scott Andrew. *A General Theory of Entrepreneurship: The Individual-Opportunity Nexus*. Northampton, MA: Edward Elgar, 2003.

Sloan, Alfred P., Jr. *My Years with General Motors*. Edited by John McDonald, with Catharine Stevens. New York: Doubleday, 1963.

Taylor, Frederick Winslow. *The Principles of Scientific Management.* New York: Harper & Bros., 1915.

LEAN STARTUP CONFERENCES

Lean Startup Conferences bring the big ideas from Eric Ries's books off the page to show how organizations are making them real around the world. We understand there's one level of learning you get from reading and another level from doing the work—and hearing how other similar organizations are interpreting and doing the work.

Whether you're an entrepreneur or a corporate innovator, you'll learn how to implement and evolve the Lean Startup methodology beyond the startup phase—to scale—in enterprise, in government, in nonprofits, and in areas you'd least expect it.

Alongside keynotes and case studies at our flagship event, Lean Startup Week in San Francisco, we offer workshops and mentoring sessions where you can have more immersive experiences, breaking off a chunk of the practice and working through it with our seasoned experts. Of course, our community also loves to network and share their stories and struggles with each other. The knowledge you come away with happens on all levels, from the inspirational to the personal.

These events are produced by Lean Startup Company, which helps entrepreneurs and innovators build better products using the Lean Startup methodology and modern management techniques. They share educational ideas, stories, and lessons year-round with individuals and companies of all sizes and sectors.

Learn more at: leanstartup.co.

ORGANIZATIONS AND CONSULTANTS

Bionic: bionicsolution.com

I've shared several clients with Bionic since its founding in 2013. David Kidder and Anne Berkwitch were integral to the development of GE's FastWorks, and have established similar "Growth Operating Systems" at several Fortune 500 enterprises. Today, Bionic is a team of entrepreneurs and venture investors who believe that very large companies can grow like startups when they adopt the funding methods and management behaviors of the startup world. Working with the CEO and his or her team, Bionic helps identify important growth opportunities and coaches enterprise entrsepreneurs as they experiment, build, and grow their businesses. They've developed a rigorous, comprehensive model for "installing" an entrepreneurial ecosystem governed by robust growth boards and a proprietary investment-decision architecture that is highly compatible with the principles and philosophy I've explored in *The Startup Way*.

Pivotal: pivotal.io

Pivotal is changing the world by building great software companies. Only Pivotal combines the best of the Silicon Valley state of mind with a business's core values and expertise to innovate and disrupt. Pivotal employs decades of industry know-how, combining traditional experience with industry-leading capabilities and infrastructure to reshape the world.

Moves the Needle: movestheneedle.com

Moves the Needle are innovation transformation architects. Its mission is to transform global enterprises by empowering people to discover and create new value for their customers.

Mark Graban: markgraban.com

Mark Graban is an internationally recognized consultant, author, keynote speaker, and blogger in the field of "Lean healthcare." He is also the vice president of Improvement & Innovation Services for the software company KaiNexus.

Strategyzer: strategyzer.com

Strategyzer's goal is to put practical tools into the hands of every business strategy practitioner.

To get there, they've assembled an amazing team of creative, technical, and business professionals from around the world. They love building products and creating experiences that benefit individuals, organizations, and society.

Corporate Entrepreneur Community: corpentcom.com

The Corporate Entrepreneur Community (CEC) is a peer-to-peer network of large enterprises sharing best practices and challenges to drive real entrepreneurial growth. The CEC facilitates the development of entrepreneurial skills through a vetted community of innovation leaders at distinguished organizations.

APPENDIX 2:
A CATALOG OF MVPs

MVP METHODS at INTUIT

For a downloadable PDF including **examples** for each MVP method, visit **thestartupway.com/bonus.**

METHOD	WHEN TO USE	TIPS	ADVANTAGES	WATCH-OUTS
1. Fast Cycle Sketch Tests This method consists of a physical simulation of an experience, often created with ordinary objects such as paper, cardboard, etc.	**For New Solutions:** Before any coding. Use to gauge customer "energy" related to the general concept (love or hate). **For Existing Solutions:** When big improvements are required to what exists today. Use to explore bold new directions (in marketing, dev, etc.)	Focus on the real behavior observed, follow the protocol. Some teams use Excel/Google sheets to make fast prototypes instead of sketches. Provide ways for the user to opt-out or "quit" the prototype. Consider recording each session.	Very cheap. Many variations can be created in minutes with just pencil and paper. Fast, no code. Fast to evolve, 4 cycles in an afternoon are possible. Can quickly iterate "live" in a session.	Look for large effect size! Small effect sizes cannot be measured. While this technique can suggest if an idea is "bad," it can't validate an idea is good. Testers often revert to "interviewing" versus observing behavior. (enforce the protocol)
2. Front Door Tests This method consists of presenting a minimal "pitch" of the customer benefit, where the customer is invited to take action to indicate interest. Often this test is in the form of a simple online landing page.	**For New Solutions:** To test if a customer desires the benefit of a proposed solution. Use this method to test marketing messages, effective channels and establish preliminary funnel metrics. **For Existing Solutions:** To determine how customers will respond to potential new features in the real world before generating code for these features.	Be sure to effectively describe the benefit behind the "door" in simple words the customer will understand. Present an obvious choice or call to action which the user must take. Require the user to provide "currency" in order to proceed, such as an email address or other information of value.	One of the cheapest and fastest methods, can be built in just a few hours using external, often free, software tools. SaaS providers offer cheap templates and measurement systems to execute these tests. Quantitative data can be generated from real user behavior.	Relies on ability to describe the benefits. Not always clear if users do not understand the benefits, or simply don't see value. Avoid focusing on vanity metrics. Don't forget to build a mechanism into the test to discover the WHY behind the behaviors.
3. Fake-O Backend Tests This method includes techniques where real people or other manual workarounds are used to mimic eventual backend or automated systems. These tests are often combined with "front door" tests.	**For New Solutions:** To determine if the solution would provide real value to the user, and what might be required to engineer the solution. **For Existing Solutions:** To determine if the solution would provide real value to the user, and what might be required to engineer the solution.	Use manual techniques, but deliver the REAL benefit to the customer as if it were an automated process. Can be flexible on attributes such as time, but not on the benefit. Consider analog outputs such as PDF documents, static images, etc., which are automatable in the future.	Somewhat cheap. Can be created in just a few hours or days. Easy to capture additional qualitative data behind customer behaviors in person. Humans and manual processes don't need re-programming. Helps determine what will need to be automated in future.	Deliver value in a manner which can be automated if needed. Be a good steward of customer data if collected. Limited ability to scale the scope of experiments and number of users in a cohort. Do not let users know they are part of an experiment!

METHOD	WHEN TO USE	TIPS	ADVANTAGES	WATCH-OUTS
4. End-to-End Tests Often referred to as a "Minimum Viable Product" or MVP, the goal is to simulate an end-to-end customer experience to learn how the customer responds. This method often combines Front Door tests + Fake-O backend tests.	**For New Solutions:** To model the end-to-end flow from customer awareness to when they receive the benefit, and how they interact with the solution over time. **For Existing Solutions:** Measure response to a proposed product enhancement in detail, to enable a relatively accurate prediction of its impact to be made.	Repurpose off the shelf technologies such as WordPress apps, email, text, conversational UI, Google Sheets, or similar "minimum" tech solutions. Plan to refactor everything that is built. Reduce "scope," but do not reduce impact, i.e. focus on a few features which have a big impact for the customer.	The experience feels real to the user. This method is a good predictor of "real world" behavior. Repeat usage can be measured over longer time horizons. Sometimes the "test" generates real revenue. In other words, the test becomes the real thing with no extra work required.	WARNING: teams almost always over-engineer. Do not over-build! Do not spend time "making it real." Measure what matters, avoid vanity metrics. Accept the fact that refactoring will be needed. If the test is "scalable," it's NOT a rapid test!
5. Dry Wallet Methods which include payment options to test revenue models. Payment options might be "Fake-O."	Use this when the revenue model or the specific pricing needs to be tested. Also good for stronger validation of ideas. (See Kickstarter)	Create as real an experience as possible to mimic the checkout process. The ability to process payments is not required, just fake it.	Since payment is a high hurdle, success is a positive indicator. Can be easily created with third-party payment systems, or forms.	Testing revenue models too early may limit the team's thinking, and negatively influence decisions by focusing on business/financial metrics.
6. Judo Methods where an existing product from a competitor or similar experience is used in place of own product.	When a similar experience already exists in the market, or customer behavior needs to be understood with a competing product.	Simply observe customers using the "Judo" product as is. Rebrand or tweak the experience by capturing, then altering screenshots.	Learn from the work of others. Minimal effort is required.	Don't simply copy a competing product. Make the effort to learn why customers do or do not love the product.
7. Analog / Retro Create a physical version of the concept, such as a PDF printout or physical prototype.	When creating a digital version will take too much time, and the content is suitable for delivery in physical formats.	Connect Analog outputs to Front doors such as forms. Try formats such as "booklets," "guides," etc, for content.	Can be very fast, since it is relatively easy to develop content. Customers are familiar with these physical formats.	Physical formats may lack ability to track usage, especially over time and repeat use.
8. Pop-Up Shop Create a physical store, pop-up shop, or "booth" which offers the proposed benefit.	Use this where foot traffic is available, and the benefit cannot be provided in real time.	Use experts or other people who might be able to provide the benefit. Include ways to ask questions or speak with visitors.	Large numbers of potential visitors in a short amount of time. Easy to ask follow-up questions and learn more.	Social nature of the pop-up can encourage bad experiment behavior such as just conversing. Don't forget to focus on behavior, not what people say.

A NOTE ON RESEARCH METHODS

Every year, I help to put on a Lean Startup Conference in San Francisco. We bring together thousands of entrepreneurs and simulcast the event in hundreds of cities around the world. It's a global celebration of what this movement has accomplished, and a chance for more people to learn about the Lean Startup method and put it into action in their organizations.

Although we've had our fair share of big-name speakers—CEOs and famous startup founders—the majority of the speakers are people you've probably never heard of. That's because we work hard to find practitioners who are willing to tell the real story of how challenging this work is in real life. (You can also see video of all past speakers at leanstartup.co.)

This book follows a similar philosophy. I have included a handful of prominent voices, but most of the stories are from practitioners. Wherever possible, I have secured permission to talk about companies and their products by name. However, one thing I have learned is that many corporate communications departments are wary of telling "lean startup" stories in public.

After all, they often involve a lot of failure. (I want to especially commend Intuit and GE for being unusually open in talking about their Lean Startup journey.)

I am suspicious of PR-driven press accounts of what innovation looks like. So for the most part, I have drawn the stories in this book from my firsthand observations of companies I've worked closely with and dozens of detailed interviews conducted by my research team.

To protect some companies' proprietary information, we have built composite stories that are carefully anonymized to preserve the confidentiality of the company in question. In every case, these stories are based on my personal observations or on direct interviews, though I have sometimes intentionally merged two or more similar stories to make it more difficult for the reader to guess the company in question.

I have tested a number of these composite stories in talks over the years. It is not uncommon for audience members to approach me afterward and, with a sly smile, tell me they know exactly who I'm talking about. In fact, usually more than one person tells me he or she can positively identify the story's lead—and then each one names a different suspect. That's because so many of these stories are archetypal; common organization structures give rise to common incentives and, therefore, common behaviors.

This approach allows me to bring you more raw details about what life is really like deep in the trenches.

DISCLOSURES

In *The Lean Startup* I attempted to give a comprehensive list of the companies mentioned in the book in which I had equity and relationship interests, as well as the network of venture firms that also create many opportunities for conflicts of interest.

In the intervening years, these conflicts have multiplied so many times over that it's impossible to list every source. Suffice to say that I have relationships with almost every company named in this book, and for many of them, I am a direct investor or we have investors in common.

In cases where this is not true, I have cited external sources for interviews and quotations. For everything else, quotes are taken from direct interviews by me and my research team. Although I have endeavored to tell these stories with each company's cooperation, I have not given anyone approval over the final text.

ACKNOWLEDGMENTS

In my memory, the writing of *The Lean Startup* was a solitary affair. And yet, in the acknowledgments to that book, I thanked eighty-nine people (I counted).

This book, by contrast, has felt like a true community effort. No doubt that's in part because it got its start from the community that developed around my Kickstarter MVP book, *The Leader's Guide*. I owe a huge debt to the nearly 9,677 people who backed the Kickstarter campaign, making possible the research that eventually led to *The Leader's Guide,* as well as everyone who joined and participates in the Leader's Guide community on Mightybell that has become a dynamic, active place for discussions about the principles in the book. I am deeply indebted to Sarah Rainone, who did much of the research and development for *The Leader's Guide.*

At the Lean Startup Company, I want to thank Melissa Moore, Heather McGough, Julianne Wotasik, and Kristen Cluthe.

Thank you to the entire team at Crown, who have believed in and supported my work thoroughly: Roger Scholl, Tina Constable, Ayelet Gruenspecht, Campbell Wharton, Megan Schumann, Megan Perritt, Julia Elliott, Erin Little, Jill Greto, Elizabeth Rendfleisch, Heather Williamson, Terry Deal, and Tal Goretsky.

If you are one of those wise authors who flips to the back of books to figure out who the best agents are, let me set you straight right now: Christy Fletcher is the best in the business. She is so much more than a literary agent. She has become a true partner to me, strategizing and improvising in every aspect of my business, always with her trademark wit and calm. I am truly grateful to her and her entire organization for building this rocket ship with me.

Also at Fletcher & Co., I'd like to thank Grainne Fox, Veronica Goldstein, Erin McFadden, Sylvie Greenberg, Sarah Fuentes, and Mink Choi.

Marcus Gosling has been a long-time collaborator, dating back to our years together as co-founders of IMVU. He designed the cover and interior diagrams for this book, as well as the cover for *The Lean Startup*. (Try to imagine how many ink swooshes this has required over the years.) He also oversaw an extensive testing campaign for the book, which required his unique blend of product and design savvy. And he did all this while carrying the load as the Long-Term Stock Exchange's head of product. Thank you.

This book would have collapsed under its own weight years ago if not for my long-suffering and highly dedicated research and editorial team: Melanie Rehak, Laura Albero, Laureen Rowland, and Bridget Samburg. Melanie Rehak in particular has shouldered the burden of this volume's evolution through so many iterations. I am indebted to her for going above and beyond the call of duty time and time again. Laura Albero, who took on the enormous task of managing the many moving parts of this project, has also been essential to its completion.

I was thrilled to work again with Telepathy, the designers behind theleanstartup.com, on *The Startup Way*'s website. Thank you to Chuck Longanecker, Arnold Yoon, Brent Summers, Eduardo Toledano, Bethany Brown, Dave Shepard, and Megan Doyle for seamlessly translating the book's concepts into a beautiful web design. Check it out at thestartupway.com.

I'd like to thank GE for giving me the opportunity to work in a new way, and for allowing me to tell the story of the amazing amount of work the company has done. Everyone who works there is truly an inspiration. In particular, I'd like to thank Jeff Immelt, Beth Comstock, Viv Goldstein, John Flannery, Janice Semper, Jamie Miller, Shane Fitzsimons, Susan Peters, Eric Gebhardt, Ryan Smith, Brad Mottier, Cory Nelson, James Richards, Giulio Canegallo, Silvio Sferruzza, Terri Bresenham, Valerie Van Den Keybus, Jennifer Beihl, Lorenzo Simonelli, Michael Mahan, Brian Worrell, David Spangler, Anne McEntee, Wolfgang Meyer-Haack, Vic Abate, Guy Leonardo, Anders Wold, Carolyn Padilla, Aubrey Smith, Marilyn Gorman, Tony Campbell, Shona Seifert, Rakesh Sahay, Chris Bevacqua, Kevin Nolan, Christopher Sieck, and Steve Bolze. Special thanks also to Mark Little.

Leys Bostrom at GE went above and beyond the call of duty to make sure every GE story and fact in this book was correct.

Intuit also allowed me to tell their story in detail, for which I am grateful. Thanks to Scott Cook, Brad Smith, Hugh Molotsi, Bennett Blank, Rania Succar, Kathy Tsitovich, Steven Wheelis, Katherine Gregg, Michael Stirrat, Rachel Church, Mark Notarainni, Cassie Divine, Alaina Maloney, Catie Harriss, Greg Johnson, Allan Sabol, Rob DeMartini, Weronika Bromberg, and Justin Ruthenbeck.

In Washington, I'd like to thank Hillary Hartley, Aaron Snow, Haley Van Dyck, Mikey Dickerson, Garren Givens, Dave Zvenyach, Brian Lefler, Marina Martin, Alan DeLevie, Jake Harris, Lisa Gelobter, Erie Meyer, Jennifer Tress, Jen Anastasoff, Eric Hysen, Kath Stanley, Mark Schwartz, Alok Shah, Deepa

Kunapuli, Anissa Collins, Matt Fante, Mollie Ruskin, Emily Tavoulareas, Vivian Graubard, Sarah Sullivan, Wei Lo, Amy Kort, Charles Worthington, and Aneesh Chopra.

I've had the help and support of people at numerous companies, organizations, and nonprofits. Many of their stories appear in the book, while others influenced my thinking deeply. All of them contributed enormously to the ideas that make up *The Startup Way*. At Bionic: Janice Fraser, David Kidder, and Anne Berkowitch. Drew Houston, Todd Jackson, and Aditya Agarwal at Dropbox. At Asana: Emilie Cole, Dustin Moskovitz, Justin Rosenstein, Anna Binder, Sam Goertler, and Katie Schmalzried. At Twilio: Jeff Lawson, Roy Ng, Patrick Malatack, and Ott Kaukver. At IBM: Jeff Smith. At Airbnb: Joe Zadeh and Maggie Carr. At Cisco: Alex Goryachev, Oseas Ramirez Assad, Kim Chen, and Mathilde Durvy. At Citi: Vanessa Colella. At Adopt-A-Pet: David Meyer and Abbie Moore. At Procter & Gamble: Chris Boeckerman. At Code for America: Jennifer Pahlka. At PCI Global: Chris Bessenecker. At Pivotal: Rob Mee, Andrew Cohen, Edward Heiatt, and Siobhan McFeeney. At Gusto: Joshua Reeves, Jill Coln, Nikki Wilkin, and Maryanne Brown. At Google's Area 120: Alex Gawley. At Seattle Children's Hospital: Cara Bailey and Greg Beach. Jeff Hunter of Jeff Hunter Strategy LLC. At Pearson: Adam Berk and Sonja Kresojevic. At the NSA: Vanee Vines, Mike Halbig, and Matt Fante. At Uber: Andrew Chen. At Telefónica: Susana Jurado Apruzzese. Suneel Gupta at Rise. Matt Kresse at AgPulse (and formerly of Toyota). At the Toyota Technology Info Center: Vinuth Rai. At ExecCamp: Barry O'Reilly. At Ligouri Innovation (and GE before that!): Steve Ligouri. Aaron Feuer at Panorama. And at the Global Innovation Fund (GIF): Alix Peterson Zwane.

I am especially grateful to my beta-test readers. Your feedback made this book immeasurably better, and I'm certain that any remaining mistakes are because I didn't listen to you enough.

Thanks to Morgan Housel, Mark Graban, Janice Fraser, Steve Liguori, Beth Comstock, Viv Goldstein, Melissa Moore, Dan Debow, Vinuth Rai, James Joaquin, Tiho Bajic, Al Sochard, Kanyi Maqubela, Dan Martell, Roy Bahat, Tom Serres, Dave Binetti, Aneesh Chopra, Marina Martin, Andrey Ostrovsky, Laura Klein, Clark Scheffy, Bennett Blank, Art Parkos, Cindy Alvarez, Adam Penenberg, Kent Beck, Charles Becker, Zach Nies, Holly Grant, Carolyn Dee, Jennifer Maerz, Ann Mei Chang, Nicole Glaros, Anna Mason, Ed Essey, Daniel Doktori, Janice Semper, Todd Park, and Tom Eisenmann.

Special thanks to: Arash Ferdowsi, Ari Gesher, Brian Frezza, Dan Smith, Greg Beach, Justin Rosenstein, Matt Mullenweg, Matthew Ogle, Pedro Miguel, Raghu Krishnamoorthy, Reid Hoffman, Samuel Hammond, Scott Cook, Marc Andreessen, Margit Wennmachers, Sean Ellis, Shigeki Tomoyama, JB Brown, Simeon Sessley, Giff Constable, Philip Vaughn, Andy Sack, Brian Singerman, Craig Shapiro, and James Joaquin.

Thanks to the entire LTSE team, whose daily commitment to change the world for the better in the face of impossibly long odds inspires me more than you know. Thanks to: Marcus Gosling, Tiho Bajic, Michelle Greene, Lydia Doll, Carolyn Dee, Hyon Lee, Bethany Andres-Beck, Pavitra Bhalla, Zoran Perkov, Amy Butte, John Bautista, and especially my chief of staff, Holly Grant, who is the mastermind of our operations and handles the incredibly difficult task of coordinating a high-degree-of-difficulty startup in three cities. (Holly also developed and modeled the "Hypergrowth Lemonade Stand" examples in Chapters 4 and 9.)

I owe a tremendous thanks to my longtime executive assistant, Brittany Hart, who has navigated the roller coaster of this journey with aplomb and skill. I am grateful to have someone I can rely on so thoroughly at my side.

At Outcast, I'd like to thank Alex Constantinople, Nicki Dugan Pogue, Sophie Fischman, Sara Blask, and Jonny Marsh.

I would like to thank Quensella and Simone for helping to make life run smoothly as I've been working on this project. Deep thanks to Irma for bringing so much joy and support to our family.

To my friends, there are many more of you than I can thank here, and I trust you know how much I value your support and kindness.

My parents, Andrew Ries and Vivian Reznik, laid the foundation for all I have accomplished here. Their unwavering support—from my ridiculous first forays into technology and entrepreneurship to my utter lack of a traditional career path—has made everything you've read here possible. As a new parent myself, I have a newfound appreciation for their sacrifices and heroism. Thank you.

I am indebted to my sisters and brothers-in-law, Nicole and Dov, Amanda and Gordon, and your rapidly growing families. I offer these thanks with much love to the next generation: Everett, Nadia, and Teddy.

To my parents-in-law, Harriet and Bill: thank you for your kindness and support and for raising a most excellent daughter.

To my incredible wife, Tara Mohr: I can't believe I have the privilege of building a life with you. Your love sustains me in every moment and nourishes my soul each day. I am so much better for having known you. Thank you.

The biggest change in my life since I wrote *The Lean Startup* is the exponential growth of my own family. To my son and daughter: Thank you for inducting me into the awesome club of parenthood. You have transformed me in ways you will never fully appreciate. Since you came into my life, I judge every opportunity by whether it is something I can be proud to explain to you someday. Every ounce of my energy is dedicated to the hope that you will inherit a better world. I love you.

NOTES

INTRODUCTION

1. meetup.com/topics/lean-startup.
2. As of May 2017, FastWorks is a trademark of General Electric Company.
3. quora.com/What-causes-the-slack-at-large-corporations/answer/Adam
-DAngelo.

PART ONE

1. vanityfair.com/news/2016/11/airbnb-brian-chesky.
2. Ibid.
3. Ari Gesher spoke at the 2013 Lean Startup Conference in San Francisco; youtube.com/watch?v=TUrkwAhv86k.

CHAPTER 1

1. wsj.com/articles/SB10001424053111903480904576512250915629460.
2. 25iq.com/2017/03/10/you-have-discovered-productmarket-fit-what
-about-a-moat/.
3. ibm.com/blogs/insights-on-business/gbs-strategy/cxos-set-sights
-back-traditional-targets/.
4. marketrealist.com/2015/12/adoption-rates-dizzying-heights.

5. steveblank.com/2010/07/22/what-if-the-price-were-zero-failing-at
    -customer-validation.

6. Jack Welch and John A. Byrne, *Jack: Straight from the Gut* (New York:
    Warner Business Books, 2001), p. 330.

7. forbes.com/sites/miguelhelft/2015/09/21/dropboxs-houston-were
    -building-the-worlds-largest-platform-for-collaboration/#58f0ccd9125e;
    fortune.com/2016/03/07/dropbox-half-a-billion-users.

8. techcrunch.com/2013/11/02/welcome-to-the-unicorn-club/.

9. forbes.com/sites/howardhyu/2016/11/25/this-black-friday-jeff
    -bezos-makes-amazon-echo-sound-better-than-google-home
    /#11dc97a66cc4; wired.com/2014/12/jeff-bezos-ignition-conference/;
    fastcompany.com/3040383/following-fire-phone-flop-big-changes-at
    -amazons-lab126.

10. bloomberg.com/features/2016-amazon-echo.

11. fastcompany.com/3039887/under-fire.

12. sec.gov/Archives/edgar/data/1018724/000119312505070440/dex991
    .htm.

CHAPTER 2

1. See AnnaLee Saxenian's *Regional Advantage: Culture and Competition in Silicon Valley and Route 128* (Cambridge, MA: Harvard University Press, 1996); Reid Hoffman's *blitzscaling* thesis (Part Three Introduction, note 1); and the TechStars Manifesto (Chapter 7, note 5).

2. The term "ambidextrous organization" was coined by Robert Duncan in 1976, in the article "The Ambidextrous Organization: Designing Dual Structures for Innovation," in *The Management of Organization Design: Strategies and Implementation*, edited by Ralph H. Kilmann, Louis R. Pondy, and Dennis P. Slevin (New York: North Holland, 1976). For more, see Steve Blank's post on lean management innovation: steveblank.com/2015/06/26/lean-innovation-management-making-corporate-innovation-work/.

3. "As companies tend to innovate faster than their customers' needs evolve, most organizations eventually end up producing products or services that are actually too sophisticated, too expensive, and too complicated for many customers in their market. Companies pursue these 'sustaining innovations' at the higher tiers of their markets because this is what has historically helped them succeed: by charging the highest prices to their most demanding and sophisticated customers at the top of the market, companies will achieve the greatest profitability." Among them are new technologies and platforms. claytonchristensen.com/key-concepts/.

4. The irony is not lost on me that these same organizations have been criticized for being slow to extend this same access to a wider pool of applicants beyond the traditional demographics of Silicon Valley. This extension is essential if we are going to make the concept of "meritocracy" mean something.

5. After these events took place, GE divested the appliance business, which was acquired by Chinese conglomerate Haier in 2016 and still operates under the name "GE Appliances." See geappliances.com/our-company.

6. If six weeks doesn't seem like enough time to save a business, note that famed startup accelerator Y Combinator is twelve weeks long.

CHAPTER 3

1. For more on the history of Silicon Valley specifically, see the following: *Regional Advantage: Culture and Competition in Silicon Valley and Route 128,* by AnnaLee Saxenian (Cambridge, MA: Harvard University Press, 1994; and "The Secret History of Silicon Valley," by Steve Blank (steve blank.com/secret-history).

2. Steve Case is chairman and CEO of Revolution LLC, and co-founder and former CEO of AOL; riseofrest.com.

3. At my first job in Silicon Valley, a banner with this motto emblazoned on it hung above reception.

4. hbr.org/2013/01/what-is-entrepreneurship.

5. Alexis Ohanian, *Without Their Permission: The Story of Reddit and a Blueprint for How to Change the World* (New York: Grand Central, 2016), p. 5.

6. quora.com/Amazon-company-What-is-Amazons-approach-to-product -development-and-product-management.

7. Jack Stack and Bo Burlingham, *A Stake in the Outcome: Building a Culture of Ownership for the Long-Term Success of Your Business* (New York: Doubleday Business, 2002).

8. With apologies to our friends in finance, who would say that this simplistic formula is not quite right: 1. We're not taking into account the time value of money; the payoff is only $1 billion in future dollars, we need a net-present-value (NPV) calculation, and 2. This is actually more like an option, which should be valued according to the Black-Scholes formula, or something similar. Granted! But these involve complexity that few practitioners understand. Some of these advanced issues are discussed in Chapter 9.

9. This is why we call it a minimum viable *product*. It's not just research or a standalone prototype. It's an attempt to serve a real customer, even if in a limited way.

10. It's important to note that this system is vulnerable to abuse. It's why the Lean Startup movement is so focused on scientific "validated learning" as a unit of progress.

11. psychologytoday.com/blog/wired-success/201511/why-financial-incentives-don-t-improve-performance.

12. steveblank.com/2010/11/01/no-business-plan-survives-first-contact-with-a-customer-%E2%80%93-the-5-2-billion-dollar-mistake/.

13. Remarks at the National Defense Executive Reserve Conference, November 14, 1957; presidency.ucsb.edu/ws/?pid=10951.

14. Most boards are composed of representatives from three groups: insiders (founders and employees), investors, and independent directors. The most common configuration in my experience is 2/2/1 for a total of five directors. For much of a startup's early life, this may be the total number of people to whom it is accountable.

15. techcrunch.com/2011/11/19/racism-and-meritocracy; startuplessons learned.com/2010/02/why-diversity-matter-meritocracy.html; startuplessonslearned.com/2012/11/solving-pipeline-problem.html.

16. journals.sagepub.com/doi/abs/10.2189/asqu.2010.55.4.543. For a discussion of the study, see sloanreview.mit.edu/article/achieving-meritocracy-in-the-workplace/.

17. mashable.com/2016/04/19/early-mark-zuckerberg-interview/#En6CWSe.EZqm.

18. I'm far from the only person thinking about this. It's an important topic not just for SV, but for society at large, as there are other flaws in the meritocracy concept that need to be grappled with. For one example, see Chris Hayes's writing on this subject: thenation.com/article/why-elites-fail and boingboing.net/2012/06/13/meritocracies-become-oligarchi.html.

19. Bessemer Venture Partners; bvp.com/portfolio/anti-portfolio.

20. forbes.com/sites/larrymagid/2012/02/01/zuckerberg-claims-we-dont-build-services-to-make-money/#149d1db5370f.

21. McChrystal, Stanley. *Team of Teams: New Rules of Engagement for a Complex World* (New York: Penguin, 2015), p. 215.

CHAPTER 4

1. jstor.org/stable/40216431?seq=1#page_scan_tab_contents; journal.sjdm.org/14/14130/jdm14130.html.

2. There is a whole separate discipline to this called "customer development," a term originally coined by Steve Blank. See startuplessonslearned.com/2008/11/what-is-customer-development.html.

3. Part of the research that went into this book came from a project called *The Leader's Guide.* In 2015, I launched a Kickstarter campaign to publish a limited-run, 250-page book aimed at helping entrepreneurs, executives, and project leaders put lean principles into practice. The campaign was backed by 9,677 people choosing from 30 different reward levels and raising $588,903. The content of the book was derived from materials I'd used in the years prior; the goal was to provide a concrete road map for leaders who want to transform their management practice in an entrepreneurial direction. After it was published, I invited every backer who'd received a copy to join a community on Mightybell, a social networking application aimed at organizing communities around common interests, and share with me their experiences of putting its ideas into practice.

4. Intuit founder Scott Cook first suggested to me that "delight" is the proper standard for the value hypothesis.

5. techcrunch.com/2012/02/01/facebook-ipo-letter.

6. pmarchive.com/guide_to_startups_part4.html.

7. medium.com/@davidjbland/7-things-i-ve-learned-about-lean-startup-c6323d9ef19c.

8. medium.com/blueprint-by-intuit/design-thinking-in-the-corporate-dna-f0a1bd6359db#.6i9u9o20w.

9. For more on MVP sequencing, see *The Leader's Guide,* pp. 156–57.

10. businessinsider.com/the-washington-post-is-growing-its-arc-publishing-business-2016-6.

11. For more on growth boards, see Chapter 9.

CHAPTER 5

1. Jeffrey K. Liker, *The Toyota Way* (New York: McGraw-Hill, 2003), p. 223.

2. *Work in process* (WIP) is defined in the seminal textbook *Factory Physics* as "inventory between the start and end points of a routing." To learn more, see *Factory Physics for Managers: How Leaders Improve Performance in a Post–Lean Six Sigma World,* by Edward S. Pound, Jeffrey H. Bell, and Mark L. Spearman (New York: McGraw Hill Education, 2014).

3. startup-marketing.com/the-startup-pyramid/.

4. This is true of startups, too, because most employees will be recruited from a legacy organization.

5. The ability employees have to leave companies and start new ones without being bound by a non-compete clause is a crucial legal protection, and this policy regime is part of what make Silicon Valley so successful. For more, see Chapter 11.

6. As Peter Drucker said, "There is surely nothing quite so useless as doing

with great efficiency what should not be done at all." "What Executives Should Remember," *Harvard Business Review,* vol. 84, no. 2, February 2006; hbswk.hbs.edu/archive/5377.html.

7. For an example of how stage-gate is supposed to work, see Robert G. Cooper, *Winning at New Products: Creating Value Through Innovation* 4th ed. (New York: Basic Books, 2011).

8. I have met many teams that backdate what they claimed was going to happen to match the new management directive that's in vogue. George Orwell would be impressed.

9. Creating this structure so that it is truly functional, rather than just another system that can be gamed, requires the hard work of building and using growth boards and other mechanisms. See Chapter 9.

10. Brian Frezza spoke at the 2013 Lean Startup Conference in San Francisco; youtube.com/watch?v=I2l_Cn8Fuo8.

11. knowyourmeme.com/memes/profit.

PART TWO

1. en.wikipedia.org/wiki/United_States_Department_of_Health_and _Human_Services.

2. fastcompany.com/3046756/Obama-and-his-geeks.

3. nbcnews.com/news/other/only-6-able-sign-healthcare-gov-first-day -documents-show-f8c11509571.

4. advisory.com/daily-briefing/2014/03/03/time-inside-the-nightmare -launch-of-healthcaregov.

5. washingtonpost.com/national/health-science/hhs-failed-to-heed-many -warnings-that-healthcaregov-was-in-trouble/2016/02/22/dd344e7c -d67e-11e5-9823-02b905009f99_story.html.

6. advisory.com/daily-briefing/2014/03/03/time-inside-the-nightmare -launch-of-healthcaregov.

CHAPTER 6

1. Cory Nelson is now the GM for gas compression and power generation products in the Distributed Power division of GE Power.

2. pmarchive.com/guide_to_startups_part4.html.

3. The exact membership of the "FastWorks Growth Board," as it came to be known, varied a little from year to year, including participation from leaders of individual GE businesses. For the initial eight pilot projects, it included Jamie Miller (then CIO), Susan Peters (Senior VP of HR),

Matt Cribbins (then VP of GE's Corporate Audit Staff), Mark Little (Senior VP and Chief Technology Officer of GE Global Research), and Beth Comstock.

4. aei.org/publication/has-government-employment-really-increased
-under-obama/; gao.gov/assets/680/677436.pdf; politicalticker.blogs.cnn
.com/2009/04/18/Obama-names-performance-and-technology-czars;
cei.org/blog/nobody-knows-how-many-federal-agencies-exist.

5. Aneesh P. Chopra, *Innovative State: How Technologies Can Transform Government* (New York: Atlantic Monthly Press, 2014), pp. 215–16.

6. obamawhitehouse.archives.gov/the-press-office/2012/08/23/white
-house-launches-presidential-innovation-fellows-program.

7. presidentialinnovationfellows.gov/faq/.

8. One of the major learnings, in fact, is reflected in the way I've told the story here. The team realized that instead of building a single device, it made more sense to conceptualize their new product as a system being sold to the customer.

9. For more on business models, see Alexander Osterwalder and Yves Pigneur. *Business Model Generation: A Handbook for Visionaries, Game Changers and Challengers* (Hoboken, NJ: John Wiley & Sons, 2010).

10. fastcompany.com/3068931/why-this-ceo-appointed-an-employee-to
-change-dumb-company-rules.

CHAPTER 7

1. Also along for the ride, doing a lot of critical and difficult legwork were Aubrey Smith, Tony Campbell, Marilyn Gorman, and Steve Liguori.

2. playbook.cio.gov/.

3. inc.com/steve-blank/key-to-success-getting-out-of-building.html.

4. Students of the scientific method may be concerned that we are not teaching teams the importance of a falsifiable hypothesis. It's true that I generally save this bit of theory for a more advanced session, but keep in mind that startup arrogance actually works in our favor here. The idea that *every single person on the planet will love my product* is the ultimate in easily falsified hypotheses.

5. davidgcohen.com/2011/08/28/the-mentor-manifesto/.

6. Supported by the Department of International Development in the UK, the United States Agency for International Development, the Omidyar Network, the Swedish International Development Cooperation Agency, the Department for Foreign Affairs and Trade in Australia, and the Department of Science and Technology in South Africa.

CHAPTER 8

1. Leigh Gallagher, *The Airbnb Story: How Three Ordinary Guys Disrupted an Industry, Made Billions . . . and Created Plenty of Controversy* (New York: Houghton Mifflin Harcourt, 2017), p. 177–8.
2. Ibid., p. 196.
3. metropolismag.com/interiors/hospitality-interiors/whats-next-for-air bnbs-innovation-and-design-studio/.
4. bloomberg.com/news/articles/2015-08-18/emc-vmware-spinout-pivotal -appoints-rob-mee-as-new-ceo.
5. usds.gov/report-to-congress/2016/immigration-system/.
6. lean.org/lexicon/set-based-concurrent-engineering.
7. businessinsider.com/ge-is-ditching-annual-reviews-2016-7.
8. Ibid.
9. wsj.com/articles/ge-does-away-with-employee-ratings-1469541602.
10. Matt Mullenweg spoke at the 2013 Lean Startup Conference in San Francisco; youtube.com/watch?v=adN2eQHd1dU.
11. obamawhitehouse.archives.gov/blog/2013/05/15/rfp-ez-delivers -savings-taxpayers-new-opportunities-small-business.
12. ads.18f.gov.
13. seattlechildrens.org/about/seattle-childrens-improvement-and -innovation-scii/.
14. a16z.com/2017/03/04/culture-and-revolution-ben-horowitz-toussaint -louverture/.
15. currentbyge.com/company.
16. fastcompany.com/3069240/how-asana-built-the-best-company-culture -in-tech.
17. Ibid.
18. give.intuitlabs.com.

CHAPTER 9

1. These can be things as simple as the percentage of customers who pre-order an MVP, the percentage of customers who agree to take part in a training program, or the percentage of customers who use an IT system (if it's an internal project).
2. quora.com/What-was-it-like-to-make-an-early-investment-in-Twitter -What-was-the-dynamic-like; nbcnews.com/id/42577600/ns/business-us _business/t/real-history-twitter-isnt-so-short-sweet/#.WKZpShCOlaU.

3. medium.com/@dbinetti/innovation-options-a-framework-for -evaluating-innovation-in-larger-organizations-968bd43f59f6.
4. paulgraham.com/growth.html.
5. Scott Cook of Intuit created the delight standard in 2007 with his one-day Design for Delight program, which eventually grew into a company-wide innovation structure. hbr.org/2011/06/the-innovation-catalysts.
6. netpromoter.com/know/.
7. slideshare.net/hiten1/measuring-understanding-productmarket-fit -qualitatively/3-Sean_Ellis_productmarket_fit_surveysurveyio.
8. These "bingo card" charts are based on my work with GE, and are used with permission from the company.
9. Those of us who have tried to build a real startup without even a part-time CFO have learned this lesson the hard way.

PART THREE

1. hbr.org/2016/04/blitzscaling.

CHAPTER 10

1. I belong to the Peter Drucker school of gurus: drucker.institute/about -peter-f-drucker.
2. fakesteve.net/2010/04/an-open-letter-to-the-people-of-the-world.html.

CHAPTER 11

1. Entrepreneurs within both the UK and U.S. governments have taken up this approach under the banner of "the strategy is delivery." See mike bracken.com/blog/the-strategy-is-delivery-again and gds.blog.gov.uk/ usds-18f-and-gds-why-the-strategy-is-delivery-video-transcript.
2. hbr.org/2016/10/an-entrepreneurial-society-needs-an-entrepreneurial -state.
3. These are just a few examples of visa programs available in other countries: startupchile.org/programs; startupdenmark.info; italiastartupvisa .mise.gov.it.
4. Steven Watts, *The People's Tycoon: Henry Ford and the American Century* (New York: Vintage, 2006).
5. medium.com/tech-diversity-files/the-real-reason-my-startup-was -successful-privilege-3859b14f4560#.1skhsmiff.

6. For more on this, see Scott Andrew Shane, *A General Theory of Entrepreneurship: The Individual-Opportunity Nexus* (Northampton, MA: Edward Elgar, 2003).

7. papers.ssrn.com/sol3/papers.cfm?abstract_id=2896309.

8. hbr.org/2017/02/a-few-unicorns-are-no-substitute-for-a-competitive-innovative-economy.

9. rand.org/content/dam/rand/pubs/working_papers/2010/RAND_WR637-1.pdf.

10. Carol S. Dweck, PhD, *Mindset: The New Psychology of Success* (New York: Random House, 2006).

11. stvp.stanford.edu/blog/innovation-insurgency-begins/.

12. steveblank.com/category/nsf-national-science-foundation/.

13. bloomberg.com/news/articles/2016-02-10/how-tech-startup-founders-are-hacking-immigration.

14. blogs.wsj.com/digits/2016/03/17/study-immigrants-founded-51-of-u-s-billion-dollar-startups/.

15. citylab.com/politics/2013/04/how-immigration-helps-cities/5323/.

16. One such example is Kunal Bahl, a graduate of the Wharton School at the University of Pennsylvania, who went home to India to found the e-commerce company Snapdeal, which is now valued at $6.5 billion and has created thousands of jobs there—but none in the United States, where he got his education. money.cnn.com/2017/02/02/news/india/snapdeal-india-kunal-bahl-h1b-visa/index.html.

17. thenation.com/article/what-if-we-treated-labor-startup.

18. thoughtco.com/intro-to-unemployment-insurance-in-the-us-1147659.

19. ncbi.nlm.nih.gov/pmc/articles/PMC2796689/.

20. UBI isn't even necessarily the only way to build a truly universal economic benefit. A federal job guarantee might achieve similar outcomes: jacobinmag.com/2017/02/federal-job-guarantee-universal-basic-income-investment-jobs-unemployment/.

21. nytimes.com/2016/12/17/business/economy/universal-basic-income-finland.html.

22. qz.com/696377/y-combinator-is-running-a-basic-income-experiment-with-100-oakland-families.

23. kauffman.org/what-we-do/resources/entrepreneurship-policy-digest/can-social-insurance-unlock-entrepreneurial-opportunities.

24. theatlantic.com/business/archive/2016/06/netherlands-utrecht-universal-basic-income-experiment/487883/; theguardian.com/world/2016/oct/28/universal-basic-income-ontario-poverty-pilot-project-canada.

25. vox.com/new-money/2017/2/13/14580874/google-self-driving
-noncompetes.

26. kauffman.org/what-we-do/resources/entrepreneurship-policy-digest/
how-intellectual-property-can-help-or-hinder-innovation.

27. forbes.com/2009/08/10/government-internet-software-technology
-breakthroughs-oreilly.html.

28. obamawhitehouse.archives.gov/the-press-office/2013/05/09/executive
-order-making-open-and-machine-readable-new-default-government-.

29. Chopra, *Innovative State,* pp. 121–22.

30. hbr.org/2017/02/a-few-unicorns-are-no-substitute-for-a-competitive
-innovative-economy.

31. site.warrington.ufl.edu/ritter/files/2017/06/IPOs2016Statistics.pdf.

32. jstor.org/stable/1806983?seq=1#page_scan_tab_contents; larrysummers
.com/2017/06/01/secular-stagnation-even-truer-today.

33. techcrunch.com/2017/06/28/a-look-back-at-amazons-1997-ipo.

34. niskanencenter.org/blog/future-liberalism-politicization-everything/.

EPILOGUE

1. bloomberg.com/view/articles/2017–04–12/here-s-one-more-thing-to
-blame-on-senior-management.

INDEX

organizational structure, 9, 11, 42–45,
    50–51, 57–62, 118–21, 125, 128,
    311
  charts, *50, 127, 316*
  outcomes of transformation, 128–34
  silos, 38, 134, 312
  underground network, 55–57, 201–3

Pahlka, Jennifer, 196
Palantir, 18, 311
Park, Todd, 140, 160, 162, 196, 203,
    289, 315, 339
PayPal, 109, 276
Peters, Susan, 376n3
Phase One (critical mass), 143, *145,*
    146–87
  common patterns, 155–56
  cross-functional teams and, 163–66
  designing an experiment, 168–74
  language for, 182–84
  measuring success and, 174–78
  motivations for, 156–57
  starting small, 159–60
  wielding the Golden Sword, 166–67
  working by exception, 178–81, 202–3
Phase Two (scaling up), 143, *145,*
    187–222
  backlash and, 205, 222
  challenges of pilot teams, 194–95
  common patterns, 188–89
  crossing the chasm, 191–92, 222
  executive champions, 198–204, 205
  growth boards for, 218, 220–22
  internal coaching for, 206–15
  metered funding and, 215–20, *218*
  resistance from within, 195, 222
  sharing information, 198
  training for, 204–5
  widespread rollout for, 195–98
Phase Three (deep systems), 143, *145,*
    223–63
  "building that airplane," 228
  compensation and hiring, 249–52
  cultural acclimation, 258–62
  departments involved, 228–48

guidance document for, 228–31
procurement systems, 252–56
second founding and, 223–31
pivot, 6, 12, 66, 76, 86, 108–12, 116,
    207, 242, 245, 279
  pivot-or-persevere meeting, 107,
    110–11, 114, 287, 288
  the pivot to oblivion, 111–15
  vision and, 66, 81–82, 108, *108,* 112
  what it is, 66, 81–82, 108, *108*
Pivotal (software company), 231–33
Presidential Innovation Fellows (PIF)
    program, 51, 162–63, 196, 252
Principles of Scientific Management, The
    (Taylor), 329–30
process, 12, 154
  Lean Startup, 89–116
  Startup Way, *123,* 123–27, *126*
product, 24, 30, 37, 52, 69, 89–90,
    118–21, 134–35, 191
  Andreessen on hypergrowth and, 157
  creating the right, 129, 150, 375n6
  cycle time, 97, 152
  distribution, 173–74
  experiments for testing, 168–74
  LOFA and, 89–93
  MVP testing, 87–90, 96–102
  NPIs, 158
public policy changes, 319–46, 379n1

Rackspace, 203
Rai, Vinuth, 169, 170
reddit, 67
Revolution LLC, 373n2
Richards, James, 234–35
RIM, 35
Rise of the Rest, 64
Rosenstein, Justin, 260
Ruskin, Mollie, 238
Ruthenbeck, Justin, 262

SafeBoda, 219
Sandberg, Sheryl, 34–35
scale, 122, *145,* 160, 223–31, 280–85
  See also Phase Two (scaling up)